REA

**FRIENDS
OF ACPL**

Brussels Versus
the Beltway

D0891078

DEC 0 4 2008

American Governance and Public Policy Series
Series Editors: Gerard W. Boychuk, Karen Mossberger, and Mark C. Rom

Brussels Versus the Beltway

Advocacy in the United States and the European Union

Christine Mahoney

Georgetown University Press
Washington, D.C.

Georgetown University Press, Washington, D.C.
© 2008 by Georgetown University Press. All rights reserved. No part of this book may
be reproduced or utilized in any form or by any means, electronic or mechanical,
including photocopying and recording, or by any information storage and retrieval
system, without permission in writing from the publisher.

Library of Congress Cataloging-in-Publication Data

Mahoney, Christine.
    Brussels versus the Beltway : advocacy in the United States and the European Union /
Christine Mahoney.
        p. cm. — (American government and public policy)
    Includes bibliographical references and index.
    ISBN-13: 978-1-58901-203-5 (alk. paper)
    1. Pressure groups—United States.   2. Pressure groups—European Union
countries.   3. Lobbying—United States.   4. Lobbying—European Union
countries.   5. Policy networks—United States.   6. Policy networks—European
Union countries.   I. Title.

    JK1118.M285 2008
    324′.40973—dc22   2007032717

∞ This book is printed on acid-free paper meeting the requirements of the American
National Standard for Permanence in Paper for Printed Library Materials.

15 14 13 12 11 10 09 08   9 8 7 6 5 4 3 2
First printing

Printed in the United States of America

Contents

Contents

Illustrations

TABLES

FIGURES

Acknowledgments

FIRST, I WOULD like to thank the 149 advocates who so graciously granted me interviews. Spending more than one hundred hours speaking with these individuals was enlightening and inspiring.

I would also like to thank the Penn State Political Science Department for supporting my research every step of the way, from a summer interviewing in Washington, to a summer interning in Brussels, to a semester studying at Oxford. Thank you to the Fulbright Commission for funding my year of research in Brussels and the Penn State College of Liberal Arts for funding a semester writing in Brussels.

This would not have been possible without the early support of the professors on the Advocacy and Public Policy Project: Frank Baumgartner, Jeffrey Berry, Beth Leech, Marie Hojnacki, and David Kimball. Thanks also to Frank and Jeff for contributing to my dissertation committee along with Donna Bahry, Suzanna DeBoef, Regina Smyth, and John D. McCarthy. Special thanks to Frank Baumgartner for his unwavering support and encouragement over the past eight years. I would never have made it from my time as an undergraduate research assistant, through grad school, and on to my academic career without his guidance, good advice, and friendship.

Thank you also to those who made my time in Belgium enjoyable and taught me a great deal: first, to Kajsa Stenstroem at DLA Piper's Brussels Government Affairs office for providing me with the opportunity to learn about lobbying in the European Union hands-on. Second, to the Free University of Brussels, which gave me an environment in which I could be happy and productive, especially to Patrick Stouthuysen, M. Theo Jans, Kris Deschower, Petra Meier, Irina Stefuriuc, Martine Van Assche, Isabelle Bedoyan, Irina Tanasescu, Marjolein Paantjens, and Dimo Kavadias.

My postdoctoral fellowship at the Moynihan European Research Center in the Moynihan Institute of Global Affairs at Syracuse University's Maxwell School provided me with the time and support to continue the analysis.

Thanks especially to Mitchell Orenstein and Peg Hermann. My faculty position in the Maxwell School has allowed me to see this project through to the book it is.

Many individuals encouraged me along the way. Thanks especially to Sharon Balmer, Matthew Boyer, Daniel Jones-White, Amanda Lynch, Julie Nungester, Leo Pongan, Nick Semanko, and Lauren Shephard. Finally, many thanks to my family—Ann and Karen Mahoney; Karen and Chuck Homer; and Nancy, Valerie, and Jack Allen—for supporting this endeavor.

Introduction

LOBBYING IS A THRIVING industry on both sides of the Atlantic. K Street is notorious in Washington as the locus of high-powered lobbyists, with the Hill as the primary object of their attention. Round Point Schuman and Avenue de Cortenbergh form the geographical center in Brussels, with lobbyists descending on Berlaymont and Parliament. Both systems involve a wide range of advocates[1] juggling for a role in the policymaking process, from beekeepers to chemical manufacturers, environmentalists to fishermen, recreational boaters to soda makers. If you can think of an interest, industry, institution, or idea, you can probably find a representative promoting its case in the two capitals.

The number of citizen groups, lobbying firms, professional associations, geographic representations, corporations, religious groups, think tanks, and foundations that are making sure their concerns are heard in the policymaking process is ever-growing in both the United States and the European Union. In both capitals, their advertisements can be seen in the major newspapers, their posters on bus stops, and their position papers in the offices of policymakers. Literally hundreds of lobbyists can be seen dashing to and from lunchtime meetings nearly every day of the year in the cafes of the Place du Luxembourg and restaurants of Dupont Circle. It seems the work of U.S. and EU advocates is nearly identical. Their aims are the same: influence public policy in their favor; their means appear indistinguishable: letters, e-mails, meetings, advertisements, demonstrations, coalitions, media outreach; and their effect seems similar: watchdog groups in both Washington and Brussels are relentless in their criticism of the influence of special interests. Are U.S. and EU advocacy comparable? Does the same process explain advocacy strategies and advocacy success in both polities?

Some observers would say no. Citing cultural differences, many practitioners and scholars argue lobbying in Brussels is a fundamentally different enterprise than that found across the ocean. Caricatures have developed of advocates in each sphere. The European lobbyist is neutral, amicable, and seeks only to provide helpful information to the EU institutions. The American lobbyist is partisan, forceful, and seeks to manipulate policy to his or her will. The exchange between EU advocates and officials is cordial and collegiate as they work together to shape policy. Interactions between advocates and officials in Washington are combative as lobbyists try to strong-arm politicians with money and threats. While these may be pure forms of the stereotype, many observers rely on some version of them in explaining U.S. and EU advocacy differences.

Euractiv, one of the main EU news outlets, published a special report on U.S. and EU lobbying, noting: "Although lobbying techniques in Brussels and Washington are often considered similar, public affairs professionals on both sides of the Atlantic are convinced that differences in 'style and substance' will remain between the two capitals. Language and national cultures are only part of the explanation. The traditional, consensus-based approach to EU policy-making and lobbying will probably continue to contrast with the highly professionalized and more aggressive U.S.-style for many years to come" (2005a).

The implicit and explicit cultural differences that underlie the descriptions of archetypal American and European lobbyists parallel the narratives told on the larger stage of transatlantic relations. A unilateral Texan cowboy, intent on bullying the world, cannot seem to get along with European statesmen during international diplomatic negotiations whether it be about Iraq, Iran, Kyoto, or GMOs. Whether it is the result of a frontier heritage or the superpower status of the United States or the acumen and reserve that come from two thousand years of war, peace, and culture on the Continent, Americans and Europeans, the stereotype goes, are breeds apart.

Is this the case for the players in the policymaking game in Washington and Brussels? Are American lobbyist cowboys and European lobbyists just more cultured? Do they differ significantly in their advocacy behavior? And if so, can it be explained by their natures? I would argue no; culture is not the primary explanatory factor. This book fleshes out that argument, develops a theory about what does determine U.S. and EU advocacy strategies and advocacy success, and provides significant empirical evidence, both qualitative and quantitative, in support of the proposition that it is institutions, issues, and interest group characteristics, not culture, that largely drive advocacy decisions and the resulting policy outcomes.

IF NOT CULTURE, THEN WHAT?

While cultural differences may appear to explain some of what we observe in the U.S. and EU advocacy communities, upon deeper investigation and systematic study it becomes clear cultural explanations are lacking. American lobbyists do not behave in the archetypal manner at all times and even appear, in some instances, to proceed in the manner thought to be typical of their European counterparts. Likewise, EU advocates engage in American-style lobbying in certain situations. If culture explained the differences, the effect of that pervading force would be felt consistently, not variably. The institutional structure of a political system fundamentally influences advocacy strategies and advocacy success and can better explain the variation in differences we see between the United States and the European Union when it comes to advocacy.

Advocacy is a process that aims to influence public policy. The process is initiated with an advocate's decision to mobilize for a political debate, at which point the advocate determines his or her position on the issue. Once the advocate chooses to engage on an issue, a series of additional decisions need to be made about the advocacy strategy, including what arguments to use, what targets to approach, what direct or inside lobbying tactics to employ, what public education or outside lobbying tactics to engage in, and which allies to work with. The process concludes when the policy debate ends, and this determines the advocate's lobbying success (many times leading to a new advocacy process because issues carry on through time). Each of these sets of decisions, or stages, of the advocacy process can be viewed as dependent variables to be explained.

Three aspects of the institutional structure of a political system are highly significant to the advocacy process: (a) the democratic accountability of policymakers, (b) the rules of the policymaking process, and (c) the nature of the media system that conveys policy-relevant messages. Considering the first aspect, how accountable political institutions are to the people should influence how advocates approach those institutions and how successful they are in influencing the policymaking process. Policymakers who are directly elected by the public to their posts are driven by the reelection motive (Mayhew 1974).[2] If they want to retain their posts, policymakers behave in a manner that will not displease their constituents to the point that they would vote them out of office. This leads advocates targeting elected officials to formulate their advocacy strategies to emphasize how the advocates' position will help (or at least not jeopardize) the policymakers' reelection chances. Such strategy influences the arguments they make; they will frame their positions as being good for the policymakers' constituents, in line with public opinion, and in line with broadly shared values, among others. It affects the targets they select, as lobbyists focus on those who share their perspective and represent geographic regions that share the advocate's values. These policymakers can more easily be convinced that supporting the advocate's position will not be detrimental to them come election time. The presence of the reelection motive also influences the tactics advocates choose to convey their policy messages. Advocates targeting the directly elected are more likely to rely on tactics that highlight the position of the public, such as grassroots and outside lobbying strategies, and signal broad-based support as coalition activity can do.

Advocates targeting nonelected policymakers have no incentive to try to maximize this type of reelection connection. Lacking the leverage that comes with constituent mobilization threats, advocates targeting nonelected policymakers formulate their advocacy strategies to emphasize the importance of the information and expertise they can share. This influences the arguments they make to nonelected policymakers; advocates will focus on the technical— contributing research, data, and sector-specific information to the policymaking process. Their targets will be determined by what institutional units need information and their tactics selected to most efficiently convey that information.

These expectations hold within and across systems. That is, within a political system that has lobbying targets that are both directly elected and not elected, their democratic accountability will drive advocacy strategies toward them. Comparing across systems, advocates targeting policymakers in systems with institutions democratically accountable through direct elections will formulate their advocacy strategies with the reelection motive in mind. Those targeting policymakers in systems without direct elections will formulate their advocacy strategies to emphasize their information provision.

The effect of democratic accountability on lobbying success—that is, whether the advocate saw his or her policy preference realized at the end of the issue debate—is a dependent variable that has to be considered at the system level since the outcome on the issue is determined by the policymaking process of the entire system. This point is made to draw a distinction with the effect of democratic accountability on strategies discussed above, which can vary within a political system. The effect of democratic institutional designs could manifest in a number of ways: groups may be more effective in the aggregate in systems *with* direct elections, they could be more successful in systems *lacking* democratic accountability, it may be the case that it is citizen groups that enjoy influence with directly elected policymakers, or, alternatively, it could be the wealthy groups that can help them get elected who are most influential. Since democratic institutional design determines the motivations of policymakers, it simultaneously impacts the advocates trying to influence those policymakers. The specific hypotheses regarding these relationships are presented in detail in chapter 2.

The rules of the policymaking process are the second aspect of a political system's institutional structure that influences the advocacy process—

both strategies and success. Policymaking rules include the institutional rules that dictate how a proposal becomes and does not become a law and what institutions, institutional subunits, and policymakers will be included in the policy debate. Since these rules determine who is involved in the political game on any given issue, the rules of the policymaking process influence an advocate's choice of targets and the selection of tactics to use to most effectively communicate to those policymakers. Policymaking rules also affect the likelihood of policy change since different rules make it more or less difficult to get legislation passed. Advocates operating under rules that minimize the probability of policy change are more likely to adopt blocking positions, while advocates operating under rules that maximize the likelihood of policy change will tend to assume modifying positions. In addition, rules that affect the likelihood of policy change can in turn influence an advocate's lobbying success. Thus, fairly mundane institutional rules are expected to have a significant impact on advocacy strategies and advocacy success.

The third and final institutional aspect critical to advocacy is the nature of the political system's media machine. Advocacy is about communicating your message to lawmakers, and in many political systems the media are a major conduit of political communications. In modern democracies the media play a critical role conveying information from political elite to the public, as well as relaying information about public opinion and concerns to the political elites (Cater 1959; Cook 2005). The strength and scope of a political system's media machine have very real implications for an entire category of advocacy activities—outside lobbying. In systems with greater media reach, advocates are more likely to work to mobilize the grassroots, place issue advertisements to inform the public of policy topics, promote news coverage of an issue, or organize protests and demonstrations. While the effect of the nature of the media system is constrained to one stage of the advocacy process, it is a critical stage since it links to the citizenry.

Institutional design is not the only force determining advocacy strategies and success in any polity; two other sets of factors also play a role: issue and interest characteristics. To understand how advocates devise advocacy campaigns and if they succeed in achieving their advocacy goals, one has to consider the nature of the issue at hand—if it is highly salient, if it is regulatory or legislative, if it is a massive initiative or a minuscule proposal, if there are high or low levels of conflict with staunchly opposed adversaries. All of these factors drive lobbying decisions and influence the success of advocates in all democratic systems. In addition, the characteristics of advocates—who they represent, their resources, their structure, their membership, among others—also contribute to advocacy strategy decisions and their chances for success. These factors are discussed in more detail in chapter 2.

PREVIOUS LITERATURE ON ADVOCACY

The subfield of comparative interest groups studies is quite small, although interest in comparing advocacy across political systems is rising, as indicated by the growing number of preliminary conference papers and research agendas. There have been a handful of studies comparing lobbying activities in the United States, the United Kingdom, and the European Union (McGrath 2005; Thomas and Hrebenar 2000; Thomas 1993), but they have been qualitative and descriptive undertakings, and have failed to look systematically at the factors influencing advocacy in the two polities.

The bulk of comparative interest group research has focused on classifying national interest group systems as either corporatist or pluralist. Using as indicators the size of groups, the number of groups, and the existence of formal structures for interest intermediation, scholars have attempted to assign political systems to various categories and typologies, including pluralist, corporatist, clientele, statist, neocorporatist, network, and elite pluralist, among others (Streeck and Schmitter 1991; Siaroff 1999; Lijphart 1999; Eising 2005). The aim of most of this work has been either to describe or to determine the relationship between interest intermediation and democracy or socioeconomic performance (Eising 2005, 3). It is not immediately clear from this literature how the various interest intermediation patterns would influence advocacy strategy selection.

Combing the large but distinct bodies of literature on U.S. interest groups and advocacy and on EU groups and lobbying, however, provides a foundation for the theorizing and hypothesis-building presented in chapter 2. In response to the thriving lobbying communities in the United States and the European Union, scholarship on advocacy in both polities has flourished, albeit separately. The extant work highlights how issues and interest characteristics are important factors determining advocacy strategies.

In the European Union, a great deal of work has been done on advocacy activity in certain policy areas: the electronics industry (Cawson 1992), telecommunications (Schneider 1992), biotech (Greenwood 1994), fruit trade policy (Pedler 1994), aviation (Van den Polder 1994), transport (Stevens 2004), postal policy (Campbell 1994), and the environment (McCormick 1999; Rucht 2001; Boyd 2002; Long, Salter, and Singer 2002). These works considered jointly demonstrate how advocacy differs depending on the policy area and issue.

Considerable research also has been conducted on various types of actors active in the EU policymaking arena: business/economic groups (McLaughlin et al. 1993; Coen 2002; Bouwen 2002; Grossman 2004), trade associations, (Martin and Ross 2001), farmers (Klandermans et al. 2001; Bush and Simi 2001), "diffuse interests" (Pollack 1997), regional interests (Keating and

Hooghe 2001), and professional lobbyists or consultancies (Lahusen 2002). Through these studies of various categories of actors, authors have attempted to uncover the advocacy practices of different types of advocates. Considering the individual pieces of scholarship jointly suggests lobbying varies by interest group—that is, farmers are more formally included in decision making on the Common Agricultural Policy, diffuse interests find it difficult to access the commission, trade associations coordinate the work of their national components. Other scholars have sought to shed light on the similarities and differences of interest groups through general surveys of a range of advocate types (Greenwood 1997, 2002; Coen 1997, 2002; Marks, Haesly, and Mbaye 2001; Kriesi, Adam, and Jochum 2005).

These earlier works on interest groups and advocacy in the European Union, taken together, demonstrate the importance of issue and interest characteristics in explaining advocacy. However, no single study has been designed that could simultaneously consider the effect of both issue variation and interest variation on advocacy strategies and advocacy success. Studies of any one issue area lack variation on issue factors. Studies of any one advocate type lack variation on interest group characteristics. Moreover, they also tend to lack variation on issue context, since advocates are studied in a general manner through surveys that do not gather information on specific issues or the political context of a case. Thus, in the EU literature, there is a lack of variation in institutions since the focus is on one polity, and a lack of variation in issues or interests depending on the topic of the case study. Regardless of the study's focus, two critical levels are always held constant.

In the United States, previous research also gives strong credence to the idea that issue and interest characteristics matter when it comes to understanding advocacy strategies and success, but this body of work also leaves out an important component influencing advocacy—institutions. In the literature on American interest groups we have not seen a systematic study of the effect of democratic institutional design because we lack variation in institutions. In the United States, rigorous empirical and theoretical work on advocacy has been thriving for decades. Group theory has developed considerably since the early work of Bentley (1908), Truman (1951), and Milbrath (1963). Volumes have been written on mobilization (Dahl 1961; Olson 1965; Walker 1983), lobbying tactics (Schlozman and Tierney 1986; Berry 1989; Baumgartner and Leech 1998), lobbying coalitions (Hula 1999; Hojnacki 1998; Whitford 2003), lobbying targets (Bauer, Pool, and Dexter 1963; Austen-Smith and Wright 1994; Hojnacki and Kimball 1998), and advocate influence (Smith 1984; Gerber 1999; Smith 2000; Tauber 1998). What has been missing is study of the effect of institutional structure on each of these critical aspects of lobbying—an unavoidable omission when the critical independent variable is constant across cases. Thus, while scholarship on American groups has greatly advanced our understanding of the advocacy process on numerous fronts, the effect of institutional design on that process continues to elude us.

Only when we move to a comparative framework, looking at advocacy activity across polities, across issues, and across advocates, can we begin to understand the full process at play determining advocacy strategies and success. This is precisely what my study does and this research design is an important departure from previous research on lobbying. Rather than holding the factors driving advocacy strategies and success constant, as is typical, the research presented here is based on cases randomly selected to cover the full range of policy activities in the European Union and the United States. The cases involve substantial variability in issue salience, scope, policy domain, and conflict. The array of advocates involved in the study ranges from trade associations to citizen groups to corporations. And of course, with the same methodology followed in the United States and the EU, the study allows comparison across institutions as well.

CHAPTER LAYOUT

This book presents the first large-scale quantitative study of advocacy in the United States and the European Union. Drawing on 149 in-depth interviews with advocates in the two capitals who are active on 47 political issues, I detail the determinants of American and European advocacy strategies and their lobbying success.

An introductory section detailing the political systems and the advocacy communities of the United States and the European Union follows this introduction. Chapter 1, an overview of the two political systems, is provided for those readers not familiar with one or the other or both polities. The structure of the governing institutions, media systems, and advocacy communities is detailed. Chapter 2 lays out the theoretical approach of the research, the framework for explaining advocacy. A comprehensive study of U.S. and EU advocacy is achieved by identifying key factors at the institutional, issue, and interest group levels and their relationship to the advocacy process. Chapter 3, Researching Advocacy, describes the research design, the sample of cases, and the advocates interviewed.

Each of the following six chapters is devoted to a single stage of the advocacy process. Each includes theoretical discussions and empirical evidence—both quantitative and qualitative—of the determinants of decisions in that advocacy stage. Chapter 4 discusses the approach lobbyists in the United States and the European Union take toward a policy debate. The differences in lobbying approaches—whether a lobbyist is seeking to promote a proposal, modify it, or kill it—depend on the institutional setting and the issue characteristics at hand, not on innate cultural tendencies. Chapter 5 looks at the argumentation strategies lobbyists employ. The findings show remarkably similar argumentation types in the two polities but demonstrate that they are used with different frequency. Chapter 6 investigates the differing targeting strategies of U.S. and EU lobbyists.

Chapters 7 and 8 present the findings regarding the tactics advocates use. Chapter 7 deals with inside lobbying tactics, those strategies employed by lobbyists in political capitals, communicating directly to policymakers (e.g., face-to-face meetings, Dear Colleague letters, and cocktail parties, and drafting legislative language.) The findings demonstrate that lobbyists in the United States and the European Union are using very similar tactical repertoires and that issue characteristics affect inside lobbying decisions in similar ways in the two capitals. Chapter 8 addresses outside lobbying tactics, those strategies that work to influence policymakers through the public, mobilizing constituents with press releases, political advertisements, and grassroots letter-writing campaigns.

Networking and coalitions are detailed in chapter 9. This chapter demonstrates the varying propensity for American and European lobbyists to create ad hoc issue coalitions and the similarity of their networking strategies. Chapter 10 considers the final stage of the advocacy process, lobbying success. The same sets of factors that explain advocacy strategy decisions also help explain who wins and loses in political debates. This chapter shows how the U.S. system tends toward more winner-take-all outcomes, with business, more often than not, seeing its goals realized. The EU system, on the other hand, tends toward compromised success, with more advocates, business, and citizen groups emerging at least somewhat victorious.

The conclusion draws the findings together to summarize the similarities and differences between lobbying in the United States and the European Union. It also discusses how these findings extend to the comparative study of interest groups more broadly.

NOTES

1. Much debate surrounds the proper term to use when studying advocacy. Interest groups, organized interests, civil society organizations, and lobbying groups all connote some type of group, leaving out the other important players in all lobbying communities, such as individual firms, institutions, and other governmental units and lobbying, law, and PR firms. The term "advocate"—any entity attempting to influence the policymaking process—successfully captures all these actor types and is therefore used throughout the text.

2. The term "directly elected" is used to distinguish popularly elected policymakers from those elected by parliaments or governmental committees.

3.1936

1
The U.S. and EU Political Systems

THIS CHAPTER BRIEFLY introduces the two polities for those readers not familiar with one or the other political system and highlights the most pertinent institutional factors for the research presented in the following chapters. The U.S. and EU political systems have a great deal in common. Both have a federated structure with some responsibilities, or competencies, resting with the central level, some with the component state governments, and other jurisdictions shared between the two (Anderson 2002; Hooghe and Marks 2003). Both have an executive branch, a dual-chamber legislature, and a judiciary (Dinan 2005). Both the U.S. and EU systems are characterized by separation of powers, with the executive, legislative, and judicial branches operating largely independently of each other. The composition of the legislature does not determine the makeup of the government as in parliamentary systems (Pollack 1997, 575; Hix, Raunio, and Scully 2003, 192; Hix, Kreppel, and Noury 2003, 318). The interest group systems in both polities are characterized by both academics and observers as generally pluralist (Streeck and Schmitter 1991).

First the U.S. system is described, including a description of the institutions, the electoral process, the policymaking process, and the nature of the media community; this is followed by an overview of lobbying in Washington. Next, the institutions and selection process of EU officials are discussed, the process of EU policymaking explained, and the nature of the pan-EU media system described. Last is a section about lobbying in Brussels.

The U.S. Political System

While the bulk of scholarship on the European Union in the past fifty years shows a system in flux, the U.S. political system's institutions have been largely stable. The primary policymaking institutions are the U.S. Congress, made up of two chambers—the House of Representatives and the Senate—the executive branch, composed of its many agencies and departments, and the White House.

The Congress is the subject of much scholarly research and the primary focus of interest group scholars. The one hundred members of the U.S. Senate are directly elected by the constituents of their states. One-third of the Senate is elected every two years for a term of six years. The 435 members of the House are directly elected every two years by the constituents in their districts. Congressional districts are drawn according to population, as determined by the U.S. census. Both chambers divide work among numerous standing committees and subcommittees.

The president of the United States is elected by the Electoral College, created to appease both federalists and antifederalists during the Constitutional Convention. Each state gets as many electoral college votes as it has senators and representatives. All the states except two, Nebraska and Maine, award all of their votes to whichever candidate gets the majority of votes in the popular election in the state. For example if 60 percent of New Yorkers vote for the Democratic candidate, all 31 electoral college votes go to that candidate. There are 538 votes in the Electoral College and the candidate with the absolute majority (270) votes wins (Kernell and Jacobson 2006). The administration that wins decides on political appointments to lead the executive branch agencies and departments.

The primary policymaking procedure is legislative, comprising four forms of congressional action: bills, joint resolutions, concurrent resolutions, and simple resolutions (Johnson 2000). Bills and joint resolutions are nearly identical and are dealt with in the same manner. Concurrent and simple resolutions are mainly used for changes to operations in the chambers or for conveying a sense of Congress. The standard process for bills and joint resolutions proceeds as follows: A bill is introduced by a member of Congress or the administration may communicate a proposal to the speaker of the House and the president of the Senate; the proposal is technically introduced by the chair or ranking member of the relevant committee (ibid.). It is assigned to the relevant committee, which will debate the proposal, possibly hold public hearings on the topic, table amendments to the proposal, and finally vote on the amended proposal.

If the bill passes out of committee, it goes to the floor to be voted on in the full chamber. In the House a simple majority is needed. In the Senate a simple majority is technically needed, but the right of Senators to filibuster a proposal—that is the right to debate endlessly—often leads to super-majoritarian outcomes, because it requires three-fifths of the chamber to invoke cloture overriding the filibuster (Krehbiel 1998). If the bill passes in one chamber, it must be passed in identical form in the other chamber. If it passes in the other chamber but differs in form or content, then there are two options:

There can be a back-and-forth negotiation between the two chambers, each alternatively voting on the amended bill from the other chamber until there is agreement; or a conference committee can be appointed with representatives from both chambers to negotiate a compromise and then both chambers vote on the conferenced bill. Once the bill is passed in Congress it is sent to the president for signing. Copies of the bill are also issued to relevant departments so they may advise the president on the issue. The president can sign the bill into law, do nothing in which case the bill becomes law after ten days, or veto the bill. If he decides to veto, Congress can overturn the veto by a two-thirds majority in both chambers.

The legislative calendar is organized by two-year "congresses." Thousands of legislative proposals, or bills, are introduced each congress but most never become law. Many die in committee, because they are voted down or not acted upon; still others die on the chamber floor, or are vetoed by the president. Alternatively, if a bill is never voted on during a two-year congress, it is automatically killed. Policy change, in short, is not assured in the U.S. system when a policy is proposed.

The executive branch is composed of numerous departments and agencies, all with various bureaus ranging from the Agency for International Development to the Commodity Futures Trading Commission to the U.S. Forest Service. Nearly every industry sector is regulated by one body or another. Regulatory lawmaking is controlled by the agency in charge of the policy area. For example environmental regulations are developed and implemented by the Environmental Protection Agency; the Federal Energy Regulatory Commission regulates the electricity and natural gas industries; control of prescription drugs is under the Food and Drug Administration. The standard process for regulatory policymaking is for the agency to release a Notice of Proposed Rule Making. Then consultations are held to which organized interests, firms, and corporations are welcome to contribute. Once the agency compiles feedback from organized interests, and revises the proposed rule, it is released.

The media have always played a central role in American politics, which led Cater in 1959 to refer to the media as the "fourth branch of government" (Cater 1959). National newspapers, television programs, and syndicated radio broadcasts convey messages to the public in a single language across the country. The media are the main communication conduit between the government and the public. The media act as observers, watchdogs, and critics of the government, conveying stories about government activity to the citizens. In fact, the media are the main source of the public's political information. At the same time, the media are also communicating to government officials and elected representatives the issues that are important to the public and the nature of public opinion on those issues (Cook 2005). Because the media are independent, they have a great deal of latitude in deciding news coverage and content and therefore play an important agenda-setting role. If advocates want to shape public and elite opinion on an issue, it is critical to engage with the media—promoting coverage of an issue, preferably in the direction of their preferences.

Advocates engage in tactics that attempt to use the media to magnify their voice. By communicating directly with reporters through phone calls, meetings, press releases, press conferences, and op-ed writing, advocates work to foster favorable news coverage. In addition, advocates can use tactics that are newsworthy in their own right to promote coverage of their position and convey the intensity of public preferences regarding an issue—activities such as protests, demonstrations, rallies, and other creative attention-getting events like hanging massive signs from skyscrapers or dressing up like detained enemy combatants in orange jumpsuits. By achieving favorable news coverage advocates get their message out to politicians and to additional segments of the public that may support their cause.

The U.S. system then is characterized by a high degree of democratic accountability through direct election of policymakers; a low probability of policy change, because the rules of the policymaking process lead to more bill death than the birth of new laws; and a high level of political communication through the cross-country media system.

It should be noted that the U.S. system is in no way an ideal type. There are numerous faults with an electoral system that is driven by money and that provides advantages to incumbents. Because of gerrymandering, franking rights, funded trips home to the district, name recognition, pork barreling, and constituency service, incumbents are more likely to be reelected than not (Jacobson 2004). These factors, combined with demographically safe districts, result in uncompetitive elections; challengers either can't compete or don't even bother to compete. However, as much as the incumbency advantage is lamented by some in the United States, it is explained in large part by constituency service and representation—it is because policymakers are held accountable that they seek to please their constituents. Because they so often do respond to constituency preferences, they are reelected in droves. When they fail to respond, they can be, and are, kicked out of office.

THE U.S. INTEREST GROUP SYSTEM

Organized interests of course have been active in the U.S. system since the country's inception. James Madison (1787) warned of the dangers of organized interests—or factions—in his call for a political Union in *The Federalist Papers*:

> Among the numerous advantages promised by a well constructed Union, none deserves to be more accurately developed than its tendency to break

and control the violence of faction. . . . By a faction, I understand a number of citizens, whether amounting to a majority or a minority of the whole, who are united and actuated by some common impulse of passion, or of interest, adverse to the rights of other citizens, or to the permanent and aggregate interests of the community. . . . There are two methods of curing the mischiefs of faction: the one, by removing its causes; the other, by controlling its effects.

The republic the Federalists called for was indeed established, but how well-controlled the mischiefs of faction have been is still up for debate. President Wilson in 1913 felt lobbyists were running rampant in the capital, especially those opposed to tariff reform. He sought to alert people to their pressure: "Washington has seldom seen so numerous, so industrious, or so insidious a body. The newspapers are being filled with paid advertisements calculated to mislead the judgment of public men not only, but also the public opinion of the country itself. There is every evidence that money without limit is being spent to sustain this lobby" (quoted in Byrd 1987).

Ernest Griffith's (1939) *The Impasse of Democracy* suggested a powerful role of organized interests. He argued that to understand politics it was not the formal institutions that should be studied but the whirlpools of activity surrounding various policy areas. "These people in their various permutations and combinations are continually meeting in each other's offices, at various clubs, lunching together, and participating in legislative hearings or serving on important but obscure committees set up within the departments" (Griffith 1939, 182). Interactions between lobbyists, legislators, and regulators were fairly informal and through these connections policy was shaped.

The works of Cater (1964) and Maass (1951) similarly portrayed interest groups as wielding considerable power in the U.S. political system. So called "iron triangles" composed of special interests, congressional committees, and executive agencies were devising policy with little outside interference. One of the most discussed iron triangles was that surrounding defense procurement. In President Eisenhower's farewell address he warned of the "conjunction of an immense military establishment and a large arms industry" and of "the potential for the disastrous rise of misplaced power" (Cater 1964, 26). Cater discusses the pervasiveness of the military-industrial complex: "Even the barest sketch of the physical anatomy of the defense-industrial complex can provoke grave concerns. It is big on a scale not even imagined by the organization men only a few years ago. It is far-reaching, affecting men's lives and thoughts to a degree that we perceive only vaguely" (ibid., 31). Truman (1951) argued that interest associations were of fundamental concern because of their great numbers and that their numbers would continue to grow as societal complexity, specialization, and group mobilization led to ever more group mobilization (1951, 60). Political scientists in the mid-twentieth century saw the role of groups as so central that group theorists like Latham attempted to understand politics writ large through groups, as he did in his *The Group Basis of Politics* (1952).

However, the dominance of the group approach began to wane. The central role of "pressure groups" was questioned by the research of Milbrath (1963) and Bauer, Pool, and Dexter (1963), which showed lobbyists to be little more than "service bureaus" assisting congressional staffers. Olson's *The Logic of Collective Action* (1965) further suppressed an intensive focus on lobbying as a central component of politics and policymaking. Group theorists shifted away from trying to explain the entire political system, to simply trying to explain the existence of groups (Salisbury 1969; Moe 1980; Walker 1983; Rothenberg 1988).

Modern interest group studies have broadened their scope, attempting to explain a wide range of interest-related phenomena, including coalition activity (Hula 1995; Hojnacki 1997, 1998; Whitford 2003); networks (Heclo 1978; Salisbury et al. 1987; Heinz et al. 1990); political action committees (PACs) (McCarty and Rothenberg 1996; Romer and Snyder 1994; Hojnacki and Kimball 2001; Wawro 2001; Wright 1985); targets (Austen-Smith and Wright 1994; Hojnacki and Kimball 1998; Hall 1998); venue shopping (Baumgartner and Jones 1993); framing (Riker 1986; McKissick 1995); influence (Gerber 1999; Smith 1984; Tauber 1998); interaction with public opinion (Smith 2000; Burnstein 2003); and outside lobbying (Kollman 1998; Goldstein 1999), among others. Indeed, as many studies documented the interest group explosion in the United States (i.e., Walker 1983; Baumgartner and Mahoney 2004), the scholarship on the subject kept pace.

Lobbying in the United States is regulated by the 1995 Lobby Disclosure Act, which requires lobbyists to register with the Senate, reporting the amount of money spent on advocacy and the issues on which the organization was active. Any hired lobbyists must also file a report on behalf of their clients. As the debate on lobbying regulation rages in the European Union, which is discussed in more detail in the next section, the topic has resurfaced in the United States as well. An editorial in late 2005 in the *New York Times,* "The Lobbying-Industrial Complex," called for a stricter system of regulation than the one currently in place:

> The founding fathers' vision of a citizen's basic right to "petition the government for a redress of grievances" has turned into a multibillion-dollar influence industry that is far too loosely tracked and regulated. The lobbyists' symbiotic relationship with lawmakers is based on their inside track as Capitol buttonholers and the campaign money trail, where lobbyists help to ensure that incumbents are enriched and their gratitude secured. . . . Clearly, it is time to enact credible controls.

Worthy proposals have been submitted for clearer electronic tracking of spending, the curtailing of congressional junkets arranged by lobbyists, and tighter controls on the leaps to private-sector riches that congressional and White House specialists routinely make. (*New York Times*, Aug. 26, 2005, 18)

Calls for increased regulation have been systematically countered by arguments that lobbying is a form of free speech. Understandably, lobbyists lobby against regulation and tend to water down controls on factions in American politics. However, they were not able to block the proposal for stricter regulations that led to passage of the Honest Leadership and Open Government Act in September 2007.

THE EU POLITICAL SYSTEM

The European Union began as a response to war. The battles that raged across the continent for hundreds of years came to a climax of destruction with World War II. Once the Allies had defeated the Axis powers, it was clear a new approach was necessary. The solution to division and war was peace through economic unity. To deal with the difficult question over the rehabilitation of the Saar, the Ruhr, and Germany generally, Jean Monnet, director of the French Modernization Plan and a crucial personality in European integration, developed the idea of a supranational European Coal and Steel Community, the ECSC. "The immediate political aim of the ECSC was to avoid the risk of future conflict between France and Germany by linking the two basic elements in their economies, the production of coal and the manufacture of steel, more closely together" (Thody 1997, 1). Monnet proposed this idea to French foreign minister Robert Schuman, and the Schuman Plan was announced on May 9, 1950, with an invitation for other European countries to join.

A stable Germany was necessary for future peace, and this view was supported by the United States through the Marshall Plan. The means by which future German aggression was to be kept in check was to ensure that the country "be linked so organically with its neighbors, and that the link should appear so evidently in the self-interest both of Germans and of all the other nationalities, that another war between the nations of Western Europe would become impossible" (Leonard 1988, 4). This was the basis for the Treaty of Paris, signed in 1951 by France, Germany, Italy, and the Benelux countries establishing the ECSC. The treaty established the supranational structures that would be reformed and revised to become today's European institutions (Pinder 1988). The ECSC was a concrete step toward European integration and, in Monnet's view, it would be a federalist, not intergovernmental, integration. When the countries decided to take part in the ECSC "all participants had to accept the principle of shared sovereignty, whatever that would turn out to mean in practice" (Dinan 1999, 24).

The Treaty of Rome, signed March 25, 1957, expanded the cooperation of the ECSC to the common market. The European Economic Community (EEC) and the European Atomic Energy Community (Euratom) came into effect in January 1958 (Dinan 1999). The Treaty on the European Union (TEU), signed in Maastricht in 1992, established the European Union (McAllister 1997). Countless histories of the European Union have been written describing the development of the institutions and the process of integration (Pinder 1988; Dinan 1999; Urwin 1995; Gillingham 2003). In brief, over the next half century, European integration continued, numerous treaties were signed, more member states joined, thousands of regulations, directives, and other types of legislation were passed, jurisdiction grew, agencies were created, institutions reformed, a common currency introduced—all leading to the supranational structure of the European Union that exists today.

The three primary institutions involved in policymaking are the European Commission, the Council, and the European Parliament (EP).[1] The Commission constitutes the first half, the Council being the second, of the dual executive of the European Union. In its executive capacity the Commission is in charge of "administering and implementing Community policy, managing the budget, and conducting external relations" (Dinan 1999, 223). The Commission also has the exclusive right to initiate legislation. The College of Commissioners is composed of one commissioner from each member state. All commissioners are considered equals. They are appointed by their member governments for five-year terms with no term limits (Dinan 1999, 215). Commission appointments and terms of office parallel the elections and terms of office of the EP.

The president of the Commission is nominated at the beginning of the Commission's term in office and approved with the rest of the commission-designate by the EP (Dinan 2005). Considered a "first among equals," the president allocates portfolios among his or her colleagues, "prepares the annual work programme of the Commission, sets the agenda of meetings of the College and is in charge of the Secretariat General" (Hix 1999, 34). The EU civil service, with an approximate staff of 17,000, further supports the commissioners' work. The Commission bureaucracy is organized into 36 directorates-general (DGs) and services; these are organizationally similar to member state government ministries. "Each DG has responsibility for policy initiation and management in a particular policy area . . . However the division of competences between the DGs is at a lower-level of policy competence than in most national administrations" (Hix 1999, 37).

In its executive capacity the Commission does not have complete control over the implementation of EU policy. The Council established a procedure known as "comitology" to monitor the Commission's executive proposals. The "comitology procedure includes three types of committees—advisory, management, and regulatory—all chaired by Commission officials but made up of national civil servants" (Dinan 1999, 228). If the Commission's plans for the implementation of a policy are not in accordance with the committee's opinions the matter is referred to the Council for a decision (Europa 2006). In addition to the standing committees the comitology procedure also includes "temporary committees of representatives of private interest groups in areas where it feels wider consultation is necessary; and committees of scientists and 'experts' give advice on technical issues" (Hix 1999, 42). The number of these committees continues to grow. "With the extension of community competences, the 'comitology' structure has been greatly expanded: there are a few thousand of these committees now" (Christiansen 1996, 89). In effect, these committees keep the Commission's power in check during implementation.

The Council, therefore, makes up the second half of the dual executive, along with the Commission, and has a role in policy implementation through the comitology process. However, it also acts as a colegislator with the EP. "The European Union has a classic two-chamber legislature in which the Council represents the 'states,' and the EP represents the 'citizens.' In contrast to many other legislatures, however, the Council is more powerful than the EP" (Hix 1999, 56). And, while the Council acts as an elected chamber, its members are not directly elected to their European posts. Some Council members are national nonelected ministers appointed by their respective national governments to oversee a given policy area who are then seconded to the supranational level at periodic intervals, monthly or bimonthly, to represent their governments in negotiations on EU policy proposals.

For example, the French government appoints an experienced French farm association advocate as its Minister of Agriculture. He acts as France's Minister of Agriculture, dealing with French agricultural issues, but also sits with his European counterparts when the Agriculture Council is convened in Brussels to decide matters in the Council. Other ministers are elected officials, elected domestically to their national parliaments and then appointed to the government cabinet as a minister. This is the format in Ireland, where the Minister of Finance is an elected member of the lower house, or Dáil Éireann. While some ministers are elected in their national political systems and others are appointed, all are appointed to their EU posts. Council members then cannot be removed from their EU office for their political decisions; they can however be removed by being removed in their own personal election if they are from a member state in which ministers are elected, or they can be removed if their entire government is removed en masse in the next national election.

The fact that they are not directly elected to their European posts elongates the chain of democratic accountability (Arnold 1990). Council ministers can be removed from their posts on account of their EU political decisions but it requires more steps than in a national setting—EU officials must act in the EU capacity, that information must get to voters, voters displeased must throw out the national government, which in turn removes the minister from his or her EU post. In addition, it is more difficult for information about their EU actions to reach domestic and local constituencies due to lack of news coverage of EU politics and lack of interest in EU issues.

Furthermore, the significance of EU decisions must be weighed against domestic political activity, which often looms larger in the minds of voters. These factors lead members of the Council, even though many are elected officials and all are representatives of elected governments, to have more autonomy in EU decision making than would be the case in national arenas. This has implications for EU lobbyists targeting those officials, as will be discussed in chapter 2. Throughout the text, when I reference how members of the Council and other EU officials are not directly elected I am seeking to highlight how they are not directly elected to their European posts by a European constituency that directly holds them accountable for their decisions regarding EU policy.

While there is officially only one Council, different sets of ministers meet in various configurations such as the General Affairs Council, made up of foreign affairs ministers, the Economic and Financial Affairs Council (EcoFin) made up of finance ministers, the Justice and Home Affairs Council made up of justice and home affairs ministers, and a number of other councils representing different policy areas. These councils decide on proposals submitted by the Commission. The presidency of the Council circulates among the member states every six months. Assisting the Council in their deliberations over submitted proposals is the Committee of Permanent Representatives (COREPER), "a highly influential committee of the member states' most senior civil servants" (Dinan 1999, 260).[2]

The Council is also known as the "Council of the European Union" and the "Council of Ministers"; it should not be confused with the European Council, which is composed of the heads of state and government of the member states and meets at regular summits.[3] The European Council deals with important and often contentious issues that could not be resolved at lower levels of governance. Often summit outcomes solve a number of political problems through package deals in which the heads of state and government concede on issues of less importance to them in order to see their preferences achieved on policies of higher priority for their country. The European Council then is the most democratically accountable body in the European Union and deals with issues of the highest importance to the Union. However, the European

Council does not weigh in on a wide range of EU policy questions that can be dealt with at lower levels of authority.

The EP, as mentioned, is the colegislator of the European Union, along with the Council. The EP currently consists of 785 members of parliament (MEPs), which have been directly elected since 1979. The elections and five-year EP term parallel the appointment and term of office of the commission. Plenary sessions are held one week a month in Strasbourg and MEPs spend the remaining three weeks meeting in standing committees and subcommittees in Brussels (Dinan 1999, 268). The parliamentary leadership includes the Bureau of the Parliament, the Conference of Presidents (CoP), and the Conference of Committee Chairs. The Bureau is composed of the EP president, the vice presidents, and the quaestors—these are MEPs who make important day-to-day administrative decisions (Composition du Bureau du Parlement, January 16, 2002). The CoP consists of the EP president and the presidents of all the party groups (Membres de la Conference des Presidents, January 14, 2002). MEPs affiliate with the party groups according to their political ideology; nationality plays no role in party composition. There are seven political groups and a group of nonattached or independent members. The two largest groups that dominate the composition of the EP are the Socialist Group (PES) and the European People's Party (Christian Democrats)/European Democrats (EPP-ED).

While the three primary EU institutions do vary to some degree in their level of democratic accountability, the EU's democratic credentials as a whole have been criticized. Weiler, Haltern, and Mayer (1995) articulated the common critique of democracy in the European Union. Drawing on academic writing, political statements, and media observations they note that the "Standard Version" of the democratic deficit laments the distance of the European Union from its citizens: the decrease in legitimacy of the European Union due to the decrease in democracy; the lack of parliamentary accountability and the shift of power from parliaments to the executive; the imbalance in power between diffuse interests, who benefit from majoritarian institutions, and specific interests, who can use money and direct lobbying to wield power in nonmajoritarian institutions; the lack of judicial control over primary legislation; the drift of policy outputs away from the median voter due to qualified majority voting; and finally the general lack of transparency across EU institutions.

Other scholars, most notably Moravscik (2002) and Majone (1998), argue that there is not a democratic deficit. They have pointed to the fact that the Council of Ministers is composed of elected officials and represents elected national governments, as do the members of the Commission. These national governments are accountable and thus EU officials are indirectly accountable through those governments. This is in addition to the MEPs who are directly elected by the European public. According to this school of thinking the European Union is sufficiently democratic.

Follesdal and Hix (2006) counter Moravscik and Majone and argue that in addition to the aspects of the democratic deficit mentioned by Weiler et al. (1995) the European Union does not deal only with issues that should be isolated from majoritarian politics or issues that are inherently uninteresting to EU citizens, and that in fact the European Union legislates and regulates on topics that should incorporate the preferences of the EU public. They also further elaborate on the shortcomings of the EP and why it fails to offset the weakening of national parliamentary control.

There are a number of factors that detract from the EP's democratic credentials. First, all member states now use some form of proportional representation in EP elections (the UK previously used a first-past-the-post system) but there remains variation in whether member states link MEPs to geographic constituencies or not. MEPs represent a geographic constituency in five of the twenty-seven member states, including Wales in the United Kingdom or Nord-Ouest in France, but those geographic constituencies do not correspond to the constituencies used in national elections (Dinan 2005, 266). The vast majority of MEPs do not represent specific geographic constituencies within their home countries. In the other twenty-two member states MEPs are elected to represent the entire country. This, of course, makes it difficult for MEPs to be responsive and accountable to the preferences of their constituents because the entire population makes up their constituency, with all the variation in preferences that that entails.

Second, the candidate lists for EP elections are drawn up by national parties, not EP political groups. This means that if MEPs want to be reelected they need to be responsive to the national party's preferences rather than the EP political group's preferences (Kreppel 2002). This is related to the third factor that detracts from the EP's democratic accountability: EP election campaigns are run by national parties, not EP political groups, and focus on national issues, not EU issues (Kreppel 2002; Dinan 2005; Hix, Raunio, and Scully 2003). These two factors taken together imply that the democratic causal chain is not functioning at the EU level. For party politics to work requires that political parties take positions on issues and make promises regarding policymaking and then, if elected, act on those promises. Voters must have knowledge of those actions (or lack of action). During the next election, voters decide whether to reelect or throw out parties based on their legislative behavior (Arnold 1990). For this process to operate at the EU level would require EP political groups to take positions on EU issues, European voters having knowledge of their legislative behavior on EU issues, and either reelecting or throwing out EP political groups and their candidates according to their record. This is not happening. European political groups are not campaigning in the member states on EU issues. As Follesdal and Hix note, "There is no electoral contest for political leadership at the European level or the basic direction of the EU policy agenda . . . the processes of electing national politicians and even the members of the European Parliament are not contests about the content or direction of EU policy" (2006, 552).

Consequently, European voters are not hearing about EU issues during EP elections because MEP candidates are not campaigning on EU issues. Compounding this, news coverage in the member states of EU issues remains low throughout the legislative term. Thus, when the next European election rolls around, European voters don't know where the European political groups stand on the issues, they don't know what they did on the issues, and thus they cannot vote them out of office if they acted against voter preferences.

This leads us to the fifth factor diminishing EP's democratic accountability: interest in and turnout for EP elections are notoriously low and continue to decrease over time (Dinan 2005, 266). Gabel (2003) analyzes Eurobarometer data and finds support for the EP to be low on a number of indicators including survey instruments asking respondents whether they think the EP's decisions are in their interests, whether the EP can be relied on to protect their interests, and whether they favor an increased role for the EP (ibid., 294).

Low interest and low turnout may be due to lack of information about the EP, to negative news coverage of the EP including stories on scandal, graft, and waste, or to the low quality of MEP candidates (Dinan 2005). Whatever the reason, research has shown that "EP elections have essentially been 'second-order national contests': fought by national parties (and covered by national media) largely on national issues rather than on European integration . . . National parties have generally convinced voters that EP elections are essentially 'super opinion polls,' and have little substantive impact" (Hix, Raunio, and Scully 2003).

In short, two of the EU institutions lack democratic accountability through direct elections of the officials to their European posts and the one institution that is directly elected is rife with democratic deficiencies. The EU system on the whole is largely not democratically accountable. Some would argue the European Union is an international organization (IO) rather than a polity and so does not require traditional democratic institutions (Moravcsik 2002). Others counter that the European Union has moved far beyond an IO to become a system of governance, making policy that reaches across the European Union and affects the lives of hundreds of millions of European citizens. As such, these critics argue, the system needs to be assessed for its democratic credentials and, they find, it comes up short.

So how is policy developed in this far-reaching polity? On issues of high politics the European Union still operates much like an IO, through intergovernmental bargaining. However, on the vast bulk of EU policy, the community method is followed, carried out by the supranational institutions in the federalist tradition. Proposals are submitted by the Commission to the Council and the EP and follow different decision making procedures—consultation, cooperation, or codecision—depending on the type of legislation. For example in the sensitive area of justice and home affairs, which includes security and policing matters, consultation is used; on issues related to the environment and the common market, codecision is used.

The EP has a different level of authority on each type of procedure. "In subjects covered by the consultation procedure, EP votes are merely statements of position. In subjects covered by the cooperation procedure, EP decisions are the basis for decision making by the other two actors" (Kreppel and Tsebelis 1999, 934). The EP has the most power in codecision; recent treaties have increased the number of policy areas decided by codecision so that today it is the primary policymaking procedure.

Codecision is a multistep process. First, the Commission releases a proposal that is usually the result of a prolonged consultation process. This proposal is commented on by the Committee of the Regions, a body representing the interests of the regions that make up the member states, and the Economic and Social Committee, a body officially representing civil society in the policy-making process. Once these bodies give their comments on the proposal it goes to first reading in the EP. A rapporteur, an MEP tasked with ushering the proposal through the legislative process, is assigned the dossier. "The European Parliament delivers an opinion at first reading. This opinion, prepared by a rapporteur, is discussed and amended within the relevant parliamentary committee, then debated in plenary session, where it is adopted by a simple majority" (EP 2004). In parallel the Council conducts its preparatory work in the Council's first reading; it finalizes its position on the proposal, including any revisions to the proposal that the Commission may have since made in response to the EP's first reading. Then if the Council approves of the Commission's proposal as amended by the parliament the process ends and the proposal is adopted. If the Council does not approve it, it adopts a common position, and the proposal goes to second reading.

In second reading in the EP the revised proposal and the Council common position are reviewed. Revisions are only allowed on topics that arose in the first reading or on topics addressed in the common position; wholly new amendments are prohibited. If the EP accepts the proposal as revised by the Council, it is passed into law. If the EP rejects the common position the process is ended. If they opt to amend the common position, this amended document is sent back to the Commission and the Council for its second reading. The Council can then accept the amended common position, or if the Council does not accept the EP amendments to the common position then the proposal goes to a conciliation committee. "The Conciliation Committee brings together the delegations of the European Parliament and the Council, and the Commissioner in charge of the dossier. The Conciliation Committee is chaired jointly by the chairpersons of the delegations from the two colegislator institutions (a Vice President of the European Parliament or a Minister of the Member States holding the Presidency)" (ibid.). The delegates work toward a compromise, release a joint text, and the act is adopted.

A great deal of effort goes into proposal development—in the form of green papers, nonpapers, consultations, revisions, white papers, and interservice deliberations—so it is perhaps not surprising that when a proposal emerges it almost inevitably becomes law. Only a handful of legislative proposals have not made it out of the codecision process. In the European Union policy change is much more likely once the wheels of the policymaking process have begun to turn.

In addition to the majority of proposals that are dealt with by the three primary policymaking procedures there are other options for EU policy. There are numerous semiautonomous standardization bodies that bring stakeholders together to hash out the details of arcane standardization issues. Standard-setting allows the common market to operate as it ensures comparability in product safety, quality, and interoperability. Two of the largest standardization bodies are the European Committee for Standardization (CEN, Comité Européen de Normalisation) and the European Organization for Technical Approvals (EOTA). In these processes as well, policy change is likely because failure to self-regulate will often prompt EU institutions to produce formal, more binding regulations.

While the media may be the fourth branch of government in the United States, and the Washington press corps a massive and tenacious body, the Brussels press corps is considerably more subdued. There are no pan-EU media and no European public (Habermas 2001, 17). Princen and Kerremans suggest that "the European Union lacks an integrated 'European Public Space.' As a result, there are no or very little European news media and European-wide debates, especially when compared with the media and public debates in the European Union's Member States" (2005, 8). Saurugger also notes that "what seems to be missing is a European demos with a shared identity, a common deliberative forum, and an open system of communication" (2005, 6; see also Michalowitz 2005).

There are a number of reasons why the EU media systems are not as large or as far-reaching as those found in the United States. First, reporters note that Brussels politics generally do not stimulate the same kind of excitement as national politics. Debates are often arcane, dealing with technical aspects of policy on topics not close to the hearts of many European citizens. For example education, health care, and welfare policies, perennially of interest to the average citizen, remain under the control of national governments. Second, the EU media system is fragmented, divided by different languages and media markets. There are few pan-EU publications but rather German newspapers, French television news programs, and Slovene radio shows. Rucht, in his study of the lobbying and protest strategies of environmental groups, notes, "Virtually all communication via mass media remains within the boundaries of national languages and discourse. Journalists located in Brussels report only for the national papers of their respective home countries" (2001, 139).

With the exception of a few Brussels-based publications that generally do not find their way out of Belgium, there is no central or pan-EU medium to convey EU messages to the public. As a result, many papers do not even cover EU policy developments. When publications do have a Brussels correspondent, their coverage of the issue is often through the national lens—interpreting EU events in light of what they mean in their specific member state. As the thriving media system in the United States has implications for the spread of advocacy communications, so too does the lack of media reach in the European Union have implications for European lobbyists.

EU advocates cannot communicate directly with Brussels-based media correspondents with the aim of transmitting a message across the whole of the European Union. Likewise, attention-grabbing events carried out in Brussels will not likely be picked up by the majority of European national media outlets. Advocates who want to pursue media-based tactics must work through their national associations or affiliates to promote coverage in national language outlets.

The EU system then is characterized by a much lower degree of democratic accountability compared with the United States due to the democratic deficit; a high probability of policy change, because the policymaking process is structured in such a way as to inevitably pass policies that are proposed; and a low level of political communication due to the fragmented pan-EU media system.

THE EU INTEREST GROUP SYSTEM

Throughout the integration process across the institutions of the European Union, organized interests have been present and lobbying at an ever-greater rate. Since the inception of the ECSC in 1951 industry interests, national interests, and Euro-federalists were actively involved in developing and implementing regulations at the supranational level. These advocates continued to push for further integration leading to the inclusion of all economic sectors in the EEC established in 1958. Even in these early years of the EC formal organized interests were emerging. The community's foremost advocate and the engineer behind the ECSC, Jean Monnet, decided to push his cause through the Action Committee for a United States of Europe, "a small, 'private supranational organization' of political party and trade union leaders. Monnet envisioned the committee as a powerful pressure group to lobby for implementation of his new initiative" (Dinan 1999, 30).

Business and industry interests continued to play a critical role in the further integration and completion of the single market. "Business interests, through the European Round-Table of Industrialists (ERT) and other transnational business associations, lobbied heavily for the single market programme by the Commission and adopted by national governments" (Hix 1999, 234). More than push for further market integration, business interests contributed to policy development much more directly. These interests worked closely with the Commission in the development of the 1985 white paper, which laid out the plans for completion of the single market by 1992. The Commission contracted "European standards organizations—CEN, the European Electrotechnical Standardization Committee (CENELEC), and the European Telecom Standard Institute (ETSI)—to develop voluntary European standards" (Dinan 1999, 357). Business interests were also consistently consulted during the process of removing internal barriers to the free movement of goods and services.

Extensive advocate activity also has a tradition in the area of agriculture, where farming interests maintained a virtually sacrosanct position in the policymaking process for the Common Agricultural Policy (CAP). Even during the push for reform in the 1980s, the "vested agribusiness and rural interests had a firm grip on the CAP and could successfully resist major reform. Farmers maximized political support for the CAP by lobbying effectively and by portraying themselves as a disadvantaged and beleaguered group providing a vital service to society" (Dinan 1999, 339). Interests pressing for CAP reform however did not relent and in the 1980s a broader range of interests became involved in the agricultural policy arena, including "consumer and environmental groups, several Member States governments, and a number of foreign governments" (Hix 1999, 252).

As the EU continued to integrate and expand its competencies, so too did the interest group community enlarge and develop. With each major treaty revision more groups were established at the EU level (Mahoney 2003b). The European institutions were reaching out to interest groups to increase their legitimacy and interest groups were reaching out to EU institutions, which were open to their input, bypassing their nation states. A positive feedback process developed; as the European Union developed competencies in certain areas, groups affected by those policies mobilized and as they engaged with the institutions and lobbied for more activity on the topic, the European Union's competencies and activities further expanded (Wessels 2000; Mahoney 2004).

By the end of the twentieth century "approximately 80 percent of all social, economic, and environmental regulation applicable in the Member States

[was] adopted through the EU policy process" (Hix 1999, 211). In response to this substantial expansion in the EU system, we now see more interests represented in Brussels, encompassing a broader range of interest types, supported by substantial resources, all from various political levels.

During the first decades of the European Union business interests were disproportionately represented in the system. This was due to the original focus of the Union—economic integration and the development of the single market. Today a larger variety of interests are represented, including professional associations, trade associations, labor unions, environmental groups, consumer advocates, patient advocates, public interest groups, regional interests, think tanks, and many others. European interest groups are representing everything from airlines, brewers, and cement manufactures, to unions, wildlife, and youth groups.

A study of the Commission's voluntary civil society registry showed business interests still dominate at 68 percent, but industry is counterbalanced by citizen, worker, youth, and education groups, which combined comprise nearly a quarter, 24.1 percent, of the lobbying community (Mahoney 2003b). The advocacy community in Brussels is vibrant and ever-growing; many joke that it is difficult to find a Belgian these days in Brussels at the countless cocktail parties and conferences as Europeans from all corners of the continent come to populate the capital. Lobbyist hotspots like Kitty O'Shea's, an Irish pub near the Commission's Berlaymont headquarters, and the cafes lining the Place du Luxembourg behind the EP provide opportune venues for the advocacy community to meet, mingle, and share information. As the weekly diary in the *European Voice* attests, there is some type of event being held by one lobbying organization or another every night of every week.

In addition to the myriad associations, also present are individual firms ranging from medium-sized businesses to massive international corporations pressing their interests before the EU institutions. The big multinationals with Brussels offices include global heavyweights, including AT&T, Coca-Cola, Dow Chemical, ExxonMobil, HP, Intel, and Sony. The number of professional or for-hire lobbyists also has flourished; in Brussels they are referred to by the ambiguous term "consultancies." Burson-Marsteller, Hill and Knowlton, and Weber Shandwick, three of the biggest, have hundreds of lobbyists representing clients before the EU institutions. Smaller and more specialized consultancies are being founded every year. While EU lobbying has had more of a public relations basis in the past, more law firms are becoming active, developing practices similar to those of U.S. lobbying and law firms.

As there is a broader range of types of interests represented in the European Union, there is also now a wide range of interests from various political levels advocating their positions. We see global interests active in EU policymaking like the World Wildlife Federation and Greenpeace. International humanitarian associations are also present and pressing the case for EU action in humanitarian crises (Hix 1999, 329). Euro-level organizations are quite prevalent in the EU interest community with transnational federations of associations in nearly every interest category. National-level interests also target the European Union in addition to or at times in place of their national governments. Numerous national-level interests have established offices in Brussels.

While the regions are represented in the Committee of the Regions (CoR), many have also begun advocating their positions to the European Union directly. "An increasing number established lobbying offices in Brussels which essentially gathered information on EC/EU initiatives to send back to the region" (Mitchell and McAleavey 1999, 178). Transnational regional associations have developed like *Dionysos*, composed of "ten French, Italian, Spanish, and Portuguese wine-growing regions" (Keating and Hooghe 1996, 226). The European Union is also targeted by subregional units and transnational organizations of subregional units like *Quartiers en crise* which "promotes exchanges among twenty-five cities on problems of social exclusion" (ibid.).

Because there is no mandatory registration system as in the United States, it is difficult to know just how many lobbyists are active. As the *European Voice* explains, "The lobbying community around Brussels is large and amorphous. The European Commission has estimated that there are 15,000 lobbyists. The EP estimates that 500 large companies have representation and that there are 200 international firms" (September 22, 2005, 25). While the European Union currently has no system of lobby registration, many have called for one based on the U.S. model. In a special report on EU lobbying by the *European Voice*, King notes "Supporters say that mandatory registration of lobbyists works in the United States, so should also work in the European Union" (2005, 24). Bounds and Dixon, in a *Financial Times* article, stated that the EP and the Commission are pushing forward with independent attempts at lobbying regulation, but the hope is to develop a joint system that includes financial disclosure (October 9, 2007). One of the most vocal proponents has been the lobbying watchdog group Corporate Europe Observatory (CEO). In addition, a coalition has been formed for the very purpose of promoting EU lobbying disclosure and transparency called ALTER-EU. As in the United States, lobbyists—mostly industry representative and lobbying firms—continue to lobby against stricter regulations.

Thus we see highly developed advocacy communities in both the United States and the European Union, so much so that regulators in each polity are seeking some control over their activities through lobbying registration systems. While the aims of American and European advocates are the same—to influence policymaking—it is not yet clear whether their methods are the same also. Do the institutional differences found between the two political systems

lead to differences in lobbying behavior? The research presented in the following chapters will seek to answer this question.

NOTES

1. A word should be said on the omission of the fourth major institution—the
European Court of Justice (ECJ). While the Court has played a critical role in policy
development and has propelled the integration of the European Union (see Stone
Sweet 2003; Fligstein and Stone Sweet 2002), individual actors cannot bring an issue
before the Court, as could be done in other polities with supreme constitutional courts
such as the U.S. Supreme Court. If individuals desire to bring suit related to European law, they have two options: (1) if it is alleged a private actor is breaking EU law,
the individual takes the matter to his or her national court, which must uphold EU
law (due to the principle of direct effect); (2) if it is alleged a member state is breaking EU law, the individual requests that the Commission begin infringement proceedings against the member state and the Commission may continue with those
proceedings, resulting in a case before the Court (Stone Sweet and Gehring, 2004;
Bomberg et al. 2003). In the first option, action is being carried out at the national
level and thus does not fall within my study of the supranational arena. In the second option, the advocacy on the part of the advocate would be directed at the Commission, not the Court, and thus would be picked up in my study as lobbying of the
Commission. Therefore, because advocates cannot lobby the Court in any direct way
(even something akin to an *amicus* brief is not an option) the Court falls outside the
focus of this research.

2. The committee actually consists of two levels: the heads of the member states'
permanent representations (or perm reps), COREPER II, and the deputy permanent
representatives COREPER I. As the European Union's competencies have expanded,
COREPER has taken over more and more of the deliberation process; "some 90 percent of decisions are now taken at the level of COREPER or below" (Edwards 1996,
135).

3. Nor should the Council be mistaken for the Council of Europe, an independent international organization.

2

Explaining Advocacy

NUMEROUS HANDBOOKS AND how-to manuals have been written in both the United States and the European Union on how to lobby successfully (Guyer 2003; Watkins et al. 2001; Avner 2002; Burson-Marsteller 2003). However, attempts at an all-purpose prescription for successful lobbying are misguided, for there is no such thing as *the* best advocacy strategy, *the* best route or access point, *the* best tactic—a successful lobbying campaign is one that is tailored to the specifics of the situation at hand. Lobbying decisions must be taken with the political context centrally in mind. As one lobbyist, in the transportation sector, interviewed in this research describes, a large number of options are available from which lobbyists can choose; the key is determining the right mix:

> When I go home to Oregon, folks say, "Oh yeah lobbyists, you go and buy fancy dinners for members of Congress and their staff . . ." but that's just not reality. The way we advocate our priorities is to demonstrate the empirical basis of our recommendations, provide facts that demonstrate the benefits from enacting the policies that we advocate, coupled with aggressive inside-the-beltway and outside-in-the-real-world public relations campaigns as well as grassroots activism and our greatest strength—constant and direct lobbying. All of those things have to be employed to be successful. Anybody that thinks you can accomplish your goals by sending in a couple of e-mails or writing a PAC check is not dealing in the world in which I have to live.

For example, some have suggested in the European Union the national route is the most effective lobbying method. However, if an EU issue involves a social dialogue overseen by the Commission and a lobbyist is back in Helsinki trying to influence the process, he will find he has selected the wrong strategy. Similarly, some in the United States have touted the power of the people and mobilizing the public. However, if the issue is a regulatory one, and a lobbyist is conducting grassroots mobilization campaigns, she will find she has selected the wrong strategy.

When to be low-key and when to go public; when to go face-to-face with elected officials and when to send letters; when to fly in your CEOs and when to fly out officials for site visits; when to rely on scientific arguments; and when to resort to symbolic arguments all depends on the design of the political system, the nature of the policy issue, and the characteristics of the interest group doing the lobbying.

This is not to say that there can be no better understanding of advocacy strategies and success than that they vary from issue to issue. The research presented here seeks to do just that: explain how the advocacy process is influenced by a number of forces. By advocacy process I mean the process by which advocates mobilize, formulate arguments, choose targets, select tactics, decide whether to work with others in an attempt to influence public policy, and ultimately whether they are successful in their efforts. Advocates are any entity that seeks to influence policymakers in a certain direction, so that entity includes interest groups, corporations, institutions, regional or geographic representations, lobbying firms or public affairs consultants, and even other policymakers if they have become champions of a cause. The advocacy process is not only the series of decisions that these various types of actors must make throughout an advocacy campaign, but also the final outcome on the issue. The questions then are: What influences lobbyists' decisions on what tactics to use, how to approach a policy debate, what arguments to use, whether to build alliances with other interests, and whether they are successful or not in their advocacy goals?

This chapter lays out the theoretical framework that underpins the research. I argue that factors at the institutional, issue, and interest group levels combine to determine advocacy strategies. The first section explains the process of advocacy in more detail; this is followed by a discussion of the three levels of factors influencing that process. First there is a discussion of the importance of the institutional design of the political system within which advocates are working. The second section details how the characteristics of the issue at hand, such as scope, salience, and conflict, influence the development of advocacy strategies. The third section describes how the characteristics of the advocate themselves—resources, membership, organization—come into play when a lobbyist is making tactical decisions.

ADVOCACY AS A PROCESS

To accurately study advocacy it is necessary to recognize what advocates do day in and day out as a *process*. Lowery and Gray note that advocacy consists

of "steps or stages required for organized interests to influence policy outcomes," which they term "an influence production process" (2004, 164).
Narrower studies looking at only one or two segments of the process cannot
hope to provide a full understanding of the character or important determinants of advocacy in a political system. If we seek to accurately explain the
process in its entirety, it is necessary to dissect the advocacy process into its
components to analyze how different factors have different impacts on the
various stages of advocacy. That is, the main determinants of a group's argumentation strategy may be different from the factors that influence its decision to ally with other organizations.

The broad concept of the advocacy process is defined through a series of
sets of dependent variables that capture each of the major stages of the advocacy process including: determination of the lobby position; formulation of
arguments; selection of targets of advocacy communications; choice of inside
and outside lobbying tactics; and decisions to forge alliances. These should not
be seen as predetermined steps proceeding chronologically in time—that is,
the decision of how to argue one's position does not necessarily precede the
decision of whom to target—but rather as critical segments of the advocacy
process. In addition to these sets of advocacy decisions there is a final stage:
lobbying success.

First, advocates must decide if they are going to mobilize for a policy debate. At times this may seem preordained; if a policy proposal promises to have
a major impact on an organized interest the advocates may have no choice but
to mobilize. Indeed many lobbyists note that they feel they are constantly
"firefighting," leaving little time for proactive advocacy. On other issues there
may be more leeway, and whether or not they organize for the fight may be
up for debate. When this decision is made, an interest's lobbying position is
defined. That is, whether they are working to promote a proposal, modify a
proposal, or block it. The lobbying positions advocates assume influence other
aspects of their advocacy strategies.

Second, advocates must devise an argumentation strategy. There can be
many ways to look at a political issue. Advocates work to develop convincing
arguments tailored to the situation at hand. They must decide whether to
employ arguments that evoke shared goals and appeal to broad audiences; are
more technical in nature, focusing on the often arcane details of policymaking;
make cost or economic claims about the impact of a proposal; reference the
feasibility or smooth functioning of the implementation of a policy; call into
question the fairness of a proposal or its discriminatory impacts; or finally that
reference the will of constituents or public opinion.

A third critical segment of the advocacy process is the selection of lobbying targets. Advocates must assess the positions of policymakers and determine
to whom they will communicate their advocacy positions. This is a decision

regarding which institutions to target—often determined by the policymaking procedure—and which officials within those institutions, influenced by the specific interests of those individuals. Lobbyists must assess if they will work to mobilize friendly policymakers, seek to sway undecided officials, or attempt to persuade the opposition to change their minds.

The next two important stages of the advocacy process are those often focused on by interest group scholars—lobbying tactics. Tactic selection is better understood by dividing it into its two distinct components: inside lobbying and outside lobbying. Inside lobbying tactics include the activities we most often associate with lobbying: face-to-face meetings with policymakers, mailing letters and position papers, drafting legislative language, attending consultations, testifying at hearings, and holding cocktail parties, among many others. Advocates must decide which mix of inside lobbying tactics they are going to employ on a policy debate. Outside lobbying tactics are those aimed at communicating to policymakers via the public. Advocates work to influence policy indirectly through press releases, press conferences, issue advertisements, letter-writing campaigns, grassroots mobilization, and other outside lobbying strategies.

The sixth stage of the advocacy process that must be considered is the set of decisions regarding networking and coalitions. Groups can opt to work alone, to casually share information with other advocates in the lobbies of hearings, or to ally as members of a formal ad hoc issue coalition. And the final stage of the advocacy process, which can be influenced by all of the decisions made in the previous stages, is lobbying success. Lobbying success is whether or not an advocate sees policy goals realized at the conclusion of a policy debate.

Advocacy is a complex process; decisions need to be made about each of these components. The specific outcomes on each of these decisions—the dependent variables—and the final outcome are the result of a number of forces at play in any democratic political system.

A CONFLUENCE OF FACTORS

How do we explain the many decisions in each stage, the outcomes on these seemingly endless dependent variables? I argue that a complex process is at play influencing the decisions of lobbyists and the results of their efforts. This claim should of course not raise much objection. Any chaos or complexity theorist would agree, as would other scholars who have attempted to step back and look at the big picture in explaining political phenomena. However, if we are to make sense of the political complexity that is driving advocacy strategies it is necessary to refine reality to its primary components.

Kingdon, building on the "garbage can model" devised by Cohen, March, and Olsen (1972), seeks to explain the outcome of agenda change with such a big picture approach. He argues there are three major process streams—problems, policies, and politics—and that they "are coupled at critical junctures, and that coupling produces the greatest agenda change" (1995, 87). Problems are the political problems that government might work to solve. Policies are the proposals the policymaking community devises to ameliorate problems. Finally, by politics Kingdon is referring to public opinion, electoral outcomes, and partisan balance. He argues that these streams operate independently of one another but that "the key to understanding agenda and policy change is their coupling. The separate streams come together at critical times" (ibid., 88).

While Kingdon makes a strong case for this model in explaining agenda change, it does not extend well to explaining advocacy strategies. However, Kingdon's approach, which considers how factors in the broader context interweave and interact to determine policy outcomes, provides a framework for theorizing.

To understand the decisions of lobbyists at each stage of the advocacy process, it is necessary to consider advocates in their broader context, and to parse that context into manageable components. In addition, rather than simply identify components in order to paint a picture with qualitative evidence, the components should be precise enough so that their relationship to advocacy decisions can be demonstrated quantitatively. To understand advocacy strategies we must consider factors at three critical levels, namely, Institutional, Issue, and Interest Group factors interweave to determine the decisions at each step of the advocacy process. How each of these levels influences advocacy decisions is dealt with in turn. For clarity the main factors used throughout this book to explain advocacy outcomes are:

- **The Determinants of the Advocacy Process**
- Institutional Level
  - The degree of democratic accountability
  - The presence of a broad-reaching media community
  - The rules of the policymaking process
- Issue Level
  - Scope
  - Salience
  - Conflict
  - Focusing event
  - History of issue
  - Type of issue/policymaking procedure

- Interest Group Level
  - Financial resources/staff
  - Membership resources
  - Advocate type
  - Organizational structure

Institutional Characteristics

To understand the process of advocacy we must consider the institutions within which organized interests lobby. Institutionalist approaches to understanding politics focus on how the design of institutions influences political behavior. As Beyers notes, "Institutionalists emphasize that institutional variability leads to incentives and constraints that influence the emergence of particular political practices" (2004, 212). But what aspects of institutional design have a significant bearing on advocacy?

How accountable institutions are to the people—or the political system's democratic institutional design—is one important factor that fundamentally influences advocacy. Institutions that are democratically accountable to the public produce a set of incentives for elected officials founded on the reelection motive. This driving force affects the strategies of organized interests who seek to influence those officials. Alternatively, institutions structured in such a way as to protect officials from having to answer to the public create a different set of incentives for policymakers who are not directly elected. The motives driving these officials similarly influence the advocacy strategies of organized interests. Thus, the accountability to citizens of institutions of any government has direct effects on the character of the advocacy process.

Direct elections—elections in which candidates are elected directly by the public—are central in democratic theory. Dahl notes that "democratic theory is concerned with processes by which ordinary citizens exert a relatively high degree of control over leaders" (1956, 3). Citizens exert control over leaders via elections, by granting or revoking elected positions to policymakers. A fundamental assumption of democracy is that policymakers want to govern and thus want to be reelected. Downs' model in *An Economic Theory of Democracy* begins with the assumption that every democratic government seeks to maximize political support; given that those with the most votes control the government, the goal of all policymakers in such systems is reelection (1957, 12). Mayhew (1974) is probably most famous for the assertion that reelection is central to understanding the behavior of members of Congress. While he recognized other goals are present—that is, power in the chamber, good public policy—reelection is required before these other goals can be accomplished. Arnold similarly begins with the assumption that reelection is the dominant goal: "Electoral calculations shape everything from legislators' roll call decisions to the strategies and tactics of coalition leaders" (1990, 6).

Policymakers want to govern, and thus want to be reelected; therefore they have to behave in a way that will get them reelected. They must make decisions that do not displease their constituents. Schlesinger, in laying out his "ambition theory of politics," argues: "In democracies the desire for election and more important reelection provides the electorate with a powerful control over public officials" (1994, 35).

When a policymaker is subject to direct elections, he or she wants to know whether constituents will support his or her vote on a given proposal. Lobbyists seeking to influence a legislator's vote then must tailor their advocacy strategy to communicate: your constituents want this, or they would support it if they found out about it and you are electorally vulnerable if you oppose it. This message can be sent through the arguments and tactics used. Arguments focusing on broad-based goals or commonly shared ideas will dominate, as will references to the constituency and public opinion. Tactics that demonstrate the support of the masses, like letter-writing campaigns and grassroots mobilization, as well as coalition formation, will be more likely.

In political systems where policymakers are not directly elected, they have no reelection motive. Bureaucrats, technocrats, and Eurocrats are appointed to their positions. They may be driven by ambition to rise in the ranks of their unit, they may be driven to develop good policy, but they are not driven to please a constituent base. As such, lobbyists seeking to influence policymakers who are not directly elected do not need to convey the will of the people or communicate what the reaction of constituents will be to a decision. Arguments and tactics should differ from those made to elected officials; in the latter case, argumentation will be more technical and tactics will focus on a one-to-one transfer of information from lobbyist to policymaker.

As suggested in the introduction, the effect of democratic accountability on success could take a number of forms. First, advocates may be more successful in a system with institutions that are democratically accountable through direct elections compared with those operating in a system lacking direct elections, because advocates who can credibly threaten electoral mobilization may be better able to sway policymakers. Indeed, the influence of special interests in majoritarian systems is one of the reasons certain policies have been delegated to insulated institutions like central banks, autonomous agencies, and bureaucracies. As Moravcsik notes: "Insulated institutions offer one the means of redressing underlying biases in national democratic representation. The most common distortion is the capture of open political processes, and thus government policy, by powerful particularistic minorities with powerful and immediate interests, who oppose the interests of majorities (often treated as 'the median voter') with diffuse longer-term or less self-conscious concerns" (2002, 614).

Second, an opposing hypothesis is feasible: advocates active in a system without direct elections will achieve higher levels of lobbying success, compared with direct-election systems, as organized interests are the only external input into a system lacking voters. This is also related to research on bureaucracies and nonmajoritarian institutions that suggests unelected regulators can be subject to capture by interest groups. As Follesdal and Hix note, "Independent regulators are highly prone to capture, primarily because they are heavily lobbied by the producers who are the subjects of the regulation" (2006, 546; see also Lowi 1969).

In a system with democratically accountable institutions, the effect of direct elections on advocacy success could follow two different lines. First, citizen groups and organizations that are in line with public opinion may be more influential because they represent the preferences of voters who will reelect policymakers (Smith 2000). However, in many modern democracies advocates point to two things that matter in politics: money and votes. Indeed votes matter; elected policymakers need individual citizens to vote for them if they want to retain their posts. But we cannot ignore the reality that money matters as well, in part because it takes money to get citizens to vote for a candidate.

Money is used in campaigns for print, radio, and television advertisements, for public appearances and travel on the campaign trail, and for political consultants to devise and carry out campaign strategy. Winning elections (and importantly reelection) takes money and money is one thing advocates can give. Depending on the laws of a political system the organizations or interests an advocate represents may be able to give money to the campaigns of policymakers and their political parties or spend money on election-related issue advertising. If money is as important as, or more important than, votes, the financial resources of an advocate become a critical consideration when one tries to understand lobbying success in light of the reelection motive. This influence is above and beyond the influence wealthy interests enjoy from being able to intensively engage in the full range of lobbying tactics. Thus a second and alternative hypothesis emerges regarding the effect of democratic accountability on lobbying success within systems with direct elections that are privately funded: the higher an advocate's financial resources, the more likely he or she is to achieve lobbying success.

In sum we see four alternative hypotheses relating democratic institutional design to lobbying success. Proceeding from the vast literature on the European Union's democratic deficit, discussed in detail in the system descriptions in the introduction, the U.S. system is taken to be more democratically accountable through direct elections than the European Union system. The four alternative hypotheses therefore are: (a) U.S. groups are more influential than EU groups on average; (b) EU groups are more influential than their U.S. counterparts on average; (c) citizen groups are more influential within the U.S.

system and compared with the EU system; and (d) monied interests are more influential within the U.S. system and compared with the EU system.

The second major characteristic of democratic institutional design that must be considered is the presence of a broad-based media system to communicate political information to the public. Lobbyists active in political systems with a highly developed news system can use that resource to their advantage for outside lobbying. They can communicate quickly and effectively to the public. In addition such a news system creates a situation in which the policymakers know the public can and will be notified of their decisions. In political systems lacking a broad-reaching media system, the means by which lobbyists can communicate policy messages and information to the public is severely limited.

Third, the rules surrounding the policymaking process influence the likelihood of policy change and this has implications for advocacy. The likelihood that proposals will pass in a political system should influence the stage of the advocacy process when advocates determine lobbying positions—whether advocates attempt to promote a proposal, modify it, or block it. Specifically, systems that have a very high probability of passage should lead lobbyists to seek modifying positions, working to make small changes in a proposal that will likely become law. In systems with a very low probability of passage, lobbyists should be more likely to attempt to block the proposal, exploiting the low passage rate so that it does not become law. The likelihood of policy change should also influence an advocate's chances of lobbying success, and that effect will vary depending on the advocate's lobbying position.

The democratic institutional design of a political system influences the motivations of policymakers and thus the types of lobbying communications to which they are responsive. The institutional characteristics of electoral accountability, the presence of a media system, and the rules of the policymaking process should influence the ways in which advocates lobby at every stage of the advocacy process as well as their ultimate lobbying success. This is tested in chapters 4 through 10. The institutional structure however is not the whole story; the characteristics of the issue at hand also influence advocacy strategies and success, as discussed next.

It should be noted that the argument that institutions drive advocacy strategies and advocacy success is not in opposition to Lijphart's (1999) work. Lijphart argues that all modern democracies can be categorized as majoritarian or consensus democracies and that variation in government forms is explained by the cultural divisions or cleavages that exist within a society. Highly fragmented societies need consensus-inducing structures to keep the polity together. More homogenous societies can afford to have majoritarian structures in which the will of the majority rules because the preferences of the majority will not be too far off from the minority. Lijphart classifies the United States as more majoritarian and the European Union as more consensus focused. I agree that Lijphart's classification scheme describes well the political systems of modern democracies, but I work to isolate what factors in the institutional system fundamentally impact advocacy strategies and success.

This book will draw on quantitative and qualitative evidence from the 149 interviews in an effort to parse whether it is cultural differences, as described in the introduction, or institutional differences that provide the strongest explanation for the advocacy outcomes we observe. At the institutional level, however, the study is only a sample size of 2, so the conclusions from the qualitative evidence will provide a significant first step in a research agenda aimed at researching the link between institutions and advocacy.

Issue Characteristics

As argued at the beginning of this chapter, the lobbying approach, arguments, targets, tactics, and alliances an advocate selects depend—and they depend in a large part—on the nature of the issue at hand. The contours of a given political fight—the scope, salience, conflict, procedure, and so forth—shape the advocacy strategies of lobbyists. Not every issue characteristic is expected to influence every advocacy stage. The issue characteristics that are likely to be the most important and the stages they are expected to affect are laid out here.

First is the scope of the issue. Does the proposal affect only a few individuals or sectors, does it impact numerous massive industries, or does the policy have ramifications for the entire political system? The scope of the issue is expected to have an impact on nearly every stage of the advocacy process. It should affect the lobbying positions advocates assume. Large-scope issues should have more momentum behind them because more actors have an interest in the outcome. Thus, advocates would be more likely to take a modifying position rather than a blocking position on issues of larger scope.

Scope should also affect targeting strategies. It becomes even more important for a supporting coalition to be large when a policy will have a significant impact on society. Lobbyists active on large-scope issues, therefore, will be more likely to target many different types of policymakers representing the full range of positions on an issue. The larger the scope of the issue, the more likely advocates are to use multiple types of inside lobbying strategies and the more likely they are to use outside lobbying tactics. Large-scope issues may be more likely to produce ad hoc issue coalitions because they require that advocates demonstrate they have a breadth of support. Finally, the larger the scope of the issue the less likely advocates are to succeed in their lobbying goals because so many other interests will be active in the debate. Policymakers will be unlikely to follow the suggestions of a given interest.

Second, the salience of the issue to the policymaking community and to the public at large is an important aspect of an issue. Similar to scope, salience is expected to influence most of the stages of the advocacy process. Highly salient issues should lead to more arguments evoking commonly shared goals and public opinion, more targeting of policymakers of different views, more use of inside and outside lobbying tactics, and more alliances with like-minded organizations. With regard to lobbying success, a pattern similar to what was hypothesized for scope is expected: as an issue is more salient to the public and the number of people watching the case increases, the likelihood of lobbying success for any one advocate should decrease.

The third issue characteristic expected to influence advocacy strategies is the level of conflict on a policy debate. Issues can be highly contentious with opposing camps battling it out; they can be less controversial, with a number of various perspectives but not viewpoints that directly contradict each other; or finally there can be issues where there is no conflict at all and one viewpoint dominates the discussion. The level of conflict on an issue is expected to influence the lobbying positions that advocates assume; the targeting strategies they develop; the level of inside and outside lobbying they conduct; the coalition activity in which they engage; and the final outcome of the case.

The fourth characteristic of an issue, focusing events, must be taken into consideration—whether or not a focusing event has occurred on the case. Focusing events are occurrences "like a crisis or disaster that comes along to call attention to the problem, a powerful symbol that catches on" (Kingdon 1995, 95). A classic example is an airplane crash that stimulates policymakers to make changes to policies regarding air safety. The occurrence of a focusing event can crystallize the need for policymakers to act and can create momentum for policy change. Thus, the presence of a focusing event is expected to influence the lobbying positions that advocates assume: If an issue has a great deal of momentum behind it, and policy change is imminent, then advocates will be more likely to take modifying positions rather than blocking positions. In addition, focusing events can affect lobbyists' argumentation strategies. Lobbyists that were lobbying on a topic before a crisis will likely alter their argumentation strategy if a relevant focusing event occurs on their case.

The fifth issue characteristic, its history, could play a role in advocacy decisions. New issues may be of more interest to the public than older, reoccurring issues. The newness of an issue could influence the ability of a lobbyist to pursue outside lobbying strategies.

The sixth and final issue characteristic that can impact the advocacy process is the policymaking procedure. In the United States procedure depends on whether the case is legislative or regulatory. In the European Union the advocacy process depends on whether the policymaking process is consultation, cooperation, codecisions, or another softer type of policy development like voluntary agreements, social dialogue, or self-regulation. Different procedures involve different bodies or governmental units in the policymaking process. The policymaking procedure is expected to affect the lobbying positions advocates assume and the inside lobbying strategies they develop.

It should be noted that issue characteristics are not wholly exogenous. It is, in part, the job of advocates to try to manipulate the definition of an issue—to frame it (Riker 1986; Baumgartner and Jones 1993; Kingdon 1995; McKissick 1995). While lobbyists are not able to mold an issue at will, skillful advocates can alter the perception of an issue. A proposed policy change that is on paper fairly small in scope could be framed as a slippery slope—a first move down a path toward major policy change that would lead to much broader ramifications. For example the Unborn Victims of Violence Act debated in the United States, which would charge a criminal who murdered a pregnant woman with two counts of murder, was understood by pro-choice activists as an attempt to give a fetus the standing of a legal person, which would have significant implications for freedom of choice in the country. The salience of an issue is of course also flexible. An organization that undertakes a massive public education campaign on a topic can create awareness of a problem and in time, if the public is convinced, increase the salience of the issue. The degree of conflict on an issue very much depends on the issue's definition. As Schattschneider argues, "The most important strategy of politics is concerned with the scope of conflict" and advocates are tasked with managing—extending or constraining—the degree of conflict (1960, 2).

While it may seem that, with all these possibilities for manipulation, it is impossible to investigate the effects of issue characteristics on lobbying, issue characteristics are not as plastic as the possibilities might suggest. Any given advocate has only so much influence on an issue's definition; thus, the global understanding of a case cannot change at the whim of one lobbyist. Issue characteristics are not completely flexible and fluid—some stability of how an issue is perceived occurs and the characteristics that emerge influence the advocacy strategy pursued by actors.

The issues in this study were assessed for the six issue characteristics laid out above at the time of the research and those characteristics are related to the advocacy being conducted at the time of the research. Some of the issues in my sample may have been more or less salient five years ago, or the degree of conflict could have changed, but this research was concerned with how the nature of an issue concurrently influences advocacy on that issue.

One more level of factors—the characteristics of the interest—combine with the institutional and issue context to determine advocacy decisions.

Interest Group Characteristics

A number of characteristics of an organized interest have the potential to influence the decisions lobbyists make throughout the advocacy process and their ultimate lobbying success. The first characteristic critical to an advocate's decision making is the level of financial resources. Schlozman and Tierney (1986) argue this is one of the most important factors because financial wealth translates into other resources, like staff, specialized researchers, and contracting hired help. Financial resources tend to highly correlate with staff size (Berry 1989). Financial resources, as measured by staff size, are expected to influence the number of inside lobbying tactics an organization employs, the level of outside lobbying, and the extent of their coalition activity. In addition, institutional factors likely intersect with resources to determine lobbying success.

Second, membership resources are also important. The size and type of organization members can affect lobbying strategies that rely on member involvement. For example, Bacheller (1977) suggests that large mass-membership groups will be more likely to use the grassroots while non-membership groups will be more likely to use the grasstops. Gerber (1999), looking at the case of interest group lobbying on direct legislation measures, also suggests tactics are influenced by membership resources as well as financial resources. The size and type of membership are expected to be most important in the outside lobbying stage.

Organizational structure is another organizational characteristic expected to influence the use of outside lobbying strategies. In the United States this influence is determined by whether or not the organization has subnational units or local groups. In the European Union this influence depends on whether the structure of the organization is federated, direct membership, or mixed, with both associations and institutions or corporations as members. Organizations with local units in the United States and national associations in the European Union are expected to engage in outside lobbying at a higher rate.

Finally, the fourth critical interest-group characteristic—advocate type— or put differently, who the actor is as an organization, is expected to have ramifications for advocacy decisions. Whether a lobbyist is representing a large citizen group, a foundation, or an individual firm should lead to different strategies. Clark and Wilson argue that organizations attract membership through different incentive systems—material, solidary, or purposive—and that the "incentive system may be regarded as the principal variable affecting organizational behavior" (1961, 130). Jordan and Halpin (2004) expand the range of incentives even further. While the organization's incentive system may not be the *principal* variable, it is an important one. Specifically, actor type is expected to play a role in argumentation strategies. Citizen groups, for example, are expected to be more likely to employ arguments that evoke commonly shared goals, while business interests are more likely to make technical or scientific arguments in support of their positions. Actor type is also expected to influence targeting strategies, inside and outside lobbying decisions, as well as coalition activity. As with resources, the expectation is that there may be an interaction between institutional characteristics and actor type to determine lobbying success.

CONCLUSION

Advocate characteristics are expected to merge with contextual factors at the issue and institutional levels to determine lobbying decisions at each stage of the advocacy process. For clarity, the advocacy process is composed of the seven critical aspects or stages of a lobbying campaign: (1) determination of the lobbying position (whether promoting, modifying, or blocking a proposal); (2) argumentation development; (3) target selection; (4) inside lobbying strategies; (5) outside lobbying strategies; (6) coalition and networking activity; and (7) lobbying success. The decisions lobbyists make during each of these stages and the final outcome are the dependent variables I seek to explain. They are determined by a confluence of factors emanating from three levels. In addition, outcomes at one stage can have an effect on decisions or outcomes at another stage. Specifically, the determination of the lobbying position can have implications for argumentation strategies, as discussed in chapter 5; tactical decisions can have implications for lobbying success as discussed in chapter 10. Such linkages can be explored by studying the entire advocacy process.

As the introduction argued, it is critically important to understand how democratic institutional design influences advocacy decisions and advocacy outcomes. This chapter has detailed how direct elections, the presence of a media system, and the rules surrounding the policymaking process are expected to influence each stage of the advocacy process. The next chapter describes the research design, which aimed to accurately assess the nature of advocacy in both polities and uncover the determinants of lobbying decisions at every stage of the advocacy process.

3

Researching Advocacy

THE PREVIOUS CHAPTER laid out the theoretical basis for the research—arguing institutional, issue, and interest factors collude to determine the nature of a lobbyist's advocacy strategy on a given political issue. Until now a model simultaneously considering the effect of the three sets of independent variables—institutions, issues, and interests—on the entire advocacy process, and tested through rigorous empirical analysis, has not been possible. This is because of the design of previous research projects studying advocacy; in each area of relevant scholarship at least one critical component was missing.

This chapter describes the research design required to successfully test the theory presented in chapter 2 and then presents the sample of issues and advocates that resulted from the data collection and that provided the basis for the analyses in the following chapters.

A NEW APPROACH

This project builds on the Baumgartner, Berry, Hojnacki, Kimball, and Leech project on advocacy and public policymaking in the United States, which was based on nearly three hundred interviews with advocates, congressional staffers, and executive branch officials active on ninety-eight issues debated during the 107th and 108th Congresses. My interview protocol, which produced the data for this project, is based on theirs and their idea that only by studying a truly random sample of issues can we draw any generalizable conclusions about advocacy. I would add that by studying advocacy in more than one polity we can better understand how institutions influence advocacy as well.

Rigorous testing of my theory requires variability across all three levels: institutions, issues, and interest groups. The most generalizable results come from a random sample of advocates active on a random sample of issues, in more than one polity, that differ on the characteristics of interest.

As mentioned, one of the most palpable aspects of institutional design that must be considered when one studies advocacy decisions is the democratic accountability of policymakers. Whether policymakers are elected or appointed should make them more or less responsive to various advocacy communications and activities.

To evaluate this expectation it was necessary to study advocacy in two political systems that differ on this important characteristic; the cases that were chosen were the United States and the European Union. There are a number of reasons for selecting these two polities. First, the two systems have similar historic development trajectories, with federalist and antifederalist tensions shaping the institutions and balance of power between the states and centralized government. Menon notes that the two systems "share several traits, including potentially comparable institutional landscapes, apparently parallel developmental trajectories, and strikingly similar institutional dynamics stemming from comparable federal structures" (3, 2005). In a detailed review of the legislative systems of the United States and the European Union, Kreppel concludes that a comparison between them may make more sense than comparisons between the European Union and its member states:

> This comparison between the two legislatures demonstrates that, despite the common assumption that the two are fundamentally different, there are some important similarities that are generally ignored in analyses of the EP that use the legislatures of the EU member states as the basis for comparison. Moreover, the similarities that exist between the EP and the House of Representatives are some of the most familiar aspects of the American legislature that are generally thought to set it apart from its democratic cousins in Western Europe, suggesting that comparisons between the EP and the parliaments of the EU member states may simply be misguided (2005, 7).

Second, the two polities have similar pluralistic advocacy communities. The debate about whether the EU interest intermediation system is corporatist or pluralist has settled on a pluralistic description of the system with numerous scholars drawing parallels to the advocacy community in the U.S. capital (Streeck and Schmitter 1991; Eising 2005; Coen 1997; Cowles 2001). In both Washington and Brussels, thriving communities of advocates are ever-growing and competing for access to policymakers, working to ensure their interests are promoted and protected in the policymaking process. The similarities of the advocacy communities have driven scholars to call for future research agendas comparing the two systems.

In Wöll's review of the literature in EU advocacy she concludes, "In all of these studies, there is a consensus that EU lobbying cannot be understood without looking at the institutions and policy context in which groups are trying to act. . . . Increasingly, scholars have thus turned their attention to cases beyond Europe to understand more about EU lobbying" (2005a, 6). She suggests a comparison with the United States as a stepping-off point. Michalowitz also makes a strong case for future European Union–United States comparisons in researching lobbying, arguing that "Firstly, the question as to why EU lobbying may be less influential than it appears from literature is difficult to answer from looking at the EU alone. . . . Since U.S. literature provides data already, it appears most useful to begin with a comparison of the European Union and United States" (2005, 2). She adds: "The availability of U.S. literature on the topic is the second reason to choose a comparative analysis of the European Union and the United States" (ibid.). And of course she notes there is the simple fact that observers—academic and practitioner alike—are increasingly making the comparison and noting similarities. These comparisons can be seen in countless news articles and reports; also common are articles on regulating lobbying, which draw European Union–United States parallels (Corporate Europe Observatory 2004; Malone 2004). In short, lobbying in the European Union and the United States appears similar. Wöll echoes that "a comparison between the two largest lobbying industries, Washington, D.C. and Brussels," is justified in that "lobbyists have to interact with a fixed set of institutions that are comparable in terms of the roles they play during the policy process" (2005a, 3).

In sum, the United States and the European Union share numerous similarities, in their institutions, norms, and lobbying communities. Moreover, the wealth of scholarly treatment of lobbying in the two systems provides a strong foundation for pursuing comparative research. For all these similarities the two systems do differ in important ways, which is why a comparative design can provide important insights into understanding the advocacy process. Specifically the two systems exhibit different democratic institutional designs.

The vast literature on the so-called Democratic Deficit in the European Union, and suggested solutions for its remedy, have been growing for over a decade (Weiler et al. 1995; Scharpf 1999; Moravcsik 2002; Follesdal and Hix 2006). A review by Follesdal and Hix (2006) coherently summarizes scholars' concerns with the EU's democratic credentials: there has been increased executive power and a decrease in national parliamentary control; the EP is too weak; there are no "European" elections—the voters that do vote in EP elections do so on national rather than European issues; and the distance between Brussels and European citizens is too great.

As discussed previously in the description of the EU political system, the policymakers of the EU institutions are not held accountable through direct elections. The officials of the Commission and Council are appointed and the members of the EP are in reality held accountable only to their national party leadership, not the public, due to national party lists and voting on national rather than European issues (Kreppel 2002; Marks and McAdam 1999; Leconte 2005).

Policymakers in the United States on the other hand, as shown by Schlesinger (1994), Mayhew (1974), Fenno (1978), Arnold (1990) and the large literature on the Congress, are keenly aware of their electoral vulnerability and strongly driven by the reelection motive. The expectation then is that reelection-minded policymakers in the United States will be more responsive to certain types of tactics and arguments when compared with the European Union, where policymakers are protected from electoral threat.

ISSUE AND INTEREST VARIATION— THE SAMPLING PROCEDURE

Drawing a random sample of issues is difficult because the universe of issues is undefined—there are theoretically an infinite number of issues that could rise to the political agenda. Using lists of introduced proposals or hearings is a faulty approach because those issues have already received a considerable level of political attention and they are institution specific. To capture issues being moved through all institutions and their subunits, as well as the issues that never fully make their way onto the active political agenda, a random sample of advocates was relied on to identify the random sample of issues.

The American actors were randomly drawn from a database created from the 1996 Lobbying Reports filed with the Secretary of the Senate compiled by Baumgartner and Leech (2001). The Lobbying Disclosure Act of 1995 (Public Law 104-65) requires lobbyists to file registrations and reports of income and expenses related to their advocacy activity. Each lobbyist must note the issues on which they were active. Thus if an advocate was active on three issues, he or she is in the lobby disclosure database of Baumgartner and Leech three times; therefore there is a type of weighting toward those advocates who are frequently engaging with the American institutions.

In the European arena, a sampling frame was developed from the 2004 registry of the EP, the 2004 Commission registry of civil society organizations (CONECCS), and the 2004 European Public Affairs Directory. The 2004 EP registry lists the individual lobbyists from each organization who have a pass to the EP, meaning an organization could be listed up to six times if it has numerous advocates visiting the EP. To ensure that those organizations with larger offices had the same chance of being randomly selected as small operations, all duplicates were deleted so that each organization is listed only once. With duplicates removed, the EP registry contains 2,098 advocates. These include civil society organizations, lobbyists for individual corporations, and hired lobbyists such as law firms, public relations firms, and consultancies.

The 2004 CONECCS database contains information on 732 civil society organizations. The 2002 version of the database was analyzed at length elsewhere (Mahoney 2003b), which demonstrates that the Commission's definition of "civil society" includes citizen groups, trade groups, professional associations, business lobbies, religious groups, research groups, unions, and associations of institutions and governmental units. Individual corporations and for-hire lobbyists are not included.

The *European Public Affairs Directory* (2004) includes information on advocates, EU officials, and permanent representations; only those offices whose primary activity is advocacy were included in the sampling frame, resulting in 2,244 advocates. All actors were included under the directory's listings of: corporations, European trade and professional associations, interest groups, chambers of commerce, national employers' federations, regions, think tanks, labor unions, international organizations, law firms specializing in EU matters, consultants specializing in EU matters, national trade and professional associations, national associations of chambers of commerce, and any organizations listed in the 2004 directory supplement on the 2004 EU enlargement. Combined, these three lists result in a sampling frame of 5,074 actors engaging in lobbying in the European Union. Duplicates were not removed, so an actor could be in the database up to three times; for example major players like the Union of Industrial and Employers' Confederations of Europe (UNICE) would appear in the CONECCS database, the EP registry, and the European Public Affairs Directory and thus, as in the U.S. sampling frame, there is a slight weighting toward those who are actively engaging with EU institutions on a regular basis.

The design consisted of randomly drawing advocates from the respective universes of lobbyists. These randomly selected actors were then sent a letter requesting an interview. Those advocates who agreed were asked to identify the issue they were most recently working on, thus forming the random sample of cases. Advocates were allowed to offer any political issue on which they were active; issues were not restricted to lobbying on only the most concrete and straightforward legislative proposals.

In the European Union there are at least three distinct policymaking processes: The community method—dominated by all three supranational institutions; the coordination method—a highly cooperative method including the Commission but being more dominated by member state governments in the Council; and the intergovernmental method—largely controlled by member states through the Council (Stubb, Wallace, and Peterson 2003). Moreover, across these broad categories there are "over thirty specific and different legal instruments and procedures at the disposal of the Union" (ibid). The European Union produces regulations, directives, recommendations, general decisions, individual decisions, opinions, resolutions, declarations, communications, and action programs (Borchardt 1999). These assorted instruments vary in the degree to which member states' governments are bound to implement them, but each can be powerful in that less-binding measures can be the first inroads into supranational control over a new policy area. For example, in the 1970s the Commission promoted a coordination method on environmental issues that evolved into a binding EU policy in 1987 (Stubb, Wallace, and Peterson 2003). Today the European Union controls more than 90 percent of the environmental policy in the member states (Greenwood 1997). Thus, advocating for a communication from the EP to the Commission to consider introducing a policy proposal may not in itself be a significant policy change, but may be the catalyst for substantial policy change in the future; thus all issues, no matter how "big" or "small," no matter what EU instruments are involved, were allowed to fall into my random sample of issues.

Similarly, in the United States a range of procedures could be the basis for an issue. The distinction of regulatory versus legislative captures the majority of variation, but within those categories are many variations; for example the U.S. Congress can produce simple resolutions, concurrent resolutions, and senses of Congress, among others. As described in detail in the review of the two systems at the end of the introduction, the legislative route is a major source of policy development and the focus of most lobbyists; regulatory lobbying, working to shape rules as they are developed by executive agencies is the other. Lobbyists work to make topics politically salient and to shape policy once the issue is on the agenda. Small legislative amendments or a nonbinding sense of Congress can be a first step to further policy. Thus, again, any type of issue, no matter the size or the degree of formal progress in the policy-making process, was accepted if identified by U.S. advocates as the issue of current interest to them.

Respondents were also asked to identify the other major players on the issue who were also interviewed, forming the snowball portion of the sampling procedure. Other major actors could be any type of actor; thus the sample includes a wide range of actor types in both polities, including citizen groups, trade and professional associations, business groups, lobbying, public relations and law firms, institutions, individual corporations, and even policymakers. Policymakers were included as advocates if they were fighting for a certain position on an issue, and engaging in advocacy activities to build support for their view. This was more often the case in the United States where members of Congress often become champions for a specific position. Congressional champions often hold press conferences, write op-eds, support and sign on to issue advertisements, organize coalitions of interest groups, devise argumentation strategies among many other advocacy tactics; therefore it is important to investigate their activities as advocates.

I carried out the American interviews during 2002 under the Baumgartner, Berry, Hojnacki, Leech, and Kimball project.[1] The European fieldwork occurred from 2004 to 2005. The response rates to my interview requests were high in both political systems: For the United States the issue identifier response rate was 51 percent and the snowball response rate was 76 percent; for the European Union the issue identifier response rate was 93 percent and the snowball response rate was 91 percent.

Interviewees were also asked about the background of the issue they were working on, the tactics they were engaging in, coalition participation, the arguments they were employing, the opposition they were facing, and the allies they found to support their cause, among others. Responses were then coded in a comparable manner for the two systems. This coding forms the basis for the empirical analyses presented in the following chapters.

ADDITIONAL DATA COLLECTION FROM PUBLICLY AVAILABLE SOURCES

In addition to data collected through the in-person interviews, information was also collected on individual organizations and issues. In the United States information on group type, founding date, membership size, membership type, and staff size was gathered from *Associations Unlimited*, an online directory of Washington organizations. For groups in the European Union, information collected from websites included group type, founding date, type of membership, and membership size. On issues in the United States, *Roll Call* and the *Washington Post* were monitored and research was conducted on the websites of the House of Representatives, Senate, administration, any relevant agencies and the Library of Congress' legislative tracking system. In the EU, the *European Voice* and *Euractiv* were monitored weekly and issues were researched using the Commission archives and EP Legislative Observatory OEIL as well as the Commission's legislative tracking system Pre-LEX. This issue research was the basis for coding of the issue variables of scope (0–impacts small sector, 1–impacts large economic sector, 2–impacts multiple sectors, 3–pan-EU or pan-U.S. impact); conflict (0–only one perspective or viewpoint on issue, 1–multiple viewpoints but not directly opposed, 2–directly opposing viewpoints); presence of a focusing event (0–absence, 1–presence); and history of issue (0–recurring or ongoing issue, 1–new issue).

A measure of salience was collected for each issue. Salience is the amount of attention the general public is giving to a policy issue. Salience is measured by news coverage. In the United States, salience is indicated by the number of *New York Times* articles on the issue during the two-year period of research. This variable was collected via LexisNexis searches. Searches were limited to the two-year time span of the 107th Congress (January 1, 2001–December 31, 2002), during which the U.S. interviews were conducted. This is selected as an *indicator* of salience; the aim was not to identify the precise number of articles covering the issues in the sample. While the *New York Times* is not read by everyone in the country, its stories are picked up by local papers, making it a good indicator of what the media are paying attention to and thus what issues the public is informed about.

LexisNexis searches of the *Financial Times* (*FT*) were conducted for a public salience measure of EU issues. Searches were similarly limited to a two-year time span surrounding the time period of the EU fieldwork (June 1, 2003– June 1, 2005); this ensures comparability between the U.S. and EU media coverage measures. Again, this source is selected as an *indicator* of salience; it is simply not possible to monitor media coverage of my sample issues of twenty-six issues in all twenty-three of the European Union's official languages in the major papers of all twenty-seven member states. Therefore the *FT* has been chosen as a measure of media attention to the issues, as it is considered an unbiased presentation of EU news; "With few exceptions (such as the *Financial Times* or the Brussels-based *European Voice*) the media invariably view European Union developments through a national prism" (Watson and Shackleton 2003).

Issue Variation

This data collection process led to a random sample of twenty-one issues in the United States and twenty-six issues in the European Union. The issues vary on a number of characteristics of interest such as the scope of the issue, salience, and conflict as well as occurrence of a focusing event on the topic or an issue being a new topic or one that was recurring with a longer issue history. Table 3.1 presents the variation on these characteristics.

To give a sense of the variety of issues, some of the cases that form the basis of this research will be briefly described (the appendix contains a full description of each of the forty-seven issues). In the United States, the sample includes issues of very large scope such as the U.S. Farm Bill, which was the renewal of the nation's agricultural policy including titles covering traditional commodities such as dairy, sugar, peanuts, and livestock, to titles on trade, credit, forestry, and energy, to rural development including chapters on rural broadband access, historic barn preservation, and even a section on rural seniors, as well as a title on agricultural research and education that covers topics such as biosecurity. In short, the 2002 Farm Bill was a massive piece of omnibus legislation affecting large numbers of citizens and involving billions of dollars. At the other extreme were very small niche issues like Effluent Limitation Guidelines for the Transportation Equipment Cleaning industry. This case concerns EPA regulations of wastewater runoff when tank trucks—used for

Table 3.1   Issue Characteristics

	United States		European Union	
	Frequency	Percent	Frequency	Percent
Scope				
Small sector	9	43	12	46
Large sector	7	33	8	31
Multiple sectors	2	10	3	12
Pan-EU/pan-U.S.	3	14	3	12
Conflict				
One perspective	9	43	9	35
Multiple but not opposing	1	5	2	8
Opposing perspectives	11	52	15	58
Focusing Event				
Absent	16	76	25	96
Present	5	24	1	3
Issue History				
Recurring	14	67	21	81
New issue	7	33	5	19
Salience	*New York Times*		*Financial Times*	
0 stories	11	52	14	54
1–5 stories	5	24	11	42
6–30 stories	3	14	1	4
31 or more stories	2	10	0	0
Total	21	100	26	100

transporting liquids in bulk—are cleaned between trips. The EPA had to regulate the amount and content of the runoff and did so through its small business office, working closely with transportation equipment users and cleaners.

There is also a great deal of variation in the salience of the issues in the sample. The case of a ban on human cloning was highly salient. The announcement of the successful cloning of a human in 2002, while never confirmed, produced a large amount of political, media, and public interest in the issue of cloning human embryos—both for therapeutic reasons as well as less likely reproductive purposes. In addition, the tireless work of paralyzed actor Christopher Reeves in support of stem cell research also kept the topic in the news. Then there are the issues of no interest to the larger public, such as the Recreation Marine Employment Act, a bill introduced to exempt small marinas from having to pay longshoreman's insurance, a type of insurance intended to protect dockworkers on large seafaring ships. Proponents pushed for an exemption from the irrelevant insurance, which they argued would improve the financial situation of small marinas, allowing them to hire more staff, which in turn would be good for small communities.

Highly charged issues also fell into the sample such as the revision of Corporate Average Fuel Economy Standards; these are regulations regarding the fuel use of vehicles and were hotly contested by environmental organizations and industry representatives. Environmental advocates adamantly argued for the need to improve vehicle efficiency in order to protect the environment and alleviate the country's dependency on foreign oil, while industry representatives countered that no additional technological changes were feasible and that lighter cars could endanger passengers. The positions of politicians came down to classic partisan divisions. Conversely, other issues had no evidence of conflict at all, so-called motherhood-and-apple-pie issues that are difficult to publicly oppose. An example of such an issue from this sample is U.S. funding for basic education in developing countries. This was a push to increase the U.S. aid budget to support K–12 schooling in the third world, with an emphasis on the importance of girls' education. Advocates of basic education argue and provide evidence of the positive ripple effects of education for developing countries.

A handful of issues were related to some type of focusing event. The Enron scandal resulted in a great deal of fallout in the business world. Three issues in my sample were framed as a response to the Enron scandal: regulation of over-the-counter derivatives, regulation of affiliate relationships, and regulation of stock option expensing. Senator Dianne Feinstein of California called for regulation of all types of financial instruments known as derivatives following the Enron scandal because many believed California's energy crisis— a series of price spikes and blackouts in 2000 and 2001—resulted from the lack of transparency in the energy trading market. Derivatives were never regulated in the past and thus became a subject of scrutiny.

The issue of regulating affiliate relationships is similarly linked to the Enron focusing event. The Federal Energy Regulatory Commission (FERC) released a proposed rulemaking for electricity and natural gas that would regulate the way large companies, with multiple subentities (or affiliates), could communicate with each other. Without such regulation, proponents argued, large conglomerate companies that own subcompanies along the production line (e.g., a natural gas company with entities controlling extraction, processing, pipeline transportation, and distribution) would have an unfair advantage, leading to a situation similar to insider trading where the CEO of such a conglomerate would have access to supply and demand information, and be in the position to manipulate supplies.

Finally, the issue of stock option expensing had been debated by academics for years, but being a theoretically tricky issue, never materialized as a political issue. Stock options are an option to buy a certain number of shares of stock in the future; because the value of stock constantly fluctuates, it is difficult to place a set value on options, and therefore difficult to expense them in company annual reports. Thus, it had traditionally been the practice to not include stock options in financial reports. However, after the clear abuse by Enron CEOs, stock options came to be seen as something manipulated and exploited by billionaire board members—to the detriment of shareholders—and more and more advocates called for federal regulation to force companies to expense their stock options in their books.

Two other issues in the sample also involved focusing events. The issue of regulation of foreign nationals and laboratories, a topic of great concern to universities, was a direct result of the September 11 attacks in New York, Washington, and Pennsylvania. The Patriot Act was created specifically to strengthen national security and generation of this act also gave rise to the issue of how strongly to regulate foreign nations living in the United States and how strongly to lock down research laboratories. The other issue rekindled due to a focusing event was the ban on human cloning. Though Senator Brownback and others had sought to ban cloning in the past, the effort had largely lost steam, until December 2002 when the group Clonaid publicly claimed to have cloned a human and that the mother of the clone had given birth to her. While the claims of this group, which also attested to communicating with aliens, were highly questionable, the suggestion that science was close enough to possibly achieve such a feat mobilized anticloning advocates to call for a federal ban on cloning for any purpose.

The full range of the legislative process is also represented in the sample. There are the first attempts to get an issue on the agenda, like the case of funding for optometric residencies. This case was so young that the potential champion in Congress targeted by the lead organization was not yet on board to make it a concrete issue. At the other end of the legislative time line was a case that was finalized during the interviewing stage, which involved including federal safety officers along with local police in a program within the Affordable Housing for Americans Act of 2002 to encourage police to reside in at-risk communities. The amendment was put forward when the bill was in committee and was accepted easily and was included in the final version of the bill. Finally, the sample ranges across the policy areas of commerce, agriculture, the environment, financial services, social services, education, energy, defense, foreign aid, infrastructure maintenance, and health.

The same high degree of variation of issue types is evident in the EU sample. An issue of massive scope is REACH, a proposal for a new regulatory system for all types of chemicals across Europe; the acronym stands for

Registration, Evaluation, Authorization, and Restriction of Chemicals. It not only impacts the European chemical industry, which would have to register 30,000 chemicals, but also all so-called downstream users—that is, all manufacturing that involves chemicals in the production process, the majority of the production industry. At the other extreme in issue size was the work of a subnational business organization to urge the Commission to produce a communication regarding the organization and operation of the organization's EU umbrella federation. The subnational organization felt there was no way to improve its condition vis-à-vis the umbrella federation other than a statement by the European Commission. Thus, this issue not only affected no other sectors, it did not even affect any other organizations or federations, save for the umbrella organization.

The European issues also varied in salience to the public. Highly salient was the Services Directive—a proposal to harmonize the services market across the European Union's internal market, to achieve a common market similar to the market for manufactured goods. The proposal would employ the "country of origin principle"—that service providers would adhere to the rules of their home country in whatever EU member states they were operating—to simplify the market in services. The goal was to enable EU citizens to compare the quality and price of various service providers and choose the optimal service provider. The proposal covered a wide range of sectors from hairdressers and nannies, to gardeners, plumbers, and electricians, to advertisers and IT support. The coverage of this EU issue was remarkable, as citizens became more and more concerned that service providers from the new member states with weaker regulations would come to the West and provide services of questionable quality for less money. The issue achieved such a level of salience that it became wrapped up in the discussions of the French and Dutch referenda on the Constitution—that a "no" vote would be a "no" to the Services Directive and a "no" to an EU that would allow weakly regulated service providers into the "old" member states.

At the other extreme is an issue that was not at all on the radar of the European public—the international negotiations surrounding the codex on fruit juices. The Codex Alimentarius is an international standard-setting system organized by the Food and Agricultural Organization of the United Nations and the World Health Organization to establish basic standards in the foodstuffs sector. The case that fell into the research sample was the standard for fruit juices, specifically what the ratio of fruit juice concentrate to water should be. The European Commission had a seat at the negotiating table in addition to the member states and thus lobbying the European Union regarding its position became a point of activity by industry. Needless to say, this is not an issue that sparked the attention of the media or the masses.

An example of a high-conflict EU issue is the case of the Consumer Credit Directive. When this directive revision was originally put forward to the Parliament and assigned to the rapporteur, no one expected it to be a hotly contested dossier; however, as debate began to unfold it became clear that the issue was rife with conflict. First, there was conflict between the institutions, with the Parliament ardently opposing the Commission's proposal, which it argued was underdeveloped and outdated. Second, there was conflict between the organized interests in which two strong camps were easily identifiable: on one side were the credit issuers, the companies and representatives of the banking industry, and on the other side were the consumer protection advocates. Thus, what at first appeared to be a simple revision of the 1987 directive became a protracted debate spanning more than four years. Many would argue that most EU issues are not nearly as contested. Other issues in the sample were of a cooperative nature, such as negotiations to set EU standards on cold storage rooms, structures used in restaurants and hospitals and similar institutions to prepare food. To ensure that cold storage rooms met similar standards of quality across the Union, EOTA was tasked with determining the proper guidelines for requirements regarding materials, ventilation, flammability, and structure strength, among others. In order to achieve this task, the competent authorities from each member state, along with expert contributors and industry representatives, discussed and agreed upon proper standards. This was not an issue characterized by impassioned politics.

While a number of issues in the U.S. sample involved a focusing event, only one case in the EU sample was linked to any type of event that crystallized policymakers and organized interests on the need to act: the issue of data retention. Following the Madrid bombings on March 11, 2004, European law enforcement cooperated to track down and prosecute those involved. Headway was made in the investigation by tracing cell phone calls made by one of the bombers. This led a number of member states to seek stricter rules on retaining traffic data—mobile calls, landline calls, and internet activity—by putting forward a proposal in the Council to require telecommunication companies to store such data in the event those data were to be needed by law enforcement. Needless to say, the telecom industry mobilized in turn, which led to heated debates about the need for such preemptive data collection and the balance between national security measures and the protection of privacy.

The full range of the legislative process is also included in the EU issue sample, from the very early stage of agenda setting—as in the case of getting public health on the EU agenda, to the end of the legislative process as in the case of regulations on live animal transport, which was decided on and concluded in the early months of my field work. As in the U.S. sample, issues from across the policy-area spectrum are included: the environment, financial services, internal market, telecommunications, energy, worker safety, foreign aid, international trade, development funds, and health.

It should be noted that the European Union does not have jurisdiction over the full range of policy issues that most national political systems do. Many EU observers commenting on the apparent lack of popular interest in the European Union have noted that the European Union does not deal with the issues that public opinion surveys show again and again to be of interest to regular citizens: education, pensions, health care. While a number of important policy areas remain the strict purview of national governments, the range of policy areas in which the European Union has full or partial control is indeed large and growing. In addition, as the issue of getting public health on the EU agenda demonstrates, advocates are creating issues even in areas the European Union does not technically control as laid out in the Treaties.

In sum, both polities produced issue samples with a wide range of characteristics. These characteristics should have important implications for the lobbying strategies lobbyists pursued and the outcomes that resulted. The relationship between issue characteristics and the various stages of the advocacy process will be investigated in the following chapters.

Advocate Variation

As described in the beginning of this chapter, the aim of the research design was to ensure variation on the institutional settings, the issues, and the interest groups lobbying on those issues. The sample of 147 advocates (sixty-five in the United States, eighty-two in the European Union) contained a good deal of variation in both polities, on a number of factors such as actor type, organizational size, and resources.[2] The variation by actor type is seen in table 3.2.

In the United States there is an even balance between citizen groups and trade associations. The other large category is members of Congress. In the United States many more government officials and representatives were named by interviewees as proponents for a particular point of view on an issue and thus they were interviewed as advocates. Most often a bill's sponsor plays an important role as an advocate for a particular perspective on an issue; often writing "dear colleague" letters to other members of Congress, holding press conferences on the Hill, having staff issue press releases, and even publishing editorials in major papers. As Hall and Deardorff argue, the importance of a congressional ally is so clear that it explains the seemingly illogical tendency of lobbyists to "lobby their friends" (2006). It is not only a bill's sponsor who acts as an advocate; mobilized members of Congress who oppose a bill or amendment behave in a similar manner.

In the European Union, on the other hand, members of the EP and Council and Commission officials were rarely mentioned as advocates. More often they were discussed as a neutral target only, or they were not named at all.

Table 3.2 Advocate Types

	United States			European Union	
	Frequency	Percent		Frequency	Percent
Citizen	9	14	Citizen	17	21
Foundations	3	5	Foundations	1	1
Union	1	2	Union	2	2
Professional	7	11	Professional	1	1
Trade	12	18	Trade	40	49
Multinational corporation	2	3	Business	5	6
Corporation	7	11	Lobbying firm	3	4
Think tank	3	5	Multinational corporation	4	5
Institution	1	2	MEP	1	1
Association of institutions	1	2	Commission	1	1
Member of Congress	14	22	EU agency	2	2
Executive branch official	5	8	Perm rep	1	1
			National governmental unit	1	1
			Regional/local government	2	2
			International institution	1	1
Total	65	100		82	100

Table 3.3   Advocate Staff Size

	United States		European Union	
	Frequency	**Percent**	**Frequency**	**Percent**
1 to 5	17	26	30	37
6 to 20	31	48	38	46
21 or more	17	26	14	17
Total	65		82	

Many lobbyists clearly stated that Commission officials asked that they not reveal that the lobbyists talked with them. Moreover, rapporteurs are assigned by the EP president to see a dossier through the legislative process. This assignment is based on party group power, not individual MEP interest in the topic. Thus in the EU sample fewer policymaker-advocates are found. Roughly 25 percent of the sample is composed of civil society groups, and about half are business, trade, and professional organizations.

Previous studies often focused on a certain type of advocate by including business, trade, and professional organizations; professional lobbying firms and public relations consultancies; as well as citizen groups, institutions, and officials, so lobby strategies of different types of actors can be compared and analyzed.

Organizational resources are also very important in lobbying strategies and there is a wide range in both samples, as indicated by the staff size of government affairs offices in Washington and Brussels. Table 3.3 presents the range in advocacy staff size in the United States and European Union gathered from interviews with advocates. U.S. lobbying offices are generally better staffed with an average of twenty-nine staff people versus an average of fourteen in the European Union. The two political systems are similar in that roughly half the offices have ten or fewer staff, but the United States exhibits a higher number of very large offices. Numerous interest-group characteristics should theoretically influence lobbying strategy decisions, including not only advocate type and resources but also membership type, size and spread, organization structure, and goals. The effect of each of these characteristics on each stage of the advocacy process will be investigated, along with institutional and issue characteristics.

CONCLUSION

The research strategy introduced at the beginning of this chapter was designed to achieve variation on institutional, issue, and interest-group characteristics, to allow study of the effect of all three levels of factors on the advocacy process. The data collection process produced such variation with a wide range of policy cases and advocates. Now that the theoretical and empirical foundations for the research have been laid out, the empirical analyses can be presented. The following chapters will investigate how the three levels of critical factors interweave to determine lobbying decisions.

NOTES

1. Advocacy and Public Policymaking Project, NSF grants SES-0111224 and SBR-9905195.

2. Two of the 149 in-depth interviews conducted were more exploratory in nature and thus are not included in the empirical analyses.

4

Lobbying Positions

MANY OBSERVERS OF U.S. and EU politics perceive a great difference between U.S. and EU lobbying *styles*. Wöll's comprehensive review of the literature in this area concludes that "all analysts seem to agree that EU lobbying is less confrontation and more consensus-oriented than U.S. lobbying" (2005b, 7). She references a number of scholars to support this interpretation, such as Coen's argument that the European lobbying style is characterized by a "low public profile" and is "sophisticated" compared to the "aggressive lobbying of Washington firms" (1999, 41). McGrath, in his comparison of European and American lobbying styles, quotes a lobbyist who suggests differences stem from culture: "I think it might also simply have to do with the natural characteristics, for here people tend to be very reserved, polite, discreet, while Americans seem to be very brash and in your face" (2000, 23; see also 2005). Thomas and Hrebenar (2000) also refer to culture: "Unlike the situation in the United States where 'defensive lobbying' is a widely used tactic, it is not in the nature of EU lobbying to stop something, to kill it" (quoted in Wöll 2005b, 12).

American lobbyists, the misperception suggests, use money, connections, and threats to strong-arm policymakers into killing legislative proposals. Self-interest is blatant in their argumentation. Everything is political; everything is partisan. EU lobbyists, the stereotype continues, are much more reserved, providing information and expertise in a neutral manner. Their argumentation focuses on the data. Nothing is political; everything is technocratic. Many have noted that in the European Union, lobbyists do not try to "kill" anything as do their American counterparts; this is attributed to the stark differences in aggressive versus compromising natures. These stereotypes are highly inaccurate.

Observers seek to explain these general patterns through simplistic cultural explanations which themselves are indicative of different approaches to lobbying fights. The dependent variable here that I seek to explain is the position lobbyists assume at the beginning of a political debate—do they seek to promote a policy proposal, do they seek to modify an existing proposal, or do they seek to kill a proposal? Lobbying behavior can be better understood by studying the variation in these specific lobbying positions, which can be operationalized and explained by a set of independent variables.

I show that the patterns of lobbying positions in the two capitals are not drastically different, especially when it comes to killing proposals, and I provide data to support this conclusion. To the extent that there are differences in the way in which U.S. and EU lobbyists approach policy debates, the tendency is due not to inherent cultural traits, but rather to democratic institutional design and the rules surrounding the policymaking process. These institutional factors affect the probability of policy change, which in turn influences the lobbying positions advocate assume.

In the United States the likelihood of policy change on a specific issue is low; a proposal may succeed or it may die. In 2004 only 306 bills were enacted into law out of the 2,764 introduced in the House and Senate; that is an 11 percent passage rate, or put differently, 2,458 proposals failed (Congressional Record 2005). Of course, many bills would not bring substantive policy change, while others are introduced for symbolic reasons, but the bill passage rate gives an indication of how difficult it is to enact a policy proposal. Advocates can more clearly come down for or against the status quo, and thus lobbyists tend to find themselves in a position fighting to promote a bill or to block it. In the European Union the potential for policy change is much higher, as is demonstrated by only two codecision proposals having failed since 1994—a proposal on takeover bids in 2001 and a proposal on port services in 2003 (Europa 2005). Again, the codecision passage rate does not cover all policymaking processes, but it gives a sense of the likelihood of policy change once a proposal is developed. Whether advocates are for or against a proposal is less consequential—in either case they must seek to mitigate the damages or promote the proposal if they support it. Thus lobbyists tend to find themselves in a position where they are working to modify the proposal. Three lobbying positions then are possible in each polity: promoting, modifying, or blocking. In the United States however, there is a higher probability of promoting and blocking and in the European Union, a higher probability of modifying.

Moreover—and in further evidence of the inaccuracy of the caricatures in the introductory paragraphs—the differences are tendencies, not absolute divergences. Variation in policy-change expectations and thus lobbying positions can be found within both polities. This variation can be explained by issue level factors. Some issues have so much inertia behind them that they cannot be killed, regardless of the polity.[1] For example in the United States, an annual budget must go through, an energy bill laying down the nation's energy policy must be agreed upon, some form of antiterrorism legislation following the September 11 terrorist attacks had to materialize. In the European Union an issue may not follow the standard codecision legislative process that so often leads to new policy, or the question of whether a certain issue falls under the jurisdiction of the supranational institutions may be contested, and thus policy change may not be as assured. The nature of the issue and the policymaking process being employed influence the probability that a policy proposal will succeed.

Thus, lobbyist perceptions or expectations about the potential for policy change are the mechanism by which institutional and issue characteristics influence their lobbying positions. This chapter seeks to highlight the role of institutions and issue factors in determining whether an advocate is in a promoting, modifying, or blocking position.

Therefore, first the relevant institutional differences between the two systems are discussed, detailing how those differences affect the potential for policy change and thus lobbying positions. The second section details how issue characteristics also play a role in shaping the policy change expectations of lobbyists and, in turn, their lobbying positions. In the empirical section, qualitative and quantitative evidence is presented demonstrating the effect of institutional and issue differences on the lobbying positions of advocates.

The lobbying positions in which advocates find themselves are critically important, not just because in the aggregate they explain the general style of lobbyists active in Washington and Brussels, but because they play an important role in determining argumentation strategies. An advocate's arguments on a given policy debate are determined by the institutional system within which the advocate is active, the characteristics of the issue, as well as who the advocate is and his or her lobbying position. Chapter 5 examines these parameters.

FACTORS INFLUENCING POLICY CHANGE EXPECTATIONS AND POSITIONS

Two institutional differences are important to understand the difference in U.S. and EU lobbying positions: electoral accountability and the rules of the policymaking process. The first tends to give American lobbyists more leverage over their policymaking targets than their counterparts in the European Union. The second creates different opportunities for initiating policy change and different inertial environments for lobbyists in the two polities. These will be discussed, followed by a discussion of how issue characteristics affect the potential for policy change within the two polities.

Institutional Characteristics

The first institutional characteristic that can affect the selection of advocacy positions is the degree of electoral accountability in the political system. If an elected official votes for a bill, and constituents disapprove of it, the official could pay for it at election time. If an elected official supports a bill approved of by constituents that official could benefit on election day. Thus, whether a bill is passed or not could have direct bearing on policymakers' careers. This provides lobbyists some leverage when they go before a policymaker to present policy positions; they can emphasize how the policymaker's constituents share similar concerns and further, that those constituents can be mobilized at election time to vote accordingly. In the European Union, this is less the case; the careers of Commission officials, Council ministers, and MEPs do not depend as directly on how they voted on any given proposal. Lobbyists in the European Union may not be able to credibly threaten to mobilize constituents during the next election to throw policymakers out who did not vote their way. This is because the chain of democratic accountability is longer—EU officials need to act, information of that action needs to get back to constituents (often difficult because of low levels of news coverage of EU politics), and then that EU action needs to be weighed against their performance in domestic politics (it will be difficult to vote out a national government that is wildly successful in bringing down unemployment because of its EU policy decisions). For these reasons it is harder for lobbyists to credibly threaten direct electoral implications for EU action.

Thus in the United States, members of Congress can be convinced that championing or killing some bills is in their personal interest. In the European Union there are no direct personal ramifications for decisions on individual dossiers, and thus policymakers have less incentive to champion a proposal or destroy it. Generally then, U.S. lobbyists may be more likely to take promoting positions if they support a bill, and blocking positions if they oppose a policy because the former stance gives them a better chance of convincing legislators to champion or kill a bill. These hypothesized relationships are only tendencies, but they are expected to be strongly reinforced by the more powerful institutional force: the rules surrounding the policymaking process. The rules of the policymaking process influence the lobbying positions that advocates assume and determine the probability of initiating a proposal and the probability of proposals making it through the policymaking process to become law.

In the United States it is relatively easy to propose a bill; any member of Congress can draft a bill and put it in the hopper and the Speaker of the House will send it to committee. Thus advocates who support a proposal can seek to promote that proposal to any member of Congress who will listen. Proposal initiation is relatively easy, so a huge number of bills are introduced every Congress. Many of these bills die in committee, some make it to the floor and die. If a bill does pass, an identical version must pass in the other chamber and if there are differences between the House and Senate versions they have to go to conference; few bills actually become law. In addition, at the end of a two-year Congress if a bill has not passed it dies and has to be reintroduced which, while easy, does take some level of political will.

In the European Union only the Commission has the right to introduce proposals, so there is no reason for advocates supporting a proposal to attempt to promote it to any EU official who will listen. There may be many MEPs sympathetic to their view, but they cannot introduce a proposal for the advocate. When a proposal for a regulation or directive does surface, much more effort has gone into its development. The process includes a multitude of steps; often there have been green papers, white papers, consultation meetings, Internet consultations with stakeholders, and the development of nonpapers, drafts, and redrafts. Once a proposal surfaces, a lot of energy has already been invested. Furthermore, there is no time line killing a proposal after a certain period: the current consumer credit directive (CCD) has been debated for five years, and there are examples of proposals being debated for much, much longer.

This leads to two different hypothesized approaches by lobbyists in the United States and the European Union. In the United States you try to kill a bill or amendment if you oppose it, and you try to make it survive the legislative process if you support it. In the European Union you would not likely spend much time promoting proposals. If an initiative has been launched by the Commission, you know that the proposal is going to materialize in one form or another; your aim is to make changes, amendments, and compromises so that it does minimum damage or achieves the highest goals. As one EU lobbyist interviewed put it: "Action by the Commission is like the weather; it doesn't really matter whether you like it, or don't like it—it just is."

These two institutional characteristics—electoral accountability and the rules of the policymaking process—lead to two different environments in which U.S. and EU lobbyists must work. In the U.S. arena lobbyists supporting a bill can more easily promote it and seek champions for it, and lobbyists opposed to a proposal are better able to try to block that proposal. In the EU arena lobbyists in support of a proposal have a difficult time promoting the launch of a new initiative and must work by modifying related initiatives. Furthermore, lobbyists opposed to a proposal must seek to modify the proposal in ways that make it less damaging to the interests the lobbyist represents.

Issue Characteristics

The nature of the issue at hand also affects the probability that policy change will occur and thus the expectations and lobbying positions of advocates. Each issue varies in the momentum behind it; that momentum is driven by focusing events, the scope of the issue, the degree of conflict, and the policymaking procedure.

Some authors have discussed the importance of focusing events in crystal-lizing the need for policy change (Kingdon 1995; Baumgartner and Jones 1993). For example, a nuclear power plant meltdown captures the attention of the media and the public as well as politicians. If a policy change could prevent such a disaster from occurring in the future, the event causes pres-sure to produce a policy change and to do so in a timely manner.

The scope of the issue could also affect a lobbyist's perception about the potential for policy change. If an issue is extremely large in scope, affecting multiple large industries or the country or the supranational system at large, a lobbyist may feel less confident that he or she could derail such a substan-tial proposal. In such a situation an advocate may have to settle for a modi-fying strategy. The degree of conflict may also play a role in lobbying position selection. Low-level conflict may lead lobbyists to follow a modi-fying position, while issues with intense conflict, where opposing camps are battling it out, may drive lobbyists to attempt to block proposals supported by their adversaries.

Finally, the policymaking procedure should matter a great deal in the po-tential for policy change and thus in lobbying positions. Some policymaking processes are more likely to lead to new policies, such as regulatory issues in the United States or social dialogue or other "soft" policy instruments in the European Union. In both cases an institution releases some version of a noti-fication to regulate, and the representatives of organized interests are invited to share in the policymaking process; while the quality of the output of these processes may be questioned, they almost always lead to a policy change. There may be a lower probability of policy change with standard legislative process, providing lobbyists with an opportunity to attempt to block the proposal.

EMPIRICAL FINDINGS

For the dependent variable in this chapter, each U.S. and EU advocate was coded as to whether they were promoting a policy proposal, working to modify a policy proposal, or fighting to block a policy proposal. Qualitative discus-sions of each type are provided as well as qualitative evidence of the relation-ship between those positions and the independent variables. Data collection for the issue-level independent variables was described in chapter 3; here data are included on the occurrence of a focusing event, the degree of conflict, the scope of the issue, and the policymaking procedure.

Institutional Characteristics

Considering the institutional hypothesis that lobbyists in the United States will be more likely to attempt to promote or block a proposal and EU lobbyists more likely to work to modify a proposal, figure 4.1 reports the percentage

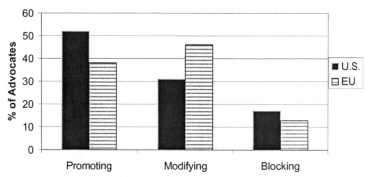

**Figure 4.1   Lobbying Positions in the United States
and the European Union**

of advocates in each polity that assumed each of the three positions: promoting, modifying, and blocking.

The evidence supports the expectations: lobbyists in the United States are more likely to promote a proposal, at 52 percent, compared to EU advocates, of which only 38 percent worked to do so. Lobbyists in the United States were also slightly more likely to attempt to block a bill, at 17 percent, than advocates in the EU, of which only 13 percent attempted to do so. Finally, EU advocates were more likely to attempt to modify policy proposals, at 46 percent, compared to their U.S. counterparts, of which 31 percent reported doing so.

In the United States examples abound of advocates seeking out congressional champions and working with their governmental allies to promote a policy. On the issues of regulating over-the-counter derivatives, funding for optometric education, exempting small marinas from longshoreman's insurance, and banning human cloning, among others, advocates were working hard to get issues on the agenda, get bills introduced, and promote them to other policymakers.

In the European Union the plurality of advocates were in modifying positions, with most advocates assuming modifying positions compared to promoting and blocking. A number of EU lobbyists attested to the inevitability of policy change as their motive for taking a modifying position. A business advocate on the CCD, a policy decided by the codecision process, noted: "On CCD in general we don't see the need for a new Directive, we are fine with the Directive of 1987. The whole banking industry didn't call for this, they all would be happy to have the current Directive stay in place. But now it is on the table so now we have to try to modify it and amend it." While all of industry was opposed to the CCD revision, none of the advocates took a blocking position; once the ball was rolling, they recognized a new policy would ultimately result and thus a modifying position was the only option.

On another issue that would have a dramatic impact on a single industry, again, manufacturing advocates did not attempt to block, recognizing that a Commission proposal indicated the institution was serious about policy change. The tire manufacturing industry lobbyists merely asked for more time to phase out cancer-causing aromatic oils from the tire production process.

Even REACH, a regulation that would have a massive impact on the chemicals industry, was not blocked out of hand by industry advocates. Instead lobbyists representing chemical manufactures, cognizant of the high probability of policy change, took modifying positions across the board. One industry advocate put it in these rather positive words: "Mostly all of industry, like us, says: workable, at reasonable cost, and proportionality. Everyone wants REACH to succeed."

Similarly on the case of the Clean Air for Europe Framework (CAFE)—a policymaking framework that would simultaneously review and revise a number of older directives that regulate nitrogen oxide, particular matter, carbon dioxide, and sulfur oxide—advocates for heavy industry that would be directly affected by the ultimate legislation were all pursuing modifying positions rather than blocking. Many lobbyists indicated that their modifying position was due to the long policy development method being employed by the Commission, which included a great deal of consultation with organized interests. A representative of one heavy industry noted: "We do support the CAFE process because it is set up to be a huge consultation, a three-year-long consultation with stakeholders, and everyone is around the table, everyone interested is really included in the discussion." With policymakers embracing the input of advocates during a three-year policymaking process, attempting to block the framework was not a viable option for lobbyists. The CAFE process was going to go forward, and it was imperative that the set of directives included under the framework be reviewed and revised. If advocates wanted to work with the Commission to modify the proposals they were welcome to do so, but if they wanted to see CAFE killed, they would have to sit on the sidelines while they watched representatives of other interests play the policymaking game.

As a final example of the tendency to modify, all of the advocates interviewed who were opposed to the Service Directive sought modification rather than annihilation because they recognized the momentum behind the Commission proposal; as one business community representative explained, "The Services Directive didn't just come out of the blue, it is the outcome of a very long consultation process that has been going on for about four years, from 2000 to 2004, in which we have been involved throughout. It is based on the idea that the internal market for services is not working, and it is not just an idea but is empirically supported by the Kok report." The Kok report, a re-evaluation of the European Union's progress toward the goal to be the most dynamic and knowledge-based economy by 2012, painted a very depressing picture and called for dramatic reforms if there were any hope of achieving some semblance of the original goal. One of its suggestions was passing the Service Directive. The Kok report and the lagging economy of the European Union throughout that period further bolstered the call for liberalizing the internal market in services and added fuel to the fire driving policymaking forward on this issue. Thus we see it is not an innate desire to be amenable that compels EU lobbyists to assume modifying positions, but rather momentum-driven policy environments.

While the findings in figure 4.1 and the examples above provide evidence of the tendency for lobbyists in the United States and the European Union to approach lobbying from different positions, the trend is far from absolute. Thirty-one percent of American lobbyists are forced to resort to modifying inevitable policy proposals. Thirty-eight percent of EU advocates were assuming promoting positions and 13 percent of EU lobbyists find themselves in situations where they feel they can attempt to block a policy proposal. The nature of the issue at hand, discussed next, goes a long way in explaining this variation in lobbying positions within each polity.

Issue Characteristics

In the United States actors on a number of issues reported modifying positions because the policies being debated had too much momentum behind them to be stopped. Focusing events are one factor that provides such propulsion to issues. None of the actors on two such issues reported taking a blocking position. One issue is antiterrorism regulations and especially how they related to student visas and laboratory security. After the September 11 attacks there was much momentum to enact laws that would prevent future terrorist incidents, and a great deal of bipartisan solidarity aided the quick passage of policy proposals like the far-reaching Patriot Act. The atmosphere was not one in which an advocacy group could be seen as working to block or kill the proposals. As one lobbyist working to modify the policy proposals noted:

> We wanted to be clear that we weren't in opposition to the tracking system, but we wanted to make sure it was workable. In this climate, it's a real challenge to work with legislation and not be perceived as being a drag on patriotism—being unwilling to do our role in the antiterrorism effort. The public relations side to that is very tricky. In fact, one of the associations we work with, they had written a letter to INS outlining a few remaining concerns with this computer tracking system as they were currently considering rolling it out. The *New York Times* had a front-page article, accused the university community of foot-dragging.

It was an unfair article, it was inaccurate. But it portrayed universities in a very unfortunate light, one that we had been trying very carefully not to be trapped in.

Similarly an immigrant rights lobbyist echoed concern about being perceived as blocking the legislation: "I think the immigrant community, after the USA Patriot Act understood that you can't be antisecurity, clearly we want to be pro-security as well . . . you can't just keep saying no, no, no to everything, because then you just aren't a legitimate actor."

Another issue driven forward by a focusing event was the debate over regulating affiliate relationship in the electricity and natural gas industries. The rules would control how entities of a large company could share information if the company had subunits (or affiliates) throughout the chain of production. The Enron scandal provided the catalyst to enact regulations that had been discussed for years. Once that process began, advocates opposed to the regulation saw no way out. As one industry lobbyist noted: "I guess no rule would have been the optimal one, at one point there were a number of people that argued well, look FERC, if you really need to do anything you don't need to do it right now, but that's politically not feasible right now, given Enron and everything else." Thus, advocates who might have worked to block the proposal were required to attempt modifications at the edges, due to the shift in political climate.

From the academic literature that documents powerful examples of policy-altering focusing events and from our own personal memories of such historical events in the news, we may be led to believe issues with focusing events are the most momentum-driven cases (see Boin and t'Hart 2003), forcing lobbyists who oppose the new initiatives into modifying positions. This is because regulators are suddenly armed with real-world evidence of the status quo policy's failure and are further supported by a public mobilized by the event.

However, this is where case-study analysis can lead us astray and why it is important to consider a larger number of issues. While focusing events do sometimes result in such a great deal of momentum that advocates are unable to assume blocking positions, this is not the norm. Of lobbyists reporting a blocking position, 45 percent of them did so on an issue without a focusing event, while 55 percent did so on an issue with a focusing event. Thus, of advocates blocking, more were doing so on issues that should have been driven forward by the powerful force of a focusing event. Some advocates who reported taking blocking positions did so on three of the five issues in the sample that had a related focusing event. One case regarded the regulation of over-the-counter derivatives, a second was the debate on human cloning, and the third concerned regulating stock options. The reason why advocates were able to block on these cases becomes apparent when we consider the other issue characteristics.

The effect of a focusing event varies; it can interact with other issue-level characteristics. The actors on the issues related to antiterrorism proposals and affiliate relationship regulations were unable to pursue blocking positions. The effect of the focusing event may have been bolstered by the policymaking procedure. The first issue involved an administration-initiated proposal and the second involved a regulatory issue, both of which are more likely to lead to policy change. Other issues with related focusing events did allow for blocking positions by opposition advocates. Those cases were (a) an amendment to regulate over-the-counter derivatives; (b) a bill to regulate stock option expensing; and (c) a bill to ban human cloning. The first was an amendment, which is easier to block than an entire bill. The other two were high-conflict topics that, as the empirical findings show, led to a higher probability of blocking strategies.

Stock option expensing was fiercely debated between regulators and large companies that would not be affected by the regulations and companies that relied heavily on stock options as part of their financial strategy. The debate on human cloning was quickly defined according to pro-choice and pro-life lines, historically diametric opposites. Thus, we see that focusing events can act as a catalyst for policy change, but other issue factors interact to determine the ultimate lobbying position advocates assume.

In the EU sample issues with related focusing events were much less common; only one case had an event related to it that propelled policymaking forward: data retention. The aim of retaining traffic data of telephone, mobile, and internet traffic is to use such data stores to track down terrorists and individuals involved in organized crime. The idea of such data retention was supported by some law enforcement bodies for a number of years, but the 2004 Madrid train bombings, and the successful use of mobile phone records to capture some of the attackers, increased support for the proposal. While support was yet again bolstered by the series of tube and bus bombings in London in 2005, this case was not one in which the issue momentum drove advocates to take more passive, modifying positions. The attempts to kill this proposal were unceasing throughout 2004 and 2005, with lobbyists of different stripes all opposing it for different reasons.

As the *European Voice* put it, "Police representatives believe it would be unwieldy; phone and internet companies estimate its cost would be prohibitive; and civil rights groups regard it as tantamount to mass espionage" (Cronin 2005, 34). Thus, the numbers for this issue variable are low in the European Union, but of the four actors interviewed who were active on an issue with a focusing event, 75 percent were blocking. As in the United States, the role of a focusing event must be considered in conjunction with other issue-level characteristics. Specifically the policymaking process in this issue was not the standard codecision process that so often leads to a new policy in the European Union, but rather a rare initiative put forward by the Council. Therefore policy change expectations of the lobbyists were lower and they knew this type of procedure could be stopped. Their decision to take a blocking position was further supported by the tension they observed between the supranational institutions—as the EP disapproved of a procedure on which they would not have equal say, and the Commission disapproved of the Council initiating such a proposal, when it should, in their view, have come from the Commission.[2] Thus, while the European Union provides an institutional setting that generally promotes modifying lobbying positions, here we see a strong blocking strategy was pursued by advocates faced with a proposal they vehemently opposed and who felt empowered by a questionable policymaking procedure.

The link between the nature of the issue and the lobbying position is strong when it comes to the level of conflict on the issue: of those advocates reporting using a blocking position in the United States, all reported doing so on high-conflict issues where opposing camps were dueling. No advocates reported blocking stances if they were active on issues with no conflict or were active on issues with multiple perspectives that were not in direct opposition. Note that it is theoretically possible to block on a no-conflict issue; for example, an amendment gets introduced with language that could negatively affect an industry, the lobbyists for that industry choose a blocking strategy, but no other advocacy organizations are interested or mobilized on that precise point—thus it would be a situation in which blocking occurred on a no-conflict issue.

When it comes to low-conflict issues in the United States, even though the institutional system is more favorable than the EU system to blocking strategies, none can be found. Thus, if advocates are working on a case where one perspective dominates or multiple perspectives are contributing to the debate, all advocates involved see modifying approaches as the most productive.

In the European Union the exact same pattern emerged; of those advocates in a blocking position, all were active on high-conflict issues while no advocates reported blocking positions if they were active on issues with no conflict at all or issues with multiple, but not opposing, perspectives. Again, theoretically, advocates could attempt to block a policy proposal harmful to their interests that did not concern other advocates; we do not, however, see any evidence of this. As in the United States, EU lobbyists find modifying strategies more effective than blocking on low-conflict issues.

Looking at issue scope, reported in figure 4.2, very few U.S. advocates are engaging in blocking strategies on large-scope issues: none reported doing so if they were active on an issue with an impact on multiple sectors, and only 9 percent of advocates reported doing so on issues with system-wide scope. Instead, kill-the-bill strategies were reserved for niche or single-sector scope

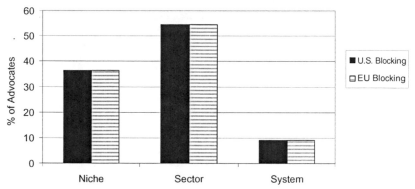

**Figure 4.2 Lobbying Positions in the United States
and the European Union by Issue Scope**

issues; 91 percent of advocates using blocking strategies reported doing so on such smaller-scope cases.

The relationship between issue scope and lobbying positions is identical in the European Union, with only 9 percent of advocates reporting blocking on large-scope issues (affecting multiple sectors or the entire system), while the majority of advocates using blocking positions did so on small-scope issues that had an impact on a single small or large sector. This was the expectation: large-scope issues, affecting and mobilizing larger numbers of organized interests, would be difficult to kill.

Finally, the policymaking procedure of an issue goes a long way in explaining the lobbyists' positions. The positions of lobbyists were correlated with three types of U.S. policymaking procedures—legislative, mixed, or regulatory. As table 4.1 shows, of those using a blocking procedure in the United States, 91 percent reported doing so on legislative issues while only 9 percent attempted to block a regulatory or mixed issue. Thus, when a case is being decided by bureaucrats, advocates find it much more difficult to take a blocking stance. This provides additional support to the institutional hypothesis that the degree of electoral accountability plays a role in determining lobbying positions, but even more important are the rules surrounding the policymaking process. Executive agencies are often mandated to pass regulations by legislative acts. So, similar to the EU system, once a proposal emerges, it will eventually be realized as a regulation. Advocates then are forced to assume modifying positions.

Within the legislative realm, however, there is still a great deal of variation (on legislative issues 21 percent are blocking, 52 percent are promoting, and 27 percent are modifying). This is in part of course explained by the fact that members of the broad interest group community want different things. However, some advocates who would like to block are forced to modify due to

**Table 4.1   Advocates Assuming Blocking Positions in the United States
and the European Union by Issue Procedure (percent)**

	United States		European Union
Legislative	91	Codecision	73
Mixed	9	Consultation	27
Regulatory	0	Implementation	0
		Social Dialogue	0
		Other	0

another aspect of the policymaking process that increases the inertia behind a policy proposal: whether the bill is an administration initiative. Within the U.S. sample a number of issues were related to large omnibus bills that are required to go through in order for the country to continue running: the 2002 Farm Bill, the 2003 Transportation Reauthorization, the 2002 TANF Reauthorization, and the 2002 Energy Bill. None of the actors active on the issues related to the first three of these omnibus bills attempted a blocking position. There was no stopping these momentum-driven bills; instead advocates worked to modify the massive proposals in ways that would protect and promote their interests.

A blocking position is possible on such a large bill if there is a singular amendment to the bill that advocates can openly criticize and attempt to kill, which was the case on the two issues related to the last omnibus bill mentioned, the 2002 Energy Bill. Two out of three advocates on both issues vigorously worked to block amendments to the 2002 Energy Bill. The first involved an amendment to regulate over-the-counter derivatives and the second involved an amendment to repeal a law that protected cogeneration facilities (PURPA: Public Utilities Regulatory Provisions Act). Advocates opposed to these amendments felt they had the ability to block the proposals from becoming part of the broader Energy Bill, and thus mobilized to make this happen.

In the European Union lobbying positions were tabulated by five policymaking procedures: codecision, consultation, implementation, social dialogue process, or other. As table 4.1 shows, 73 percent of blocking positions are on codecision. Those advocates that assumed blocking positions during consultation procedures have been discussed already—all having been on the issue of data retention. Finally, no blocking was attempted on social dialogue processes, implementation issues, or those procedures falling under "other," including fund applications, standardization procedures, and international negotiations. The policymaking process on these issues was of the type whereby some new policy would result—it was up to lobbyists if they would take part in the process and share their contributions, or stay on the sidelines while policymaking carried on without them, but blocking the process was not an option.

Advocates attempting to block proposals under the codecision policy-making process involve three issues: a directive for services of general interest, a set of directives related to alcohol advertising, and an amendment to the Packaging and Packaging Waste Directive, which would institute a PEI requirement on industry. While codecision so often results in some form of new policy, the first two issues were very early on in the policymaking process, and thus advocates felt there was still a chance to halt the process. The first was just a shadow of an idea, in the white paper phase, which would still require years of consultation and drafting before a formal proposal for a directive came out of the Commission. As such one company lobbying on the case was hoping it would disappear and was working to make that happen. It felt that if it blocked at such an early stage, perhaps the interest would dissipate and consultation would never get under way.

The second issue was similarly very upstream in the policymaking process; industry continued to try to block any type of formal regulation since they had implemented and were monitoring alcohol advertising via a self-regulation system. Industry advocates argued that as long as self-regulation did not lead to failure, no hard policymaking instruments were needed.

In addition to the earliness in the legislative process the type of proposal also plays a role. That is, as U.S. lobbyists could block amendments to omnibus bills, EU advocates could similarly attempt to block discrete amendments to large directives being decided by codecision. The third issue on which EU lobbyists assumed a blocking strategy was the PEI indicator on the Packaging and Packaging Waste Directive. The lobbyists attempting to kill the PEI proposal sounded much like their American counterparts when in a blocking position; one advocate described how the amendment was defeated:

> The main debate was on an amendment on PEI—Package Environment Indicator. Ultimately it didn't go through, the amendment on PEI got through the Environment Committee but it didn't pass plenary . . . I tell people we got a little help from Silvio Berlusconi on defeating the amendment in plenary. The vote was to take place on the 1st of July 2003, that happened to be also the first day of the Italian presidency. As it is tradition that the head of the state that is taking over the presidency say a few words to the Parliament, that day Berlusconi was to speak for a maximum of a half hour. But that wasn't what happened. After an exchange with an MEP from Germany, where Berlusconi—in one of his

attempts to be funny—said that maybe he would be a good person to play the role of a Nazi official in a new movie coming out. The German MEP was outraged and some fierce words went back and forth lasting well over an hour, so the first vote didn't happen until 1:00, and voting was supposed to have begun much earlier, most MEPs were figuring on being finished by 2:00 and going to lunch, but by 2:00 they weren't even through the first sets of votes on some very important measures regarding biotech. After those votes were all complete people started trickling out of the chamber. By the time the vote on the amendment on PEI came up there weren't enough people left to pass the amendment, so it failed, and we won the day. Thanks to Mr. Berlusconi.

Because it was an amendment to a larger directive, lobbyists opposed to the concept saw that there was a chance that this specific policy revision to the broader directive could be blocked, and thus mobilized to do so.

CONCLUSION

This chapter has provided strong evidence that institutions affect the expectations of policy change among lobbyists and thus the lobbying positions they assume. U.S. lobbyists were more likely to assume promoting positions and somewhat more likely to assume blocking positions, as it is easier in the U.S. system to introduce an initiative and to kill it once it has been proposed. This is due to both the rules surrounding the policymaking process and the need for policymakers to account for their positions on issues in the next election. In the European Union advocates were more likely to assume modifying positions because of the rules of the policymaking process that lead to an inevitability of policy change once an initiative is launched.

This analysis has also demonstrated the importance of systematically investigating how institutions influence advocacy. Trying to understanding lobbying positions without regard to the policymaking rules of the political system would result in an incomplete model, at best, and possibly a highly inaccurate explanation of why differences in lobbying positions occur. The stereotypes described in the beginning of the chapter are a case in point. Lacking a detailed analysis of the role of institutions on lobbying approaches, many observers of U.S. and EU advocacy have accounted for the differences with cultural explanations. American lobbyists behave as brash cowboys crushing legislation they dislike. European lobbyists are much more mild mannered and simply try to modify policy proposals. The data presented here should put these caricatures to rest. U.S. and EU lobbyists do not differ dramatically in their tendency to kill proposals, and the differences in promotion and modifying approaches can largely be explained by the rules of the policymaking process.

Moreover, within each polity variation in position selection remains, and that variation is explained by the character of the issue at hand. The evidence presented in this chapter demonstrates that while there are institutional differences between the United States and the European Union, advocates in the two polities respond in similar ways to issue factors. First, in both polities all advocates in blocking positions were active on high-conflict issues, while no blocking was found among advocates on low-conflict issues. Second, the size of the issue also proved important. The findings showed attempts to kill proposals to be less likely on large issues and more common on smaller-scope niche and single-sector issues, in both Washington and Brussels.

Third, the policymaking procedure plays a large role in determining the lobbying position of advocates in both systems. In the United States lobbyists are more likely to block on legislative proposals than on regulatory initiatives, and even more so on issues that are not large omnibus bills put forward by the administration. In the European Union lobbyists are more likely to block on codecision and consultation policymaking processes, especially if it is very early in the process or is on an amendment to a policy being decided by these two policymaking methods. Finally, a focusing event can influence the amount of momentum behind an issue. The relationship between focusing events and the probability of policy change is complex, interacting with other characteristics of the given issue. It seems if the other issue characteristics suggest a modifying position for opponents of a policy, the presence of a focusing event can reinforce that strategy.

Thus, we see evidence that factors at both institutional and issue levels are important in determining the selection of lobbying positions. This provides support for the theory presented in chapter 2, and for the idea that to understand the stages of advocacy we must consider the broader context that advocates are working within. In addition, it is also critical to study all stages of the advocacy process—outcomes at one stage can affect decisions and outcomes at other stages. The lobbying positions advocates assume have important implications for the arguments they use. The difference between the rhetoric of why a proposal should be promoted, cease to exist, or be modified is considerable. Chapter 5 considers the role of lobbying positions in determining argumentation strategies along with other critical independent variables at the institutional, issue, and interest group levels.

NOTES

1. The term "inertia" is used here following the literal physics definition: "a property of matter by which it remains at rest or in uniform motion in the same straight

line unless acted upon by some external force"—*Merriam-Webster's English Dictionary*. Thus, if an issue is driven forward by some factor, there is an inertial force propelling it forward.

2. This was the ultimate result in late 2005 when the Commission devised its own draft proposal to replace the Council's initiative.

5

Argumentation

ADVOCACY AT BASE is argumentation. While there can be a great deal of variation in how and to whom various policy arguments are communicated—as the following chapters will detail—it is the arguments themselves that are fundamental to advocacy. This chapter will consider the determinants of argument selection. The theoretical expectations are presented first, followed by the empirical findings, presenting a mix of quantitative and qualitative evidence regarding the character and determinants of argumentation in the two polities.

FACTORS INFLUENCING ARGUMENTATION

In some ways the selection of an argumentation strategy may seem obvious. If a proposal will damage a lobbyist's economic sector, the lobbyist would argue it will damage the economic sector. In reality, argumentation is much more complex; if a lobbyist wants to be successful in his or her lobbying campaign, it is imperative to think about the best way to frame the argument and which dimensions of the policy debate to emphasize.

While every argument has its own nuances, a number of universal dimensions can be identified and quantified. I distinguish six important types of arguments that are frequently seen and that capture the essence of lobbyists' argumentation. The use of these argument types forms the dependent variables of this chapter. Each interview was coded as to whether the lobbyist, in explaining the argumentation strategy, mentioned using arguments that (a) evoked broad commonly shared goals—motherhood-and-apple-pie arguments like "this is good for the family, community, children, sick people, elderly people, the environment, education, public health, and so forth"; (b) were highly technical in nature; (c) referenced the cost or economic impact of the proposal; (d) referenced the feasibility of the proposal or the current policy; (e) referenced the discriminatory nature or fairness of the proposal;

and/or (f) referenced constituency or public opinion. These categories are not mutually exclusive—an advocate could use a number of different types in an advocacy campaign. For example a lobbyist could claim that a proposal was bad for an economic sector and further argue that a policymaker's constituents would be opposed to the proposal.

It should be noted these broad categories are derived from the literature on lobbying, from following insider news sources on political issues, and inductively through the 149 interviews. These are argument types common on both sides of the Atlantic. On the one hand, it may seem futile to attempt to create a typology to capture argumentation, which is so broad and so rich; in some ways the endeavor inevitably leads to some degree of arbitrariness. On the other hand, argumentation is fundamental to advocacy and it is necessary to try to get some handle on describing it as well as investigating the various determinants of argumentation selection. Thus, rather than ignore a difficult topic, I attempt to work toward a better understanding of argumentation by providing quantitative and qualitative evidence about these broad and recurring lines of argumentation. Having established the rational for this typology of argumentation, we now turn to the discussion of how the three levels of institutional, issue, and interest factors are expected to play a role in argument selection.

INSTITUTION, ISSUE, AND INTEREST GROUP FACTORS

The different institutional environments of the United States and the European Union should lead to different use of the six argument types. In the United States, where policymakers are directly accountable to the public, lobbyists should exhibit more use of the first argument type, those evoking commonly shared goals as well as the last argument type, constituency or public opinion arguments. Policymakers who are highly accountable to the public should be more susceptible to arguments that make claims about commonly shared goals or the opinion of their constituents. It might also be reasonable to expect more economic arguments in the United States, as the U.S. arena includes bills appropriating federal funds.

From the EU policymaking literature we would expect more technical arguments to be made in Brussels (Bouwen 2002; Stubb, Wallace, and Peterson 2003; Kohler-Koch 1994). Technocrats or Eurocrats as they are often called should be more receptive to arguments referencing scientific data, legal precedent, or other research findings.

Not all issue characteristics are expected to have a role in determining argumentation; however the salience of an issue should play an important role in which arguments a lobbyist selects for that policy debate. The more salient an issue, the more likely a lobbyist is to employ constituency and commonly shared goals arguments. The less salient an issue, the more likely a lobbyist will rely on technical arguments, which do not translate well into sound bites for the evening news. The other issue-level factor that may play a role in argumentation is the presence of a focusing event. However, it is not that a certain type of argument is expected on issues with a focusing event but rather that there is likely to be a change in argumentation, a shift in which dimensions of the debate are being highlighted. This aspect of issue-level influence on argumentation is investigated qualitatively.

At the interest group level, the type of advocate should play a role in the selection of argumentation types. As the work of Rothenberg (1988) as well as Snow and colleagues (1986; Benford and Snow 2000) suggests, the positions an organization takes can affect whether or not it retains its members. Thus, the type of membership an organization represents may rule out the use of some types of argumentation while promoting the use of others. Citizen groups should be more likely to employ commonly shared goals and constituency arguments, while businesses should be more inclined to make technical and cost arguments. Another interest group–level factor that must be considered in understanding an advocate's argumentation strategy is the advocate's lobbying position, described in chapter 4. A lobbyist in a promoting position should be more likely to make shared goals arguments, linking the policy to concepts commonly held in high regard by the public. If a lobbyist is in a blocking position, feasibility arguments should be more likely.

EMPIRICAL FINDINGS

The argumentation strategies reported by respondents were coded according to the six categories (a–f) outlined above. Here is a more detailed description of the types of arguments under each argument category.

- Commonly shared goals arguments—This category includes arguments referencing concepts such as "good for families," "good for democracy," "good for the environment," "good for education," and so forth. As the "motherhood-and-apple-pie issues," they are positively viewed concepts that the large majority of the population would support, and that would be difficult to be publicly against.
- Technical arguments—This category includes arguments that are scientifically technical, detailing the scientific data supporting or opposing a proposal. It also includes arguments that are legally technical arguments based on previous case law or legislatively technical arguments, which make the claim that a technical change in legislative language is needed. This category can also include technical arguments that are very sector

specific, arguments that technically detail how a process works in a certain sector or how a regulation would affect the details of a sector's
operations.

- Cost or economic impact arguments—This category is fairly straightforward and would include arguments that claim a proposal or policy is
good or bad for the economy or would result in costs or savings to the
government or to private actors.
- Feasibility of a proposal or the workability of current policy—This includes arguments that a new proposal would not work or could not be
implemented as well as arguments that the current policy does not work
or that it is working fine and no new policies are necessary. This is different from technical arguments, which are more scientific or complex.
Very simple feasibility arguments can be made; for example, "This regulation cannot be implemented because it would require technology that
does not exist."
- Discriminatory nature or fairness of the proposal arguments—This includes arguments that a proposal or current policy affects some groups
more than others, or that a proposal or policy will level the playing field
or otherwise improve the equity of policy effects on citizens.
- Constituency or public opinion arguments—Arguments in this category
often are direct references to the constituency of a policymaker or references to the broader public or public opinion polls on the topic at hand.

INSTITUTIONAL CHARACTERISTICS

As expected, advocates arguing their position in the United States are more
likely, at 71 percent, to invoke shared goals that would be supported by the
majority of the electorate than are their counterparts in the EU, of which only
50 percent reported using such arguments, as seen in figure 5.1. Lobbyists in
the United States are also more likely to make constituency-based arguments:
12 percent of U.S. advocates make reference to voters in their argumentation
while no EU lobbyists reported doing so. This is still surprisingly low from a
U.S. perspective where we might assume everything is framed in reference to
constituents. However, taking a random sample of cases results in more cases
not on the public radar— the majority of political issues are not. As you will
recall thirty of the sixty-five U.S. advocates were working on issues with no
news coverage; on these types of issues advocates may not be able to credibly
argue that either the public or a specific legislator's constituents have an opinion on the topic.

Another expected trend, that U.S. lobbyists would be making cost or economic arguments at a higher rate than EU lobbyists, is also borne out in the
empirical findings. Fifty-two percent of U.S. advocates make reference to the

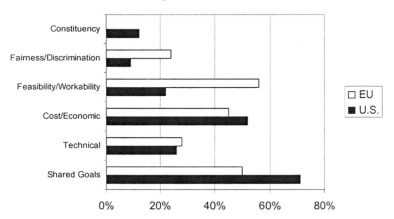

**Figure 5.1   The Use of Various Argument Types in the United States
and the European Union**

cost of proposals to the government or to private actors or refer to the economic impact on a sector or the economy at large, while only 45 percent of
EU lobbyists do so. The data on technical arguments are not extremely strong;
EU lobbyists do register as using them more than U.S. lobbyists, but only
slightly, with 26 percent of U.S. lobbyists doing so and 28 percent of EU lobbyists reporting using this type of argumentation.

The two other argument types for which there were no clear theoretical expectations—Feasibility or Workability and Fairness or Discrimination—are
both more common in the European Union. More EU lobbyists, 56 percent,
reported using arguments that referenced the feasibility of a proposal or how
well a policy was working, while only 22 percent did so in the United States.
More EU lobbyists also used arguments that referenced fairness or discrimination; 24 percent reported doing so while only 9 percent did so in the United
States. The findings show evidence of differential use of argument types in the
two polities, which is in line with expectations based on the different institutional characteristics.

While advocates in the United States and the European Union use the six
types of arguments with varying frequency, the similarity of their substantive
arguments in each category is striking. The ubiquity of these argument types
in the two polities is demonstrated through the words of the lobbyists.

SHARED GOALS ARGUMENTS IN THE
UNITED STATES

As described, arguments that invoke shared goals promote support for or protection of a commonly shared idea. A wide range of ideas are so held; across

the twenty-one issues in the United States sample arguments were made invoking the shared goals of protecting or helping children, the disabled, patient groups, the environment, and public health, as well as those that referred to promoting the security of all citizens.

One citizen group advocate engaged in the TANF reauthorization debate described its argument evoking the shared goal of helping disadvantaged disabled welfare recipients. The lobbyist and those in her coalition were arguing against strict requirements for all welfare recipients to get back to work:

> In this case, there are several arguments, but the bottom line would be, we need you to pass a bill that is going to assist people with disabilities and not leave them out in the cold. There are multiple arguments underneath that. How do you do that? That's why we need strong funding; we think there needs to be more funding in the TANF program. . . . So our main goal is to get in there with the staff, make sure that they understand what the issues are, what the population is about, sort of putting a face on. Because these are people who really can't come to the Hill themselves and talk. We're not going to get welfare moms up to the Hill. We're certainly not going to get people with disabilities easily up there to talk to the staff. So we have to do it for them.

This type of argument relies on tapping the conscience of policymakers to do what is right. In addition to citing the need to help disadvantaged groups, such as the poor, the disabled, and patient groups, advocates in the U.S. sample also spoke of more broad-reaching commonly held goals, like education. Trade association representatives were arguing for the need for strengthened math and science education in the United States, highlighting the positive effects math and science education have for the nation.

The shared goal of education was not only invoked domestically but also on international issues. Advocates active on the issue to increase U.S. funding of basic education programs through foreign aid also cited the importance of education, and the spillover effect of education. A congressional staffer advocating increased aid for basic education described the importance of education:

> It is the most basic of all, there are so many studies that have shown, particularly educating girls, that there is a domino effect on all sorts of other economic indicators. When a woman is educated, her children are healthier, she is more productive, she brings home more money for her family, the children are more likely to go to school, specifically her daughters are more likely to go to school . . . , and the numbers I think this winter are 110 million children out of school and the majority of those are girls, so there are huge disparities.

As education is a commonly held concept to promote, so is protecting public health and the environment. On the debate to revise the Food Quality Protection Act, an executive branch official who strongly advocated maintaining the current policy stated simply: "We felt these changes to FQPA would undermine the agency's ability to protect the public health. Protecting public health is an unquestionably important goal; simply stating that it is endangered can be a powerful argument."

A number of the U.S. cases had environmental aspects, and many lobbyists on those issues were making shared goals arguments that referenced the need to protect the environment. A lobbyist for an environmental organization described her arguments on the transportation reauthorization debate, which would determine how federal money was spent in the transportation sector. Her organization was advocating the concept of SMART Growth (promoting public transportation choices rather than urban sprawl) and she explained how their shared goal argumentation approach is effective: "We care about SMART growth because we care about clean air and clean water. So it often comes back to clean air and clean water, and quite frankly you know healthy children resonates with the public a lot better than, 'Hey, build me a new urbanist community,' so you go with what works."

These examples paint a picture of how U.S. lobbyists go about employing arguments that invoke shared goals. Citing concepts or groups that no politician could oppose is one effective way to garner support for a policy position. It is the most common argumentation type in the United States, where 71 percent of advocates reported using a shared goals argument. It is also common in the European Union, where 50 percent of lobbyists reported using it.

SHARED GOALS ARGUMENTS IN THE EUROPEAN UNION

Appealing to the hearts of policymakers is not limited to referencing vulnerable human groups; this technique is also used by animal rights advocates. One lobbyist on the live animal transportation debate demonstrated this and also went further to link animal welfare claims with arguments about human safety, another commonly shared goal: "Long transport times are terrible for animals, they suffer without rest, food, or water. Also, it is a health risk; after outbreaks of avian flu and other diseases, it is clear that long transport times, which make animals ill, are dangerous for human consumption."

Safety claims arose on a number of issues, such as the debate about the use of aromatic oils in tire production. While one side was arguing the carcinogenic properties of the oils, a consultancy representing the other side was also referencing human safety: "When these oils are removed it can be shown that performance decreases, especially on traction in the rain . . . there are other aspects of safety as well, to the drivers. And they are needed in certain types of specialty tires, like bulletproof tires."

Not only were claims about specific threats to human health common, but more generally advocates of increased legislation in the field of public health were making shared goals arguments in support of their position:

> What vision do we want for the future of the European Union—we believe in a social European Union that gives citizens rights, protects their well-being. . . . Public health needs to be an important priority for the European Union, they should be legislating in this area, and we try to make clear that (1) public health is not bioterrorism; (2) public health is not just communicable diseases; and (3) public health does not just involve DG health, public health involves DG trade, DG internal market, DG environment—public health affects all those areas and should be considered in all legislation.

As in the United States, advocates who support foreign aid to developing countries made references to the common desire to help needy nations. A lobbyist for a humanitarian group described his organization's arguments regarding the development heading in the European Union's Financial Perspectives. He called for a need-based approach rather than a geopolitical one: "So they are ready to dump a ton of development aid into Pakistan, even though Pakistan isn't the poorest, or the most in need, this is for political reasons, because they think Pakistan will be more stable or more influenceable—but they aren't deciding on a needs-basis—we should be funding those countries and regions that are in the greatest need."

These examples demonstrate the types of arguments lobbyists make when they are attempting to appeal to commonly shared goals and to the hearts of policymakers. This type of argument however is not always the most effective. Some issues involving mundane or arcane topics and claims about the welfare of society may not be relevant.

TECHNICAL ARGUMENTS IN THE UNITED STATES

Arguments can be technical in nature if they are highly scientific, legalistic, sector specific or focus on the details of legislative language or definitions. A number of advocates active on the issues in the U.S. sample founded their arguments on science. A lobbyist for a scientific professional association described the position on the issue of antiterrorism regulations on laboratories and agents (viruses and bacteria) after September 11:

> So we are providing scientific input into which agents should be on the list that are to be regulated, we are also providing advice on biosecurity

levels commensurate with the risk of the agent, and not just have one level of security for all of the agents because all of the agents are not the same in terms of their risk—some agents like Ebola are more difficult to work with and have different biosafety levels and also the levels should be tailored to the level of agent risk.

The issue of antiterrorism measures has a multitude of dimensions: how best to regulate dangerous agents was one aspect that required technical positions. Similarly the debate over a ban on human cloning is heavy with moral and political dimensions, but a more scientific approach was taken by some advocates active on the issue. As one citizen group described its argumentation strategy:

And then the whole question of "Do you really need to do it now?" because most of the science is struggling around whether embryonic stem cell research will even produce viable therapies, put aside clonal embryos so there is a genetic match with the patient, but can you produce them, can you solve the problem of tumorgenicity and lack of control over differentiation so that you get the kind of cell time you want? . . . So our position was, continue with embryonic stem-cell research but not cloning and if you can overcome those two obstacles you start to build the case that maybe clonal embryos are needed, but for right now the case, we feel, can't be made, because you don't even know if this approach is really even a viable one.

Some technical arguments are not based in the hard sciences but rather in the technicalities of a sector. Lobbyists on both issues concerned with regulation of financial markets relied on arguments about the technical complexity of their respective financial instruments. A lobbyist for the financial services industry explained their position on the regulation of over-the-counter derivatives:

It's a hard concept to understand but our point was because of that you shouldn't deal with an issue as complicated and as far-reaching as over-the-counter trading of derivatives and swaps in the context of an amendment on a larger energy bill, without having a full hearing on it and actually looking into the specifics and making sure that there aren't unintended consequences associated with the action you might take that would cause the market to react negatively and thereby further erode consumer confidence.

These examples demonstrate how U.S. lobbyists use technical arguments to gain support for their positions, very often to stall policy change by arguing a situation is so complex that more time and debate are needed before any new policy is put in place. Similar strategies are found in the EU.

TECHNICAL ARGUMENTS IN THE EU

Arguments based in hard science make up the bulk of the technical arguments being employed in the European Union. On the case of the CAFE framework every advocate active on the issue was employing technical science-based arguments. As a trade association lobbyist described the arguments regarding the regulation of the size of particulate matter (PM):

> PM is very central to CAFE; we believe that the scientific debate is not complete and we feel that the 2.5 is based on a decision by the Commission, not based on data. We aren't reacting to the proposal to the point of opposing it but we want to highlight the uncertainties with it and we want that uncertainty to be reflected in policy. The knowledge of PM2.5 is not solid. PM in terms of effects is unknown; there are conflicting studies, especially as to whether there is a threshold effect, so it should be run with brackets. Without having a 100 percent positive basis, we shouldn't be making policy on it. We think there should be a range.

Science-based arguments also arose on the issue of industry self-regulation of alcohol advertisements. Advocates for stricter regulations of the alcohol industry discussed health studies that they use to support their argumentation strategy:

> This has the support of I think almost all politicians except those from Spain, France, Italy, and Portugal; they say alcohol is healthy, it is good for your heart. But that isn't really true, it is only so with a lot of qualifications—like you are a male over the age of fifty or a woman over forty and only have one drink every three days, and you are at risk of heart disease. And it isn't the wine that is good for you, it is the alcohol, so the same would go for beer or other drinks. We should not be trying to make health claims about the health benefits of alcohol; we should be trying to reduce consumption. Europeans are the biggest drinkers in the world and so we also have the highest rates of alcohol-related harm.

As in the United States, also present in the European Union are technical arguments about the technical specificities of an economic sector. A trade association involved in international negotiations with the United States on the Codex regarding fruit juices relied on technical arguments as to why the standards of juice concentration (measured by the Brix value) should be set at a particular level:

> Our main argument was the 11.2 is the Brix level of oranges in the south of Europe, so the 11.2 is the natural level. We collected data, through our members, at the request of the Commission, on the natural Brix level

of our oranges; they found that 11.2 was the natural taste of oranges, so we argued that is the natural level. The United States said you have to respect the Brix values of the exporting country, but to that we responded—who has to drink it—the value should reflect the taste of the consumers, and here consumers are used to the taste of 11.2. If the standards were set at 11.8, consumers might not like it so that could depress the consumption of juices.

Also reported by lobbyists in the EU sample were legalistic arguments. Lobbyists can make legal arguments when previous case law or legislation can be referred to in support of their position. Human rights lobbyists active on the drafting of the EU annual budget were pushing for a redefinition of the External Relations heading and the Development heading. They argued that developing countries, as defined by the OECD, should be moved under the Development heading rather than External Relations. Their argument, however, wasn't simply that it was good for countries in need but rather that legal precedent demands it be so:

> Our key message is that the new Constitution considers these countries developing countries, the budget has to be in line with the Treaties, with the Constitution. This is a very strong argument because it cannot be countered; the budget has to be in line with the Treaties. And at the Commission, which is supposed to be the guardian of the Treaties, they can't really argue against it.

Scientific, legal, and sector-specific technical arguments highlight the expertise the lobbyist is bringing to the debate and provide substantiation to the positions of lobbyists.

COST OR ECONOMIC ARGUMENTS IN THE UNITED STATES

Some government proposals impose costs on private actors, others provide funds to private actors, some policies would strengthen the economy, and others may have negative unintended consequences for the health of the economy. And for each economic effect, there is a separate argument. Advocates in the United States sample made claims about the cost of policies to businesses, to farmers, to consumers, and to government, as well as arguments about the economic impact of proposals both domestically and internationally.

The most ubiquitous, and stereotypical, are industry arguments that a proposal will cost business. One example is by a manufacturing lobbyist on the Farm Bill case taking the position that American companies were unable to make a profit and thus had to close down U.S. operations due to high prices.

Price support programs aimed at increasing the return to farmers also resulted in an increase in the price of raw materials for food producers:

> The sugar program was not reformed and that's a national disgrace. Sugar sells for five cents a pound in Canada and Europe and in this country it costs about twenty-eight cents a pound. And all the candy companies in Chicago are moving to Mexico, Lifesavers announced the day after the Farm Bill was signed that they were going to move from New York to Canada where they can get five-cent sugar. So you have all these jobs going overseas all because . . . the farmer comes first.

Cost to business is often discussed in terms of factory moves, lost jobs, and costs to consumers. The cutting of funding to large road-building contractors is discussed by a pro-transport congressional staffer as an issue of jobs: "The worst thing that was done this year is the administration sent us a budget that slashed over eight billion dollars from this year's level and I've heard that for every billion dollars it's about forty thousand jobs, so you do the math—that's a lot of people out of work."

Opponents of cogeneration facilities highlighted the cost to consumers, not the cost to the electricity companies themselves, which pass the cost on to the consumer:

> We've also talked primarily about the cost to consumers about PURPA. The PURPA contracts are probably costing consumers about eight billion dollars in above-market prices every year. At one point in time when we were getting more cost information from our companies before the electricity market got competitive, we estimated PURPA was probably costing thirty-six to forty billion dollars in higher electricity prices, and that's simply money that consumers just don't need to be paying for these contracts.

Not all economic arguments are negative; many make claims that a proposal will help the economy, such as the Recreation Marine Employment Act. A congressional staffer for a member in support of the measure argued, "This is a pro-jobs bill, not an industry special interest bill. Small mom and pops are going out of business because they can't afford this insurance." This type of argument that combines a cost argument and references to small business can be a powerful one because small business is considered by some to be a motherhood-and-apple-pie sort of concept.

A similar economic group that blends the lines between economic arguments and commonly shared goals arguments is the protection of the family farm group. An energy industry representative active on the wind energy tax credit issue didn't base his arguments on the benefit to electric companies but rather on the benefit to small farmers: "We argue . . . that it's good for the small farmer and that it could help save the family farm. If a farmer can make two hundred dollars per acre from harvesting and a windmill only takes a little bit of land, a quarter-acre, and they are going to get paid three thousand dollars per quarter-acre, then they say, 'Okay, sign me up.'"

Finally, economic arguments are not limited to domestic considerations; lobbyists in Washington also consider the global economy and international trade. As a company lobbyist active on the Farm Bill illustrated:

> Then there's a trade argument too. There's a new trade round to try to lower agricultural trade barriers, the United States has generally been supportive and the lead country driving toward that effort, but this huge farm bill, in the eyes of everyone else around the world signals an about-face with respect to the notion of lowering trade barriers. So you know, we tried to point out that if you really do want to lower trade barriers you're sending the exactly opposite signal, which may make it impossible for you to have a successful trade round.

Thus we see a wide range of cost arguments claiming positive and negative effects of government policies. This is in addition to the various claims made by advocates active on issues where they were seeking federal money like the cases of Medicare funding for optometric graduate education, funding for a replacement EA-6B Prowler, basic education, funding for K–12 math and science programs, and cystic fibrosis funding.

COST OR ECONOMIC ARGUMENTS IN THE EUROPEAN UNION

In the European Union direct and clear references to the cost of a proposal to industry are more common. All of the business community advocates who were active on the data retention debate made clear arguments that the proposal was going to cost the sector, as a telecom industry representative illustrates: "What they are asking for is so large and vast in scope and so it will be very costly. And with the amended proposal there is supposed to be a cost reimbursement, but even then the cost reimbursement couldn't cover the expense. And thus the argument: 'We'll be ruined and everyone will leave Europe.'"

Other advocates do develop the cost argument further, linking the cost to business to additional secondary consequences. A trade association promoting a continuation of a reduced value added tax (VAT) in the construction sector made the link to jobs: "We kept saying, over and over, that this is good for the economic sector, that it will create jobs. It doesn't work really in the Commission—they don't believe it will have an effect—but we haven't changed our argument, we just keep saying the same thing."

A telecom company monitoring the implementation of telecoms' liberalization linked the cost to alternative provider companies to consumer choice:

> People forget. It was only ten years ago when incumbents ruled the market, but people forget how bad it was; in 1984 it took nine months to get a phone from British Telecom, you pretty much had to know someone in the ministry to get a phone, and they used to say—it takes nine months to get a phone and when you get it you can have it anywhere as long as it's in the hallway! It was really like that, and we try to remind people how bad that was and that if regulations for liberalization are too weak that could kill the alternative providers and we'd be back to the monopolies.

As in the United States, the line between cost arguments and shared goals arguments is blurred when advocates reference small businesses, which have a privileged position in the realm of industry. A trade association monitoring the implementation of the automobile industry liberalization directive referenced the danger to small businesses if the implementation were not done properly: "We try to highlight the influence the legislation could have on the market. For example there are 250,000 small companies in Belgium that do car distribution and repair, the aftermarket industry. I go and say I speak on behalf of all these firms, and all the employees they employ, and try to explain the real-world impact this is going to have, how it endangers these small companies."

Economic arguments are not limited to sector-specific cost claims; some advocates highlighted the benefit of a proposal to the systemwide economy. This was especially so on the Services Directive, which would have implications across a wide range of sectors. One business organization active on the issue explained the position they were taking: "We echo the Commission— this directive will potentially be the biggest boost to the internal market since the Euro. The internal market is completed in manufacturing; now it is time to turn to services." More creative economic arguments could also be detected. A citizen organization active on the fight to increase EU legislation in the area of public health also made broad systemwide economic arguments:

> More and more we are using an economic approach. When we did the annual report this year it was the first time we included figures on what this means economically. We are adding that more and more and when we send our report to Barroso we highlight that this is not just about being nice and caring, this is hard facts and economic impact. If you have this many children suffering from childhood obesity, they are going to be suffering from cardiovascular disease and they are more or less going to be disabled when they should be at their prime—we might lose a

generation to these types of diseases; these are people who are going to be suffering, out of work, and it is going to have an economic impact.

Finally economic arguments were not limited to the EU internal market; lobbyists also referenced international trade in their arguments. A trade association on the live animal transport debate referred to international trade: "But our main argument is competition—don't put requirements on us if you don't put them on our traders in other countries. These are the World Trade Organization arguments, these additional layers of regulations make it so much more expensive for us to produce compared to our competitors. And we make a distinction between citizens and consumers. Citizens may say they want the regulations but the consumers don't want to pay for it, so they wind up buying the competition which doesn't have the requirements."

Thus, there is a wide range of economic arguments in the European Union, including those that reference cost to individual sectors and those that reference the potential economic benefit to specific sectors and the entire internal market. In addition, cost and economic arguments are not limited to industry and representatives; citizen groups are also relying on the power of economic arguments.

FEASIBILITY OR WORKABILITY ARGUMENTS IN THE UNITED STATES

In both the United States and the European Union the rationale for incorporating organized interests into the policymaking process is often to garner information from practitioners: to gather advice on what will work, what will not, and how a proposal could be improved so that it can be more smoothly implemented. As such, advocates often reference the feasibility of a new proposal or discuss the workability of current policy—either that it is working and nothing need be changed or else that it is ineffective and new policy is therefore needed.

References to the feasibility of a new proposal are often negative: this proposal will not work. All of the industry advocates on the stock option expensing issue were making this type of claim; as one IT company representative explained: "There is no real unambiguous way to expense stock options; there are several different theories on how to expense them but there is a very gray area in forcing a company to expense something that can change over time. . . . It is a very uncertain and risky way to do things when no one can even agree on how to do it."

A disability advocate active on the reauthorization of TANF welfare policy also made a feasibility argument, specifically that the way the proposal was currently written would be ineffective:

I should mention in the House bill with regard to this issue of treatment counting as work, they had included what was in the president's bill which allowed three months to count as work and that's substance abuse and rehabilitative services, a sort of broad catchall, and that was troubling because mental health services per se were not mentioned and rehab isn't an appropriate term—these people have disabilities that are chronic and can't necessarily be rehabilitated. So there were only three months provided and we say this is highly inadequate, a completely ridiculous amount of time.

But positive feasibility arguments are also present in the argumentation strategies of the advocates in the U.S. sample. An environmental lobbyist active on CAFE argued that the proposal to increase the fuel economy of cars was feasible:

> So, basically the industry is barely meeting the current standards. And what we know, because we've done pretty extensive analysis, as have the National Academy of Sciences and other folks that we work with in the automotive and engineering world, is that the industry has technology available to them, existing, affordable, off-the-shelf technology—it's not even advanced, super-duper technology—that would bring the fuel economy of cars and trucks up to about forty miles per gallon by 2012 or so. That's just using existing technology that we know they have. And we know they can do that affordably.

Finally there are the references to the workability of current policy. In the case of PURPA reform, utility representatives opposed to the continuation of PURPA argued that the current policy simply does not work: "We've primarily been arguing that PURPA basically has failed in its objective. PURPA was designed to promote diversity in fuels, for example one of its objectives was to bolster renewable energy resources, it's done a dismal job of that—most PURPA facilities are not using renewables." Thus they argued policy change was needed.

Alternatively the effectiveness of current policy can be used as support for arguments that a program should continue. Lobbyists in support of the wind energy tax credit argued that the current policy was a success and thus should continue: "We're clean energy, it's a renewable resource. Since the tax credit was enacted in 1992, wind energy has gone from twenty-two cents to four-and-a-half cents a kilowatt hour, a clear case of government–private partnership actually working, and making it not just reasonable but feasible."

Organized interests arguing whether a policy will or will not work provide important information to policymakers about the feasibility of implementing a proposal; the same types of arguments arise on the other side of the Atlantic.

FEASIBILITY OR WORKABILITY ARGUMENTS IN THE EUROPEAN UNION

As in the United States, EU lobbyists put forth both positive and negative arguments about both proposals and current policy. Industry advocates on the data protection case made two types of feasibility arguments. First, they claimed that the proposal will not work; as one trade association lobbyist explained:

> I've given up the principle—on fighting good vs. bad. The issue is quite emotive. The other side says, "all we want to do is catch criminals" and that is a hard argument to argue against . . . who doesn't want to catch criminals. So I'm trying to turn our argument into total frustration: "We are the Internet guys, we know the Internet probably better than anybody, and we don't have any idea how to implement what you are asking us to do." Technically it is impossible.

The second feasibility argument, that the current system that is in place to liaise between operators and law enforcement works fine, was noted by another lobbyist on the case as follows:

> Our starting point is that the current situation works well: every time we have interacted with the police they say that we have cooperated and that our work has been appreciated. We keep the information we have to for billing, in line with the data protection laws, and we share it when it is requested of us. Then on an ad hoc basis we keep information for longer periods of time if there is a formal request from law enforcement—when they ask us to keep information on a certain suspect—and when that happens we do it because there is an injunction against us to do it so we are not breaking the data protection rules. If it works under the current situation then why change?

All of the industry advocates on the debate over a PEI on the Packaging and Packaging Waste Directive revision underlined again and again the unfeasibility of the proposal. One trade association put it simply: "We do not support PEI, we cannot see how it would work in practice. Either it wouldn't work or there would be a different indicator for each product and that obviously would be untenable." A business association active in the debate provided additional support: "Also, it was not technically feasible. The Dutch looked at their situation, they put together a consultation and it failed—they brought together all the right groups to the table, and for two years and a lot of money it proved undoable."

Arguments about the feasibility of new proposals were not all negative; some advocates referenced the success of similar standing policies as evidence of the feasibility of new proposals. A citizen group active on the REACH debate referenced the success of a data-sharing program for chemical testing data in Germany as proof that the new EU proposal would work: "The main way to do that is through data sharing—data sharing is key, they have been doing it in Germany, which is one of the biggest chemical markets. We say if it works in Germany we can do it on an EU scale, or even a global scale."

Another lobbyist constructed a similar argument suggesting that the current success of harmonization is evidence of the future success of the new Service Directive proposal:

> I stress the question on the principle of origin isn't and never was and never will be a question of it working—if an adequate level of harmonization is achieved, it will work, it *IS* working, but it requires member states to trust each other. Now, we can debate if there is harmonization— that is, legislation has to either be identical or equivalent—and the United Kingdom is okay with a minimum and the Nordic countries want a harmonization at a higher level—but as long as there is harmonization it can work, does work, and has been working.

Lobbyists also argued their opposition to a new proposal by claiming the current policy in place was sufficient but that it simply wasn't being implemented. A business association active on the PEI debate made just this type of argument—that the current policy would work if it were to be implemented:

> Our main point was that the proposal was unnecessary. The existing directive already obliged industry to produce the results they claimed would be produced by the PEI. This was just another clear example of another layer of regulation that wasn't needed. Before we discuss new rules why don't we make sure the current laws are being enforced. Which they are not—it is an empirical fact that the current rules are only being implemented in France and the United Kingdom. In Germany no one is going around monitoring if packaging is compliant with the directive. In many of the member states they are refusing to enact it.

Whether it is claims about the success of current policy or arguments that an advocate's insider knowledge allows him or her to detect the potential failure of a policy, feasibility and workability arguments provide policymakers with some insight into the potential shortcomings of policies.

FAIRNESS OR DISCRIMINATION ARGUMENTS IN THE UNITED STATES

Arguments referencing the fairness of a proposal may be rather abstract references to the concept of fairness or more specific about which group is being unfairly affected. A woman's rights advocate on the human cloning debate referred to how low-income citizens were unfairly neglected to the advantage of the wealthy who would be benefiting the most from stem cell research:

> And then another thing was the whole issue of equity and social justice; how we should be spending resources, even though one could argue this is investor money that might not be spent somewhere else. Well those investors will find something else to invest their money in that might be much more useful and get them a profit. So there is this question about social justice and equity and if you're going to be working with technology, which only a few rich and the elite would have access to. You have every example in the book to look at now, expensive therapies, all the reproductive technologies, everything they've developed has hardly been used by low-income individuals.

A congressional staffer on the same case highlighted the inequity of the burden of clonal stem cell research on women:

> We also argue that the process exploits women who would have to donate the eggs. There are all these diseases; ALS, Parkinson's, late-onset diabetes—they say this research could help cure sufferers. But if you took all the people in this country with all those diseases, to cure them you would have to harvest so many eggs. The process is still so inefficient, you need so many eggs to get one viable clone. In one superovulatory harvesting you get twenty to thirty eggs at a shot. For all of those diseases then, you would need 110 million women to donate, that's every woman between the ages of eighteen and twenty-five, to donate twice. That's asking a lot of every woman in the country. Plus superovulatory drugs, which are used in the process, may be linked to cervical cancer. So it could be dangerous. And clinics and labs are paying thousands of dollars for women's eggs. ACT was paying four thousand dollars and some have paid as much as ten thousand dollars. So if you were actually going to use therapeutic cloning, you'd be exploiting women and in particular poor women.

Less profound equity arguments can also be seen, however. A policy advocate arguing for the inclusion of federal officers along with local officers in a federal housing program made a simple equity argument, saying that it was unfair to exclude federal safety officers if local safety officers were included.

FAIRNESS OR DISCRIMINATION ARGUMENTS IN THE EUROPEAN UNION

Arguments focusing on the fundamental equity of certain groups in society can also be seen in the European Union. On the Service Directive debate, a union lobbyist called for the need to protect foreign workers: "We believe that it is imperative to avoid a situation where the principle of origin gets used as a way to block people from working in another country; it could be used in a way that is protectionist or worse, antiforeigner, and considering the rise of right-wing parties in many European countries, that could be dangerous." A trade industry association highlighted the need to protect Western European workers from being unfairly pushed out of jobs by new low-wage workers from Central and Eastern Europe:

> When a factory moves overseas, like to Thailand for cheap labor, they go away—the unemployed workers back home don't see it. But when cheap labor comes in to a construction site, you have cheap labor inside the fence and angry unemployed higher-wage workers outside the fence, and that leads to high-level tension, and we don't know if we could control the riots that would begin. Also it is just very unfair, if a factory decides to go to Thailand for cheap labor, with that cheap labor you have to take everything that comes with that, like bad infrastructure, low-educated workers, etc. But if you bring cheap labor into a developed country, you get the best of both worlds—cheap labor and a good infrastructure situation, and you don't have to pay for it. It just isn't fair.

A final fairness argument commonly found in the European Union is references to equity between member states. A citizen group advocating more EU legislation on public health made such a point in its argumentation strategy: "The situation is so different in different countries: if you have cancer in France or the U.K. you are less likely to die, less likely to suffer, and this is unfair, and there needs to be an EU level of standards and we go from there. This is our fundamental argument."

CONSTITUENCY OR PUBLIC OPINION ARGUMENTS IN THE UNITED STATES

Lobbyists in the United States know that linking their position to public opinion can be a powerful tool when communicating to publicly elected policymakers. Some lobbyists make explicit electoral threats, while others make more implicit references to public opinion. An example of the more explicit type can be seen in this quotation by an immigrant community advocate active on the antiterrorism legislation after September 11: "So one of our tactics is to say that [our ethnic] community is growing and there are a lot of native foreign and U.S. citizens and [our] vote is very important, and if you keep screwing us like this you're not going to get our votes, so that's something our community can do."

A research institute engaged on the human cloning debate made a more implicit electoral argument by referencing public opinion polls: "We would always start out with the first: we've never done this, we've never created life for the purpose of destroying it, we need to have a national debate on this, and just look at the polls, they're already against you, why do you want to do this when the country does not want you to do this."

The aim of these arguments is to link policy positions to the preferences of voters and thus make clear that the decision a policymaker makes on this given issue could have an effect on their success in the next election. It is not surprising then that we see no use of constituency or public opinion arguments in the European Union. Institutional differences clearly play a role in argumentation selection. More shared goal, constituency, and cost arguments are being used in the United States, while more technical arguments are being used in the European Union. There remains a great deal of variation to be explained in each of the polities.

Issue Characteristics

As discussed in the theoretical section of this chapter, the salience of an issue to the public is hypothesized to play a role in argument selection. In the United Stares the relationship between salience and the use of shared goals and constituency arguments is remarkable, as reported in table 5.1. This table shows the percentage of advocates using each argument type on issues of each level of salience. So, for example, 67 percent of advocates active on low-salience

Table 5.1   Advocates Using Each Argument Type by Issue Salience in the United States

	0 stories	1–5 stories	6–50 stories	51 or more stories	N	Percent
Shared goals	67	79	55	90	46	71
Technical	23	21	27	40	17	26
Cost/Econ	57	50	73	20	34	52
Feasibility/ Workability	10	29	45	20	14	22
Fairness	7	0	9	30	6	9
Constituency	3	7	18	40	8	12
Total N	30	14	11	10	65	100

Note: The last column represents the average use of each argument type regardless of issue salience.

issues used shared goals arguments while 33 percent did not (the percentages of advocates not using an argument type are not reported in the table). Similarly 90 percent of advocates working on the most salient issues used shared goals arguments while only 10 percent did not.

So, as the salience of the issue increases we see that the percentage of advocates using shared goals arguments increases, from 67 percent on the least salient issues to 90 percent on the most salient issues; constituency arguments trend from 3 percent to 7 percent to 18 percent to 40 percent, as the national news coverage increases from no coverage to one to five stories to six to fifty stories to fifty-one or more stories.

Lobbyists active on issues that are being followed by the public on the nightly news understand that their arguments need to be understood and received by a broad range of people. Broad shared goals arguments are one way to do just this. On the case of antiterrorism legislation, advocates for immigrant communities needed a broad-reaching message if they were to combat the hypersecurity atmosphere that engulfed Washington after September 11. Immigrant advocates attempted to appeal to the nation's sense of multiculturalism and remind citizens and policymakers of the history that built the country. They argued:

> We are a nation of immigrants and 99.999 percent of them are not dangerous—these are people who come here because they want to be with their family members or they want to study here or they want to work here. We need their labor, we should recruit them because we don't have enough people to do that work because Americans aren't taking jobs at that level. These are people that come here because they want to work and they want to contribute. And we do clearly need a complete overhaul of our immigration system, but not from an antiterrorist perspective.

Proponents of stem cell research active on the human cloning debate framed their position as one of pro-life, but pro-adult human life. In this way they attempted to appeal to the large majority of citizens who could sympathize with patients suffering from diseases: "We argue that the potential for developing cures and therapies for people that are walking around now, desperately in need of help, outweighs what the people on the other side are claiming—that a couple of cells are a human life of an equivalent weight in value [to that] of a walking-around human with enormous physical and mental problems which could be addressed if these therapies were developed, if these stem cells could be used. It is very much a health and curative argument." Highly salient issues require broad arguments that the majority of issue observers can relate to and potentially embrace.

The hypothesized relationship between low salience and more use of technical arguments is not supported by the empirical evidence. This is likely because the nature of the issue—whether there are highly technical dimensions to the topic—also plays an important role. Two issues that were low salience, but which were highly complex, were the objects of technical argumentation. These types of arguments were necessary because of the complexity of the subject matter. For example, the issue of revising the Food Quality Protection Act involved detailed scientific discussions on pesticide limits and the methodology of EPA review, lending itself to technical argumentation. Another low-salience issue on which lobbyists were making technical legalistic arguments was the Recreation Marine Employment Act. Advocates of the bill were required to focus on the detail of the definition in the legislative language and reference previous language in OSHA regulations regarding boat size.

Thus we see issue salience plays a role in argument selection in the United States, specifically in the use of shared goals arguments and constituency arguments. The relationship between salience and the use of technical arguments was weaker, likely colored by the technical complexity of the issue.

In the European Union, as salience trends up, more lobbyists reported using more shared goals arguments, but the trend is slightly weaker: 50 percent of lobbyists reporting employing shared goals arguments on low-salience issues and 57 percent on high-salience issues. As in the United States, advocates on highly salient issues want to make arguments that have a broader appeal as seen in table 5.2. A trade union advocate on the Service Directive developed an argument promoting the welfare of the worker, a goal difficult for anyone to oppose: "We have nothing against an internal market in services but it

Table 5.2   Advocates Using Each Argument Type by Issue Salience in the European Union

	0 stories	1–2 stories	3 or more stories	N	Percent
Shared goals	50	40	57	41	50
Technical	38	15	27	23	28
Cost/Econ	47	45	43	37	45
Feasibility/Workability	41	8	53	46	56
Fairness	28	20	2	20	24
Constituency	0	0	0	0	0
Total N	32	20	30	82	100

Note: The last column represents the average use of each argument type regardless of issue salience.

cannot be done at the expense of the worker, of working conditions, and it cannot be done in a way that leads to unfair competition, which will just lead to a race to the bottom."

As in the United States, the link between low salience and the use of technical arguments seems to depend on the technical nature of the issue. Technical arguments showed up on issues that were not salient but were technically complex, such as the debate on the CAFE framework. One trade association described their fairly high-tech argumentation strategy:

> The legislation requires data sets—estimations of the level of emissions in the future, since it will be for 2010 to 2020. The United Nations air quality model (called RAINS) proposes certain patterns of emissions. We spent two years developing data sets, talking with emitters of VOC, we gave data and position papers. The Commission starts from an energy consumption scenario, estimating emissions from energy consumption. We say that approach is wrong. There are so many parameters, you can't just rely on energy consumption. Even if consumption does grow—it is so difficult to estimate what the impact will be on emissions. First, the economies aren't going to grow the same all over the world, they are growing faster in some countries than others; second, you don't know the source—industry is surely declining in certain areas while transport and heating are increasing due to population growth. We say you should ask sectors—there are technological changes, some things get outdated, new technologies arise; a sector-focused approach would be more accurate. It is very complicated.

When argument use over differing levels of salience is compared in the United States and the European Union we see some additional evidence of institutional effects. Holding salience constant we see that the differences between the United States and the European Union are much starker for highly salient issues. For example, shared goals arguments are used by 90 percent of U.S. advocates compared with only 57 percent of EU advocates on highly salient issues. This makes sense—advocates targeting elected policymakers in the United States know their broad-reaching arguments will be all the more powerful on topics that the public is following in the news. Forty percent of U.S. advocates use technical arguments and constituency arguments on high-salience issues, compared with only 27 percent and zero percent in the EU for those same argumentation categories. Advocates in the European Union on the other hand are much more likely to use feasibility arguments: 53 percent on issues that are highly salient compared with only 20 percent in the United States. Advocates in the European Union are also more likely to make cost and economic arguments compared with their U.S. counterparts: 43 percent on high-salience issues, while only 20 percent of the U.S. advocates evoke financial concerns on issues of great concern to the public.

Another important point is the different patterns in argumentation combination as issue salience increases. In the United States as issue salience rises advocates use more types of arguments; that is they add more frames or dimensions to their argumentation strategy. The only type of argument that drops out as salience increases is cost and economic arguments. Advocates in the European Union on the other hand appear to shift their focus as issue salience increases, with technical, fairness, and cost arguments all dropping off. This may be more evidence of institutional effects on argumentation strategy. In the United States, as salience increases advocates attempt to reach as many policymakers as possible with numerous arguments. In the European Union, advocates shift the dimensions of debate from arguments that work better on niche issues to arguments that are more credible on highly salient issues.

The United States and the European Union exhibit a great deal of similarity in the substance of their argumentation. In addition, in the aggregate their tendency to use technical, cost, and economic arguments are also comparable. However they do differ in significant ways especially in the use of arguments referencing shared goals, feasibility, and constituents—and these differences become even clearer on issues that are highly salient. Because high-salience issues often loom larger in the minds of political observers and academics, this might be one reason why transatlantic lobbying differences are perceived to be greater than they are in empirical reality.

FOCUSING EVENTS AND ARGUMENT CHANGE

As discussed in chapter 3, only one EU case had a related focusing event—data retention—and this did not appear to have any impact on the argumentation strategies of the advocates active on the case, for they continue to focus on the cost and feasibility of the policy. In the United States on the other hand, a number of cases had related focusing events and a good deal of qualitative evidence suggests that those events had real impacts on the arguments being put forward on those debates.

The terrorist attacks on September 11 introduced a general security concern into countless policy debates that at first glance would have no security dimensions. For example the debate over financing the water infrastructure system across the country, previously a debate about deteriorating water pipes, became one including references to bioterrorism and securing the fresh water supply. As one environmental advocate explained: "And everyone is using new arguments since September 11, I've been reading articles that suddenly everything is a security issue. What happened is, I think after September 11, there was a lot of focus particularly on drinking water security and safety. And what we've simply said is that this underscores that these are very important local government services and there is a public health dimension." In addition, lobbyists on energy-related issues began evoking the "dependence on foreign oil" reference and advocates from cogeneration to wind energy to biomass all argued their industries were a solution for the U.S. addiction to Middle East oil.

The other focusing event that had an impact on a number of the issues in the U.S. sample was the Enron scandal. Regarding the case of regulation of stock option expensing, a topic that had been on and off the political agenda for a number of years, a lobbyist discussed the focusing event effect:

> The other kind of argument is I think more time-specific, due to all the recent activity with Enron, Worldcom, the accounting irregularities, the fraud, that's in the news—a lot of people attribute the accounting fraud and other corporate misdeeds to stock options. And that goes like this: companies began to give out stock options in larger and larger numbers beginning in the early 1990s and that trend increased for the rest of the decade, and that gave an increasing incentive to executives to inflate the price of the shares of their company, because if the price went up then their stock options became more valuable. . . . These options have been "free" in the past but they've provided this incentive that has caused a number of company executives to engage in illegal or improper activities.

Thus we see that some characteristics of the issue have an impact on the arguments lobbyists select. Highly salient issues call for arguments that could be widely accepted and thus shared goals arguments are often selected. Technical arguments work better on less salient issues, but there must be some technical aspect to the policy debate. Finally, if a focusing event occurs on an issue midstream, a reassessment and revision of an advocate's arguments may be necessary, so that these arguments are relevant to the new political climate.

INTEREST CHARACTERISTICS

While the political context goes a long way in explaining argument selection, it is necessary also to consider the advocates themselves. As expected in both the United States and the European Union different types of advocates are more likely to employ certain types of arguments. Specifically citizen groups in the United States are more likely than business to use shared goals arguments; 100 percent of citizen groups reported using this type of argument while only 56 percent of business groups and corporations did so.

Table 5.3   Use of Arguments by Lobbying Position
in the United States and the European Union

	Block	Promote	Modify	N	Percent
			United States		
Shared goals	55	82	60	46	71
Feasibility/Workability	27	21	20	14	22
Total N	11	34	20	65	100
			European Union		
Shared goals	18	81	37	41	51
Feasibility/Workability	91	48	55	46	58
Total N	11	31	38	80*	100

Note: Two cases are missing because they were active on implementation.

Similarly citizen groups are the most likely to make constituency-based arguments; while only 12 percent of all advocates reported using this type of argument, 40 percent of citizen groups did compared to none of the business lobbyists. Technical and cost arguments on the other hand are the purview of industry lobbyists, with 44 percent and 88 percent of corporate lobbyists reporting using them, respectively. This is a much higher rate of use than citizen groups—none reported making technical arguments and 30 percent reported making cost or economic arguments.

In the European Union we see citizen groups very likely to employ shared goals arguments, 94 percent compared to the 30 percent and 43 percent of industry lobbyists of the trade associations and hired consultancies. As in the United States, industry lobbyists were the most likely to make technical and cost or economic arguments.

The findings in table 5.3 show a relationship between lobbying positions and the types of arguments advocates make. In the United States, as expected, advocates in promoting positions are most likely to use shared goals arguments that will reach the broadest audience. In addition, lobbyists in blocking positions are the most likely to make feasibility arguments, 27 percent compared to lobbyists in promoting and modifying positions. In the European Union we see the same pattern but it is even stronger. Lobbyists in promoting positions are most likely, at 81 percent, to use shared goals arguments. Of lobbyists in blocking positions we see the most use of feasibility arguments, 91 percent, compared to lobbyists in promoting and modifying positions, of which only 48 percent and 55 percent report using that type of argument.

CONCLUSION

The evidence presented demonstrates the role of both political context and advocate characteristics in argument selection. The democratic accountability of a political system matters in advocacy argumentation: the more accountable the more likely lobbyists are to develop arguments that invoke commonly shared goals and reference public opinion. The more policymakers are distanced from the masses, the more likely lobbyists are to rely on technical, scientific, or legalistic arguments. We also found they are much more likely to formulate arguments about the feasibility or workability of a policy. It should be noted that advocates are not necessarily lobbying for more common good policies in democratically accountable systems or for technical policies in less accountable systems, but rather that they *frame* their goals in different ways depending on their audience. By considering institutional design and taking into account the motivations of the argument recipients—that is, policymakers—a more complete model of argumentation is possible. The institutional system is an important force driving advocates to frame their positions in certain ways.

However, we also saw a great deal of similarity in the content of the arguments put forward by American and European advocates. In this way, more evidence is brought to bear on the similarity of advocates operating in democratic systems. The qualitative data presented in this chapter underscore the inaccuracy of the cowboy versus compromise stereotypes. U.S. advocates are not advancing threats to support a position or face losing campaign support. European advocates' argumentation repertoires are not constrained to technocratic jargon and legalese. Advocates on both sides of the Atlantic are drawing on similar arguments about the effect of a proposal on society, the public's opinion on the topic, the innate fairness of the initiative, and the economic impact of new policies, as well as the more technical details and the feasibility of the proposal.

A growing phenomenon is the advancing of the exact same arguments on the exact same global issues. More and more issues are being debated in both arenas, often simultaneously. Issues such as international intervention in Darfur, Sudan; implementation of the Kyoto protocol; mobilization of a peacekeeping force in Lebanon—are all instances in which advocates in both Washington and Brussels were working toward a common goal. They were simultaneously putting pressure on their policymakers to respond in a similar way to a global problem, and in some instances for U.S. and EU officials to work together, as in the case of a Darfur intervention. In cases like these, growing international advocacy networks allow advocates to share data and talking points to support their arguments. They can even draw on each other's success to put added pressure on their targets—arguing a step has been taken forward in the other arena, why not here at home?

Not only are advocates advancing similar arguments but they respond in similar ways to contextual cues. Advocates in both polities choose to make certain arguments on certain types of issues. Highly salient issues better lend themselves to constituency and shared goals arguments. Low-salience issues can be argued along technical lines, but only if there is some complexity to the debate. Focusing events can change the nature of debate if they happen at some point in the middle of the policymaking process.

Actor type and lobbying position are the final factors that weave in with the political context to determine argumentation strategies. Citizen groups are more likely to use shared goals and constituency arguments while industry interests employ more technical and economic arguments; these patterns hold in both polities. Advocates in promoting positions use shared goals arguments and those in blocking positions are more likely to use feasibility arguments.

Thus, we see evidence that not only the full model—with three streams of factors flowing together to produce advocacy outcomes—but also the stages of the advocacy process influence outcomes at other stages. Not only do lobbying positions influence arguments, but the selection of argumentation strategies likely influences lobbying success. This question is left to explore in chapter 10.

6

Lobbying Targets

THE EARLY SCHOLARLY works on lobbying in America painted a picture of unbridled power of special interests dictating the nation's public policy. Cater (1964) detailed the uncontested influence of the sugar lobby and military–industrial complex. Advocates for sugar producers and defense manufacturers were portrayed as largely dictating legislation in these areas due to their tight relationship with policymakers in their respective iron triangles. Maass (1951) described a very similar situation in the area of water policy. Lobbyists in short were wielding considerable influence in the policymaking process. Bauer, Pool, and Dexter's (1963) study flipped this common understanding of lobbying on its head—their research showed lobbyists were talking to people who agreed with them, who would vote their way anyway. Surely this could not be Dahl's (1957) definition of power—getting someone to do something that they would not otherwise do. If they were talking to friendly policymakers how could they be said to influence the positions of those policymakers?

Debate continued throughout the next three decades, with some arguing that lobbyists were trying to convert policymakers who were of another opinion and sway those who were undecided, and that lobbying of friendly policymakers was only to counteract communications from enemies (Austen-Smith and Wright 1994). Others argued that yes lobbyists were, as Bauer, Pool, and Dexter (1963) suggested, working with like-minded policymakers, but that this could be useful. Hall (1998) maintained that motivating allies to become champions is a fundamentally important aspect of lobbying. Hojnacki and Kimball (1998) suggested that lobbyists do target their allies first, but they move beyond friends to lobby undecided policymakers when resources are available. Still others argued that "who is with you and who is against you" is endogenous and depends on which dimensions of debate rise in salience (McKissick 1995).

The question of whether lobbyists are targeting friends, foes, or fence-sitters in the United States remains unanswered. But on the other side of the Atlantic the question has never even arisen. This is perhaps not surprising; the targets of lobbying on a given issue are much more constrained in the European Union. Differences in institutional structures between the two polities lead to very different targeting strategies. In the United States, lobbyists approach a more flexible system, where additional venues can more easily be pulled into a policy debate and where the full membership of the U.S. Congress is fair game. In the European Union targets are more predetermined; the institutions involved on a given procedure are more fixed, and the number of MEPs that can have significant influence on a dossier is much lower.

Institutional differences lead to such great differences in targeting strategies that the appropriate questions regarding targeting differ for the two polities. Therefore, this chapter will detail the differences between U.S. and EU targeting, providing qualitative and quantitative evidence of the drastically different targeting options faced by U.S. and EU lobbyists. Then the analysis diverges, addressing separate questions relevant to each polity.

For the United States this analysis seeks to weigh in on the long-standing debate about the nature of lobbying: how much of it is persuading policymakers with alternative positions and how much is mobilizing friendly policymakers. For the European Union, where targets are largely predetermined at the supranational level, there is much less variation to explain and thus the discussion of EU targeting strategies is briefer; detailing the specific targeting arrangements for each EU issue does not give us much of a theoretical handle on target selection. That policymaking procedures drive target selection is a fact of EU policymaking; however, a point of flexibility for European advocates is targeting member state governments when lobbying the Council.

THE DIFFERENT TARGETING POSSIBILITIES IN THE UNITED STATES AND THE EUROPEAN UNION

It is possible to draw parallels between U.S. and EU targeting. For example in Washington bill sponsors and cosponsors are the key legislative targets and in Brussels it is the rapporteurs and shadow rapporteurs. In both systems committee leadership is an important lobbying target. However, while it is possible to make comparisons in name, the targeting options for lobbyists in the two arenas are drastically different. Specifically, lobbyists in the two polities have diverging levels of flexibility when it comes to approaching policymakers on a given issue. In the United States lobbyists have more latitude to draw policymakers into a debate; in the European Union targets are much more predetermined, set by institutional rules.

To get a sense of the differences between the two, the number of distinct bodies that the advocates reported targeting was coded (committees, subcommittees, agencies, DGs, etc.). The results are quite similar: in the United States the mean number of targets was 3.43 with a maximum of sixteen. In the European Union, the average number of targets is 2.89 with a maximum of fifteen. While EU and U.S. lobbyists are targeting roughly the same number of bodies, American lobbyists are targeting more individuals within those bodies. This is most evident in the Congress, where lobbyists on average mentioned six members of Congress by name whom they were targeting.[1] In the European Union the rapporteur and possibly the shadow rapporteurs (unofficial rapporteurs assigned by each party group to monitor a proposal) are the main targets, 30 percent of U.S. lobbyists mentioned targeting five or more members by name, some targeting fifteen and twenty, and these are just those they mentioned by name during the interview; the actual number of targeted members is most likely much higher. American lobbyists have more flexibility to approach individual policymakers and this freedom translates into a higher number of members being the object of lobbying attention. However, qualitative evidence further clarifies the picture.

While the Commission is the sole purveyor of policy proposals in the European Union, in the United States any member of Congress can introduce a bill, as discussed in chapter 1. This fact makes all 535 members potential targets for lobbyists seeking a sponsor to introduce their bill. In addition, party cohesion in the United States is famously weak; members vote their conscience, not the party line. This means that advocates need to lobby members for their support on votes; targeting the party leadership alone is not enough. This need to gain sponsors and supporters leads lobbyists to approach a large number of members of Congress—and not just those who have jurisdiction as defined by institutional rules.

The extent of targeting is not captured as well by the quantitative evidence as it is by the lobbyists' descriptions of their targeting. One U.S. professional association active on the debate on antiterrorism legislation explained: "Oh we worked with many staff, the Kennedy staff, the Feinstein staff, Senator Gregg's staff, Senator Frist's staff, Senator Leahy's staff, Senator Biden's staff, there are a lot, many people we worked with." A trade association lobbying on the water infrastructure case noted: "We created a water infrastructure caucus and we got more than eighty members to sign up for it. We had the chairman and ranking members of the Water Resources and the Health subcommittees in Energy and Commerce and Transportation Infrastructure. They were the founders of the water infrastructure caucus. All their names began with B so we called them the killer Bs. Sometimes you have to use humor to get interest in this kind of thing."

An environmental organization active on the Farm Bill described a similar working method: "We did a lot of work with Harkin's office, Lugar's office, Colin Peterson in the House, Mike Thompson of California, McHugh of New York, half the Ohio delegation, Senator Frist of Tennessee, it goes on and on and on, I could name you forty more members if I got the books out."

U.S. lobbyists use state interests, district interests, and personal interests to gain the support of policymakers. A trade association on PURPA repeal described how it played on the personal experience of members and the situation in their states: "Obviously if we're talking about trying to get cosponsors we're going after members from states where PURPA has been a problem; unless for just philosophical reasons someone just thinks PURPA is a lousy idea, you tend to go after members of Congress where they've had a problem because they are going to be more sympathetic."

On the wind energy tax credit issue, a company lobbyist described a similar strategy, using geography and state interests to select targets, in addition to the institutionally dictated targets on the responsible committees:

> Mark Foley, who is our congressman in Florida and also a member of the Ways and Means Committee, took up the bill. In the Senate, Chairman Grassley, now ranking member Grassley, introduced the bill this Congress. All the members from Iowa, North Dakota, South Dakota, and then some of the other states we have projects in are very supportive. In the Senate that's very helpful because that means the entire Democratic leadership team—Harry Reid has a project in Nevada so we work with him. Senators Dorg and Daschle and Conrad of North and South Dakota and then Grassley and Baucus in Montana. And obviously anybody that has to do with Finance in the Senate or Ways and Means in the House, so that means Bill Thomas, Jim McCreary, Mark Foley, and then you have to look at leadership in the House too, Delay and Hastert, and we try to get some Democrats to support it as well. I mean it's got to be pretty broad, we try hard.

As this quote illustrates, U.S. lobbyists are approaching a wide range and large number of members of Congress.

Making a link to the businesses or economic problems a member has in his or her state or district is not the only hook. At times members of Congress will be interested in a policy proposal because of personal experiences. For example many champions of federal funding of cancer research have been personally affected by the disease. Two champions of basic education are another example; they visited communities in developing countries through an NGO coalition-sponsored trip and became personally engaged in the issue.

A professional association lobbyist explained how its targeting strategy reached out to members on the basis of state interests, committee jurisdiction, and personal interest:

> If you pull out a directory of Congress, the members of the subcommittee on Health and Human Services—Senator Patty Murray of Washington is very interested in science and technology-related issues because of the state and Seattle. Senator Harkin, Congressman Regula, Congressman Boehlert of New York, chair of the science committee, and Congressman John Boehner of Ohio, chair of the education committee. Congressman Wicker because he's on that subcommittee. And there are a number of others; I'd have to get out a list. They are both our targets and our champions—it depends on how much we've already educated them or how much they already know . . . Congressman Vernon Ehlers of Michigan, a physician and Congressman Rush Holt from New Jersey, another physician, clearly are in support of science. They will be champions in the House on this issue.

Thus we see advocates in the United States have a wide range of targets available to them. Advocates have a number of methods by which they might mobilize members of Congress including state, district, and personal interest. Once members decide to be champions for a cause they can be critical in getting an issue on the agenda by introducing a new bill or amendment. When proposals are on the table, champions continue to be vitally important in building a coalition of support, by writing Dear Colleague letters and encouraging other members to support the measure. Advocates are not restricted to approaching only the responsible committees.

In the European Union the Commission initiates policy proposals, Treaties dictate in which areas they do this, and institutional rules dictate which directorate general has control over a dossier. The responsible committees in the EP are equally predetermined. The rapporteurs appointed to usher dossiers through the codecision process are not engaged out of personal interest but rather through a party group appointment system. The president of the EP decides which committee is responsible for a dossier; then the party groups, who are assigned a number of points at the beginning of the year based on their strength, buy the dossier for their party group. The party group that acquires the dossier then assigns the dossier to one of its members on the relevant committee.

These institutional realities result in a fairly fixed set of targets for EU lobbyists. A trade association active on the live animal transport debate said its strategy of targeting the health and agriculture directorate generals was dictated by institutional jurisdiction: "DG SANCO was responsible on this so we gave our opinion to them and that was based on our study. We met with the DG

Services—SANCO but also Agri because there was an interservice consultation on this." A similar rigidity can be seen in the Parliament, as one trade
association's description of its targeting on REACH exhibits: "The responsible
committee in the EP is the Environment Committee. We haven't really gone
there lately, it just popped up again. We know the key MEPs that you need to
talk to and we know their assistants. When you work in the area on these topics
you come to know who you need to talk to."

Another trade association on the same issue alluded to a similar constraint
in targets: "We can't meet with everyone in the EP, the Commission is easier
in a way, it is about one hundred people maximum that are involved on this,
but in the EP it is over seven hundred. So we focus on the rapporteurs; not
all MEPs are interested."

The organizations active on the CCD all described the same focus on the
institutionally defined targets: "We knew the rapporteur in the first reading,
we had meetings with him. And we now know who the rapporteur is going
to be during the second reading so we are gong to be visiting that office as
well. With the changes there has been a change in the Committee responsible,
now it is Legal Affairs and Internal Market. We had good discussions with
Medina, an MEP on the legal committee."

The data protection case is an odd one in that the initiative came from the
Council rather than the Commission. But even though the issue departed from
standard operating procedure the targets were still fairly well fixed, and advocates needed to adjust to that new situation. As a trade association representative explained, "It is different for us for lobbying; the main actors are
different. It's not even the usual people in the Council we meet with; usually
we meet with the telecoms or maybe economics people but this is law enforcement, they don't think they need to consult industry. Telecom ministers understand our concern, but that's not who's in charge."

Thus we see across the institutions, the specific lobbying targets are defined
for EU lobbyists, providing little room for flexibility in choosing targets that
might be more sympathetic to an advocate's cause due to common personal
or geographical interests. And we see very different environments in which
American and European lobbyists need to operate. In the United States advocates have much more leeway to select and approach targets based on interest. In the European Union targets are much more predetermined by the
institutional rules, forcing lobbyists to go where the process requires.

U.S. TARGETING: FRIENDS, FOES, OR FENCE-SITTERS?

Who are lobbyists' allies and who their enemies? And how does a lobbyist decide which of them to approach? While partisan tension in America seems to

be ever growing in recent years, a member's political affiliation is not enough to determine if he or she will support or oppose a lobbyist's position. The characteristics of the issue at hand largely determine who allies and enemies are. McKissick forcefully argues that whether a member of Congress is a friend or foe depends intrinsically on what issues the member takes to be at stake—"and the definition of the issues at stake is endogenous to the process of deliberation" (1995, 5).

Whether a member supports a position is not simply defined by his or her political party. The position a member of Congress ultimately takes on an issue depends on the salient dimensions of debate. A conservative Republican may not support an environmental proposal on the argument that it is good for the environment, but if a proposal simultaneously promotes rural economies, he or she could very well become a champion. Riker (1986) traced such a shift in the terms of debate in the case of transporting nuclear waste; Baumgartner and Jones (1993) in the cases of nuclear power, urban affairs, and auto safety; and Fritschler (1975) in the case of tobacco policy.

Depending on how the issue comes to be defined a given member may be in the supporting or opposing coalition. Moreover, on some issues there may be no opposition at all—issues that are framed as motherhood-and-apple-pie issues are topics or proposals that no elected politician could be publicly against. In short, friends and foes are not predetermined, the characteristics of the issue at hand play a major role in determining who will support an issue and who will not.

While the possibility for issue redefinition, or to use Riker's term "heresthetics," is present throughout the life of an issue, at some point there is stability in the salient dimension of debate; the issue is defined as being about one subject rather than another, the degree of conflict is established—whether the issue is something no one is against or whether it is a topic on which people are polarized. At this point it becomes possible for advocates to determine where policymakers fall on the continuum of support—friend, fence-sitter, or foe. The decision then remains: whom to target. Whether lobbyists communicate only with friendly policymakers or if they reach out beyond friends to fence-sitters and foes as well depends on the characteristics of the issues and the advocates themselves.

Specifically, the larger an issue is in scope, the more likely advocates will target more policymakers, likely moving beyond friends to undecided and opposed members of Congress as well. In addition, the more salient an issue the broader support lobbyists need to amass. Therefore, the more salient an issue, the more likely lobbyists are to approach policymakers of each position. Each of these hypotheses is investigated quantitatively below. Finally, one would expect the less conflict on the issue, the more targets an advocate would approach but this is difficult to show empirically because on issues where there is no conflict, there are no foes and thus advocates would appear to be only targeting friends. They may in fact be targeting more policymakers but those policymakers would all register as friendly or perhaps undecided if they were simply lacking information on the nonconflictual proposal. The relationship between the level of issue conflict and targeting is therefore explored qualitatively.

In addition to the issue characteristics playing a role in determining an advocate's targeting strategy, characteristics of the advocate are also expected to contribute to target selection. First, the organization's resources should matter: the better staffed an advocate's office the higher the capacity to approach a larger number of policymakers and the more likely he or she should be to target friendly, undecided, and opposed members of Congress. Second, the type of group may also be important. Ideological citizen groups may be less likely to target foes than more pragmatic trade and business associations. These expectations are tested below.

EMPIRICAL FINDINGS ON U.S. TARGETING

Each advocate was coded as to whether he or she targeted friendly policymakers who supported the advocate's position, undecided policymakers who were not yet clearly for or against the advocate's position, and finally policymakers who were in opposition. All advocates active on legislative issues are targeting friendly policymakers as Bauer, Pool, and Dexter found in their study more than four decades ago; 80 percent are targeting undecided members of Congress, and 30 percent are targeting members of Congress that they know to be opposed to their position.[2] Creating a cumulative measure of whether an advocate approached only friends, friends and undecideds, or policymakers of all three positions provides another view of the results: 20 percent were focusing only on friends, 50 percent were reaching out to friends and undecided legislators, and 30 percent were reaching out to all types of legislators. Thus it is most common to mobilize friends and attempt to sway those in the middle.

An environmental advocate active on the CAFE standards issue explained how members are broken down according to these categories:

> I think you put people kind of into groups. You say, these people are definitely with us. These people are very likely against us, or definitely against us, because they've basically said they will lead the fight against us or they've come out in the press, or told us directly, that there's no way they'd ever support higher standards. And then you've got all the folks in the middle. And you spend a lot of time understanding what makes them tick, and what kinds of arguments you can make that might be persuasive. I mean, that middle, it's that middle group. You try to

whittle down that middle group. You try to get people hopefully into the support column, and hopefully not characterized as definitely against you. But yeah, you spend a lot of time working on that middle group of people and answering the questions that they have.

While the middle group is critical, it is the friendly legislators who are fundamentally important to swaying them. Hall argues that mobilizing friends to be champions is central to lobbying, that lobbying is a "legislative subsidy" by which lobbyists subsidize friends—"making it possible for the legislator to expend greater effort advancing a policy objective they have in common with the group" (1998, 1). Indeed, this is much the situation many of the lobbyists described; as an advocate active on PURPA reform explained: "What is now S. 2439 really started during the House debate last summer. We realized we were going to lose and so the folks from biomass and I went over and started talking with Feinstein and Kennedy's people. Even before the house vote was done. And we've literally spent untold hours in one little conference room in Kennedy's office hashing through some of this stuff, again and again and again. Most recently we did about six hours three weeks ago."

A citizen group active on TANF reform described a similar process of long hours providing support to congressional staff: "We've been meeting with Senator Baucus's staff . . . and Senator Rockefeller's staff for a number of weeks, every week, to talk about our concerns and to work out how they could get some of them addressed in their bill." Nearly every advocate interviewed discussed their friends, their champions in Congress, how they provide figures, reports, materials, and work hours to assist congressional staffers. In return they hope the member will work to support their shared policy goal.

Bauer, Pool, and Dexter suggested it was simply uncomfortable to talk to policymakers that were in opposition, thus most lobbyists spent their time communicating with the more amenable legislators who shared their views. This can be seen in the responses by some advocates; for example, a company lobbyist active on the Farm Bill stated: "We had a few champions, not very many, to be honest, John Boehner, Representative Cal Dooley, Senator Richard Lugar, Pat Roberts, Chuck Hagel. I used to work for one of them, not a very big group; again we focus on having a few key relationships rather than knowing everybody, too many people either don't like us or like us but don't want to be seen liking us."

Targeting foes can indeed be unpleasant, perhaps that is why only 30 percent of advocates reported doing it, or perhaps because they perceive it to be wasted effort. A congressional staffer active on the stock option expensing case noted that there was little reason to try to convince members aligned with the IT industry: "The high-tech companies were vehemently, I mean to the point of hysteria, opposed." When a member is leading the fight for the other side, lobbying them may seem futile. An environmental advocate active on the Transportation Reauthorization expressed the type of exasperation that can come with facing enemies: "So there are a lot of other reasons but the environment has become the scapegoat on this and there is pressure to do some kind of federal regulation streamlining the environmental review process. And so we've gotten into a few fights already with the majority staff on the T and I [Transportation and Infrastructure] committee, Mr. Young's staff, and it's quite obvious we're not buddies."

If lobbying foes is so unpleasant, why do advocates do it? Some described a situation in which they still thought they could change some minds, like an advocate working on the TANF reauthorization: "The Republicans are going with the administration but we'll keep trying to get support and when we show them the numbers some people who might have gone with the administration are going to say this is just going to kill our state." An educational advocate active on antiterrorism legislation went directly to the opposition, lobbying to change the mind of the member that wanted to impose a total moratorium on student visas: "The challenge then was to work with her to demonstrate that a moratorium would probably create more harm than good in terms of the overall national needs, but that we would be willing to work with them on other approaches and reporting and requirements, and a willingness to assist in getting this computerized system up and running."

Others recognized that they would not likely change any minds but that it was their democratic duty to incorporate the other side's views into the debate. A professional association active on the human cloning debate described how it went with its organizational members to visit legislators, just to make sure its constituents' voices were being heard: "We knew going in that some of the people we were visiting, their bosses were sponsors of the Brownback Bill, and we knew we weren't going to get anywhere with them but you need to let them know that there are people in their state that don't support that position on the subject and they need to hear from everybody. So, whether or not they are in favor of or oppose a bill, it didn't matter if they had a member here that was from their state, we got them in to see their member." A cumulative variable was tabulated by a number of issue and interest group characteristics to more systematically consider when lobbyists decide to go beyond their friends to target their foes and undecided legislators as well.

Table 6.1 reports the relationship between targeting strategies and the scope of the issue and the salience of the issue to the public. Both hypotheses receive support. Advocates move beyond lobbying friends and fence-sitters to targeting foes as well, as the scope of the issue gets larger. While only 16 percent of advocates target foes on small-scope issues, this rises to 35 percent for issues affecting large sectors, and to 40 percent for issues affecting multiple sectors or the entire system. Similarly, as the salience of an issue rises the more likely lobbyists are to extend beyond their safety zone to target members of Congress in the opposition. Only 14 percent of advocates are approaching foes on low-salience issues, increasing to 31 percent, 45 percent, and 50 percent as the issue is covered by more news stories in the national papers.

As mentioned in the theoretical discussion, a third issue characteristic that plays a role in targeting is the level of conflict on the issue. Noncontroversial issues often have no foes at all, and the only ones that can really be said to be undecided are those that have not yet received enough information about a proposal. This was the case on a number of issues in the U.S. sample. Advocates on issues like funding for a cystic fibrosis clinical trials research network, funding for better math and science education, inclusion of federal safety officers along with local officers in HUD development projects, tax credits for wind energy production, and an exemption for recreational marinas from longshoreman's insurance—faced no opposition from any member of Congress. As one lobbyist on the wind energy issue succinctly noted: "No, nobody was opposed to it, not at all." Or as a preservation advocate active on the Transportation Reauthorization explained: "We don't have a body of anti-preservation in Congress. There isn't anybody out there—because of the nature of our issue—that is ready to tear down landmarks or jeopardize or isolate them. So we're dealing with levels of awareness of the preservation issue here."

Citizen groups calling for more international aid for basic education also faced no foes: "No one's against education, it's just the budget issue. It is very

Table 6.1   **U.S. Targeting Strategies by Issue Characteristics**

Scope	Friends Only	+Undecided	+Foes	N
Small sector	26	58	16	19
Large sector	0	65	35	17
Multiple sectors	20	40	40	10
Systemwide	40	20	40	10
Salience				
0 stories	23	64	14	22
1–5 stories	15	54	31	13
6–50 stories	18	36	46	11
51 or more stories	20	30	50	10
Total – N	11	28	17	56
Total – percent	20	50	30	

Note: Advocates active on regulatory issues are not included in this analysis.

rarely challenged, it is more 'well we certainly agree with you but there's not enough money to go around for good causes.'" On issues where conflict is low, and foes don't exist, advocates can target a large number of members of Congress, capitalizing on the universal appeal of the topic.

Thus, the evidence supports the argument that the issue context matters when determining the targeting strategy but who the advocate is as an organization should also figure into the equation. Contrary to expectations regarding the influence of actor type on target selection; ideological citizen groups are not avoiding foes but rather approaching them at the highest rate. While only 30 percent of advocates target foes on average, 60 percent of citizen groups did so. Foundations, government advocates, and the business world appear to largely prefer the friends plus fence-sitter targeting strategy. There is little evidence to support the expected relationships between staff size and targeting strategies, as seen in table 6.2. Mid-sized offices are the most likely to target undecided and opposed policymakers. Both the smallest offices and the largest offices are most likely to extend beyond their friends but only to those on the fence.

Lobbyists are not always reinforcing the staff of friendly legislators nor only spending their resources trying to convert foes. The targeting strategy of the U.S. lobbyist depends on the scope and salience of the issue, the degree of conflict on the topic, and the type of organization the lobbyist represents. As discussed in the introduction, these calculations and decisions are not part of the lobbying process in Brussels. The decision is not whether to lobby friends or foes but which member states to target if an advocate decides to approach the Council.

Table 6.2   U.S. Targeting Strategies by Interest Characteristics (percent)

Type	Friends Only	+Undecided	+Foes	N
Citizen	10	30	60	10
Foundation	0	63	38	8
Trade	25	50	25	16
Corporate	25	50	25	8
Government	29	57	14	14
Staff				
1–5	20	53	27	15
6–20	23	39	39	26
21 or more	13	67	20	15
Total – N	11	28	17	56
Total – percent	20	50	30	

Note: Advocates active on regulatory issues are not included in this analysis.

EU TARGETING: WHICH MEMBER STATES?

As the first section of this chapter explained, the flexibility of EU lobbyists to select their targets is limited; which DGs have responsibility in the Commission, which MEPs are in charge in the Parliament are largely predetermined in codecision policymaking. In addition, venues are equally fixed for non-community method policymaking. Whether it is social dialogue processes, standardization setting, or international negotiations the appropriate targets are dictated by institutional rules and norms.

An exception can be found in the Council. If advocates decide to lobby the Council—and not all do as the next chapter details—lobbyists can play on member states' interests, in much the same way American lobbyists play on state interests. This is not something that can be shown well empirically, but qualitative evidence can demonstrate the relationship. In case after case, in which EU advocates opted to approach the Council, we see instances of advocates drawing on national linkages. For example, a citizen organization pushing for stronger regulations on alcohol advertising found an ally with Poland because the country has a growing problem with alcoholism. A humanitarian organization working for EU action against child trafficking found support from Italy, a country designated as a transit country where trafficked persons are moved from developing countries into Western Europe. On another case, industry representatives opposed to the revised CCD joined forces with the Spanish representation whose country's credit market relied on house-to-house marketing of credit cards, a practice that would be banned by the new directive. Advocates can use member state interests, concerns, or problems as a means of entrée for discussing the issue and to rally the member state's EU representatives to support the advocate's position.

A lobbyist active on the data retention case and in opposition to the new proposal was attempting to target member states based on interest and play them off against the member states that were introducing the initiative in the Council: "We're talking to a lot of people, trying to keep the communication channels open. We've talked a lot with the Germans and the Austrians since they are against it. They are against it because it would be unconstitutional under the German system, they have a strong privacy rule, and Austria has a similar tradition. The Finnish are also skeptical, but they might come around to an amended version, so we are going to try to play that German card, since it is third pillar it has to be unanimous." As the issue had to do with police and judicial cooperation in criminal matters it required unanimous support of every member state. Therefore, on this issue getting one member state to agree with the position would have been enough to derail the initiative.

Similarly, an advocate promoting the continuation of a policy that would allow member states to reduce the value added tax (VAT) in the construction sector was working to target member states that were benefiting from the policy such as France. They were pushing the countries that were benefiting from the reduced VAT to fight back against Germany, which did not want to allow the possibility of a reduced VAT because the national government would be lobbied too vigorously from their domestic construction associations to reduce the VAT in Germany.

The EU association lobbyist explained their position: "Since it is voluntary anyway—Germany is blocking the sovereignty of the other members. If Germany doesn't want to implement it, they don't have to, but don't stop other member states from doing it if it is what is best for them. So we are going to try to talk with the other member states and see if we can get them to put pressure on the opposing member states."

On the Clean Air for Europe (CAFE) framework, industry advocates worked to gain support from member states that would have the hardest time implementing the new regulations, as one lobbyist explained: "There are very different views in the various member states; everyone supports CAFE in general, they are all positive. But some member states aren't that happy with how they've been modeled. . . . On more specific things like changing the rules regarding the size of particulate matter from ten to 2.5 PM, some like Sweden say, 'Yes let's do it,' and others are saying, 'Come on, we just started with the ten, now we'll have to change, think about the cost,' and that is countries like the Netherlands."

Which member states will be supportive is very much based on the specific aspects of the issue at hand. Lobbyists need to familiarize themselves with the case before them, get up to speed on the current situation in the member states, and assess which countries will support their position and which will be opposed. However this process is only necessary when lobbyists opt to target the Council. As the next chapter details, the majority of EU associations operating in Brussels are not targeting the Council due to the extremely restricted access to the institution. Moreover, those that do are largely working through their national associations. When organizations take the national route all member state associations are communicating the same message to their capitals, lobbyists in Brussels are not undertaking strategic target selection. Thus, this one possibility for target flexibility is suppressed by the general difficulty in lobbying in the Council and the tendency for a unified-country approach via the national route.

CONCLUSION

American and European lobbyists face very different targeting environments. The U.S. system allows more policymakers to play key roles in the policymaking process. Thus, advocates target a large number of members of Congress, and appeal to them with linkages to state, district, and personal interests.

Advocates in the U.S. system have more freedom to develop tailored targeting strategies and to mobilize friendly policymakers to become champions for their cause. The nature of the issue at hand and organizational characteristics combine to determine their targeting strategy: whether they will mobilize their allies, sway the undecided, or work to persuade the opposition. Advocates tend to extend beyond their comfort zone to target undecided and opposed policymakers on issues that are large in scope or high in salience, and if the advocate is representing citizen interest. The institutional system of the European Union presents advocates with a much more fixed set of targets. Rapporteurs and responsible DGs are predefined once an initiative is underway. Some leeway is found in the Council, where advocates can attempt to play the card of member states' interests.

This chapter has presented support for the proposition that institutional design is a fundamentally important consideration when one seeks to understand who the advocates target and why. The evidence further reinforces the idea that institutional design, issue characteristics, and interest group factors all contribute to decisions throughout the advocacy process. This stage of the processes of advocacy—target selection—especially highlighted the importance of institutional structure.

Thinking about targeting as a stage in the advocacy process highlights how decisions at one stage can affect outcomes at another stage and even how the arrows of causation can go both ways, especially if an issue is considered over a longer period of time. First, the targets selected can influence the arguments that advocates use. If an advocate in the United States decides to target friends and foes on a given issue he or she may very well emphasize different arguments when talking to the two audiences. For example an advocate of wind energy on the wind energy tax credit case noted that when speaking to green-minded Democrats he emphasized the benefit of his industry to the environment, but when speaking to midwest Republicans he focused on the benefit to farmers in their districts.

In the European Union, while the relevant players are set by institutional rules, advocates target their arguments depending on the party group or committee in Parliament. A citizen group active on the REACH chemical legislation noted that when talking with members of the PES—the socialist party group—they emphasized the effect of chemicals on workers and occupational health and brought data from trade unions; when talking with members of the consumer protection committee they emphasized arguments about the dangers of chemicals to consumers. Countless examples of this type of targeted argumentation can be found across the 149 interviews, demonstrating that targeting decisions influence argumentation decisions.

Taking a longer-term perspective, the arguments advocates use can shape the way an issue is framed or understood, as the work of Riker (1986) and

Baumgartner and Jones (1993) demonstrate. Over the long term, as advocates use certain arguments, emphasizing certain dimensions of debate, new institutional units and venues could come to have jurisdiction over a topic. Therefore, decisions about argumentation strategies at one point in time could effect decisions at another point in time at another stage of the advocacy process—that of target selection.

NOTES

1. The number of individual members of Congress that each advocate mentioned by name was coded. The mean on this variable is 5.9 with a standard deviation of 12.32.

2. Nine advocates reported targeting only "neutral" policymakers, officials who cannot be said to be ideologically supportive of or opposing lobbyist positions; all nine of these actors were active on regulatory issues. Results are not presented for this category of targets.

7

Inside Lobbying Tactics

KNOWING THE ARGUMENTS and the primary targets of those arguments is not enough; advocates also will have to decide on the most effective way to directly communicate their message to policymakers. This is the world of inside lobbying; it is the day-to-day life of advocates in Washington and Brussels.[1] It involves participating in hearings, consultations, and stakeholder meetings; drafting legislation and amendments; sending position papers, letters, and faxes; meeting with policymakers one-on-one and with their staff; organizing cocktail parties, seminars, and conferences; orchestrating lobbying day fly-ins of high-level membership, and arranging visits by policymakers to the field; and many other nuanced versions of these tactics.

A number of previous studies have demonstrated the immense size of some advocates' tactical toolboxes (Schlozman and Tierney 1986; Kollman 1998; Berry 1989; Baumgartner and Leech 1998), but how do the tactical strategies of lobbyists in Brussels and Washington compare? Do institutional structures shape inside strategy selection? How do those structures combine with issue characteristics and interest group factors? This chapter details the hypotheses regarding the relationship between inside lobbying and the characteristics of the interests themselves and their political context. The first section discusses theoretical expectations, followed by empirical analysis. A comparison of inside lobbying in the United States and the European Union includes analysis of direct lobbying, other inside lobbying tactics that advocates use in addition to one-on-one contacts, and alternative lobbying routes. The second portion of the empirical section analyzes the relationship between issue and interest characteristics and insider tactics, including multivariate analysis to parse out the effect of the sets of independent variables on inside lobbying tactic selection. Discussions of outside lobbying tactics and coalition activity are addressed in later chapters.

INSTITUTIONS, ISSUES, AND INTERESTS: FACTORS INFLUENCING INSIDE TACTIC SELECTION

When does old-fashioned shoe-leather lobbying by Brussels or Washington representatives cut it, and when is it necessary to take it up a notch and fly in experts and CEOs, organize a cocktail party, or arrange a site visit for policy-makers? The political context of the issue at hand, coupled with the resources of the advocates themselves, determine the answer.

Which institutions are activated on an issue depends on the policymaking procedure of the case, and is therefore an issue-level characteristic and will be discussed in more detail here. However, it is not just which institutions, but the design of those institutions that should influence inside lobbying strategies. The democratic accountability of those institutions to the public should influence the level of direct lobbying. Institutional systems characterized as open and accountable should exhibit higher levels of direct lobbying and a broader range of inside lobbying tactics, as policymakers in those systems are driven by the reelection motive to be receptive to communications from advocates about the views of their constituents. Thus, advocates in the United States are expected to display higher levels and a broader range of inside lobbying tactics.

In addition, the role of democratic institutional design should also be perceived within a polity by investigating inside lobbying across the primary political institutions of the political system. Thus in the United States, the U.S. Congress, the most open and accountable of U.S. institutions, should be the object of more inside lobbying than executive agencies or the White House. In the European Union, the Council, the most nontransparent and unaccountable of EU institutions, should be the object of the least amount of inside lobbying.

Turning to the second level of factors that determine inside lobbying strategies, issue salience should influence inside tactic selection. Specifically, issues that are highly salient to the public may drive lobbyists to use more and a broader range of inside lobbying tactics, so that they can communicate their positions to policymakers who know the stakes are high. Larger-scope issues that affect a large segment of society may lead advocates to engage in more inside lobbying tactics than smaller issues.

The third and final issue characteristic to consider when it comes to inside tactic selection is the policymaking procedure. As mentioned, different issues are decided according to different decision rules. While there are many fine distinctions, in the United States these differences can broadly be captured by a typology of regulatory versus legislative issues. In addition, some issues cannot be clearly categorized as strictly regulatory or strictly legislative; for example sometimes it is critical to lobby an agency for a letter of support in a legislative debate and other times it is necessary to lobby for legislative language to push an inert executive agency to action. In the European Union the categories of policymaking are broadly categorized by: consultation, codecision, social dialogue, implementation monitoring, or "other," which captures the myriad other policymaking instruments available in the European polity.[2]

At the interest group level, financial resources are fundamentally important; liquid assets allow for the use of a larger number and array of insider tactics (Smith 1984; Schlozman and Tierney 1986) as well as more expensive tactics. Resource-rich advocates should be more likely than resource-poor groups to engage in costly tactics such as flying CEOs and experts into the capital, and arranging informational trips for legislators. In addition, resource-rich advocates also should be able to engage in a broader range of insider tactics. The role of financial resources in inside tactic selection will be investigated with the resource indicator of staff size.

EMPIRICAL FINDINGS

Advocates were asked about the inside lobbying strategies they used. The advocacy strategies described in the interview transcripts were coded as to whether or not the U.S. advocates directly lobbied congressional leadership, committee leadership, committee members, or rank-and-file members; whether they sent letters, position papers, or reports to congressional offices; whether they testified before congressional committees; and whether they drafted legislation or strategized with members of Congress or their staff, including vote counting, coalition building in Congress, writing Dear Colleague letters, and the like. Regarding executive branch lobbying, advocates' responses were coded as to whether they had direct contact with agency officials, submitted comments to agency consultations, testified at agency hearings, or drafted regulatory language. In addition interviews were coded as to whether lobbyists had written or direct contact with the White House.

Coding also included noting whether groups mobilized their elite members (grass tops), organized lobbying days when elite members are brought into Washington for a coordinated lobbying event, or whether visits to the field were arranged by advocates. Other miscellaneous tactics were also coded: research dissemination, event organization, outsourcing lobby-related work, working through national associations, court activity, working through the U.S. states, or whether they pursued any innovative/outside-the-box strategies. Outside lobbying strategies were also coded; these are considered in the next chapter. Similarly, coalition activity is discussed in chapter 9.

In the European Union a similar set of inside lobbying tactics was coded to indicate whether lobbyists directly lobbied the Commission, the Council, and the Parliament and the level of that contact (high-level leadership, committee or unit leadership, or low-level officials); whether advocates strategized, testified, submitted comments, or wrote letters to the Commission, the Council, or the Parliament (each institution being coded for each tactic). Coding also included whether elites were mobilized or brought into Brussels and which institutions were the targets of those efforts, and whether officials from each of the institutions were invited to the field for site visits.

The routes of influence advocates pursued were recorded: whether they worked as or through a Euro association at the EU level, the national level, or the subnational level; whether they worked as or through a national association at the EU level, national, or subnational level; and finally, whether they worked as or through an international (i.e., global) association at each of those three levels. For example, a pan-European association could lobby a national government directly, flying Brussels representatives to a national capital, or it could work through one of its national affiliates at the national level. Finally, whether advocates engaged in any of the following was coded: research dissemination, event organization, outsourcing lobbying-related work, court activity, or whether they pursued any unique tactics.

What determines which tactics are selected from this multitude of lobbying tools? Data are presented that demonstrate the effect of institutional, issue, and interest group factors on inside lobbying decisions.

INSTITUTIONAL CHARACTERISTICS

The effect of institutional design on direct lobbying tactics can be investigated by analyzing lobbying in the Congress, regulatory agencies, and the White House in the United States and across the Commission, Council, and Parliament in the European Union. As discussed, the policymaking procedure of the issue determines in large part which institutions are activated during a given policy debate. If an issue in the United States is a purely regulatory one, the likelihood that an advocate will engage in face-to-face lobbying of Congress is low. Thus, comparing the level of lobbying of executive agencies versus congressional offices is necessarily colored by the sample of issues. However, because the samples are random, and therefore representative of the universe of issues in each polity, it is possible to investigate the relative frequency with which lobbyists use each of the various inside lobbying tactics in each of the institutions in each polity.

First, data on direct lobbying tactics are presented. Direct lobbying tactics are tactics in which advocates seek to communicate their positions directly to policymakers. This is followed by an investigation of other inside lobbying strategies that are not clearly targeted at a specific institution. Finally, an analysis of U.S. and EU advocates' tendency to pursue alternative routes to influence policymakers is presented.

DIRECT LOBBYING IN THE UNITED STATES AND THE EUROPEAN UNION

The more democratically accountable system should exhibit higher levels and a broader range of inside lobbying tactics—elected policymakers have a stronger incentive to listen to organized interests representing various configurations of constituents. Organized interests can mobilize the public in electoral campaigns—in reaction to policymaking decisions—meaning the careers of policymakers, to some degree, are influenced by Washington lobbyists. Lobbyists therefore use this leverage to communicate their positions on various policy debates.

Generally the majority of direct communications in the United States are directed at the legislature, whereas in the European Union they are targeted at the executive, as seen in table 7.1. Lobbyists in the United States are using more of the tactics at a higher rate; more American lobbyists are sending letters and position papers, strategizing with members of Congress, and drafting legislation.

In the United States, it is clear that face-to-face lobbying is predominantly focused on Congress, with 84.6 percent of interviewees reporting having arranged meetings with members of Congress or their staff. Of members of Congress, meetings are most often with committee leadership; 77 percent of advocates mentioned having done so—least often (14 percent) with party leadership. While personal meetings are the major route by which to communicate one's message in the House and Senate, the sending of letters and position papers comes in second, with 63 percent of respondents noting that they provided their positions on paper. White House officials were by and large not the target of direct lobbying, with only 18 percent of lobbyists mentioning any direct communication with White House staff. Written communications are even rarer; only 6 percent of advocates mentioned using them.

In the European Union, every direct lobbying tactic is used to the greatest extent in the Commission, then the EP, and then the Council, as seen in table 7.1. Regarding face-to-face lobbying, 94 percent of lobbyists mentioned arranging meetings with Commission officials, while 62 percent did so with MEPs and only 39 percent with Council ministers and staff. Within the Commission, where personal meetings were most common, official submission of comments to Commission consultations was also very common; 62 percent did so during their advocacy campaign. In the EP, again it is the personal meeting—that classic shoe-leather lobbying—that predominates, with 62

Table 7.1 U.S. and EU Direct Lobbying Tactics

	Frequency	Percent
Congress		
Face-to-face		
Party leadership	9	14
Committee leadership	50	77
Committee member	29	45
Rank & file	44	68
Letter, sent position	41	63
Strategize with MC	21	32
Draft language	24	37
Testimony at hearing	14	22
Regulatory Agency		
Face-to-face	18	28
Submit comments	7	11
Strategize with official	2	3
Draft language	4	6
Testimony at hearing	1	2
White House		
Face-to-face	12	19
Letter, sent position	4	6
Strategize with official	2	4
Total	65	100

	Frequency	Percent
Commission		
Face-to-face	77	94
Letter, sent position	44	54
Submit comments	51	62
Strategize with official	36	32
Draft language	14	17
Testimony at hearing	25	31
European Parliament		
Face-to-face	51	62
Letter, sent position	25	31
Submit comments	20	24
Strategize with MEP	4	5
Draft language	11	13
Testimony at hearing	18	22
Council		
Face-to-face	32	39
Letter, sent position	8	10
Submit comments	5	6
Strategize with official	0	0
Draft language	0	0
Testimony at hearing	2	2
Total	82	100

percent of advocates reporting have done so; this is followed up by sending letters or position papers, which 30.5 percent included in their action strategy. The Council is generally not a target of direct communications by Brussels lobbyists. Only 39 percent of lobbyists mention arranging face-to-face meetings and even less, 10 percent, mention sharing their positions via letter or position paper.

Testifying at EU Commission consultations is more common than before the U.S. Congress. The rate of testifying before the EP is identical to the rate of congressional testimony in the United States; 22 percent of advocates in both polities reported having been asked to testify before congressional or parliamentary hearings.

Drafting legislation on the other hand is slightly more common in the United States; 37 percent of lobbyists mentioned it as part of their legislative advocacy activities, compared to 30 percent in the combined figures for the EP and the Commission. This might speak to the notion some U.S. observers have of Washington—that K Street lobbyists are writing legislation. However it is important to note that while lobbyists may report drafting legislation as part of their advocacy strategy, it does not mean that that language is being included in the final versions of public law.

Elite mobilization is more balanced in the European Union. It is targeted at the Commission and the EP to a fairly high extent and at some level toward the Council, as seen in table 7.2. In the United States it is targeted principally at Congress. Elite mobilization occurs at a higher rate in the European Union than in the United States, contrary to the hypothesis that more tactics would be used by more U.S. lobbyists. Only 15 percent of U.S. lobbyists mentioned mobilizing elites to target members of Congress, whereas 49 percent of EU lobbyists targeted the Commission and 25 percent targeted the EP. As chapter 8 will show, mobilization of the masses is a different story, but when it comes to mobilizing elite members, national directors, or organization experts, Brussels-based lobbyists have found the tactic more critical in their advocacy strategies. This may be due to the intense need for national linkages, which can be facilitated by having important members from various member states communicate with EU policymakers.

More site visits are arranged in the United States; 14 percent of advocates reporting fly-outs of members of Congress or regulators, compared to 4 percent in the European Union. Fly-ins however are much more common in the European Union, with 77 percent reporting some type of elite Brussels visit, in relation to the 17 percent of U.S. advocates bringing members to Washington. Again, this may be due to the importance that lobbyists place on building a national connection with policymakers, best done by using national association leaders.

Table 7.2 U.S. and EU Elite Mobilization Tactics

	Frequency	Percent		Frequency	Percent
Congress			**Commission**		
Grass tops	2	3	Grass tops	0	0
Mobilizing elite members	10	15	Mobilizing elite members	40	49
Fly-ins/Lobby day	10	15	Fly-ins/Lobby day	37	45
Fly-outs/Site visits	8	12	Fly-outs/Site visits	1	1
Regulatory Agency			**European Parliament**		
Grasstops	2	3	Grass tops	0	0
Mobilizing elite members	0	0	Mobilizing elite members	21	26
Fly-ins/Lobby day	1	2	Fly-ins/Lobby day	19	23
Fly-outs/Site visits	1	2	Fly-outs/Site visits	2	3
White House			**Council**		
Grass tops	0	0	Grass tops	0	0
Mobilizing elite members	0	0	Mobilizing elite members	9	11
Fly-ins/Lobby day	0	0	Fly-ins/Lobby day	7	9
Fly-outs/Site visits	0	0	Fly-outs/Site visits	0	0
Total	65	100	**Total**	82	100

NONDIRECT INSIDE LOBBYING IN THE UNITED STATES AND THE EUROPEAN UNION

Face-to-face and direct institutional lobbying are not the only tactics that comprise the inside lobbying toolbox. A number of other tactics are also available to lobbyists seeking to influence policymakers. Events are one such tactic, perhaps more in line with traditional (or stereotyped) notions of lobbying. Lobbyists can get policymakers' attention and convey a great deal more information by organizing events like breakfasts, dinners, cocktail parties, or conferences. The planning of issue-related events is much more common in the European Union than in the United States, with 37 percent of respondents reporting doing so compared to only 6 percent in the United States (see figure 7.1).

The occurrence of events may be less common in Washington due to the rather strict rules requiring the reporting of money spent on lobbying by the Lobby Disclosure Act and strict House and Senate ethics rules regarding gifts (Maskell 2001). By these regulations, the amount of money advocates can spend, for example, on wining and dining or on gifts is restricted, but advocates are able to organize workshops related to issues. Four American lobbyists reported organizing some type of event described as roundtable meetings.

In the European Union, on the other hand, much more elaborate event organizing was evident. As one NGO lobbyist described: "We held a cocktail, with a coalition of NGOs—to welcome MEPs and to tell them that REACH is one of the most important proposals they will deal with in their term. There were about thirty MEPs there—a mix of both new and old MEPs." An industry lobbyist described a counter-event on the same issue—the chemicals regulation REACH—in which MEPs were invited to a cocktail party, during which

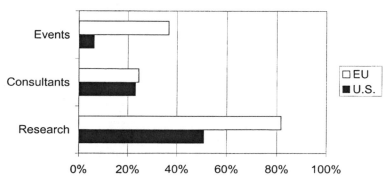

Figure 7.1   Use of Events, Consultants, and Research in the United States and the European Union

pieces of restored art were on display along with descriptions of how chemicals were used in the restoration process. In addition to conveying information during events, if advocates publicize the function in their association newsletters, organizations can demonstrate to their members that they are doing something. Some advocates noted that this also figured into their decision to hold an event.

Sometimes it is necessary to outsource work related to a lobbying campaign—whether a small staff is stretched too thin, or a special need requires expert advice; advocates can opt to hire consultants. The tendency to do so in the United States and the European Union is nearly identical: respondents reported 23 percent and 24 percent, respectively. In the United States these consultants ranged from legal advice to research assistance to hired lobbyists to lawyers to help draft legislation and submissions. These hired hands were thought to be helpful by one-fourth of the lobbyists interviewed; however, within the Washington advocacy community there is a perception that a hired lobbyist cannot effectively represent an advocate's interest.

As one university representative described it: "We do periodically engage consultants, but we are careful that those consultants don't actually go out and lobby directly on our behalf. They basically write guidance and strategic thinking for us, but we do our own lobbying. It's our view that most of the issues we work on are supported by members of Congress . . . and we're our own best advocates, rather than sort of a hired K Street lobbyist coming in on [our] behalf." Not only do lobbyists fear that their message, presented by a hired hand, would not be well-received, they also question the degree of trustworthiness of lobbying firms. An energy corporation lobbyist argued that hired lobbyists have an incentive to not finish the job, because it will lead to future contracts with the same client. These perceptions may lead advocates to avoid contracting lobbying firms.

In the European Union a similarly negative view surrounds consultants to some degree. In addition to the concerns described earlier—that policymakers do not have a good opinion of hired hands and that they may have an incentive to shirk—an EU banking industry lobbyist also notes that they simply don't have the specialized knowledge required to successfully lobby for a given industry, making the process inefficient: "We don't use consultants; consultants are not well-informed about our industry—our members know the figures the best. With the consultants there is a cost, of course, and there is a delay. We have to react very quickly, in the past you had three to six months, it was very relaxed, now you have six weeks. If you go to a consultant you have to first decide what consultant to use, then do a tender, then decide what mandate you are going to give the consultant—it takes time, and there isn't always the time."

In both polities one of the primary types of consultants that advocates hire is research entities, institutes or specialists that can conduct original research for the organization to include in its lobbying campaign. While some organizations opt to outsource such research projects, many others choose to do them in-house, or rather to use publicly available information from international organizations or from other organizations with which they work closely.

Research is mentioned as being critically important by lobbyists in both the United States and the European Union, but almost twice as many EU lobbyists noted using research as part of their lobbying strategy. This may be in part due to an inability of EU advocates to link arguments to a constituency to influence policymakers and thus advocates must resort to technical arguments based on data. In addition, the oft-cited shortage of Commission and EP staff renders the institutions more reliant on external research than in the United States, where Congress has its own research corps and individual members of Congress have staff orders of magnitude larger than MEPs.

In the United States 38.5 percent of lobbyists conducted original research in-house, while 24 percent noted using external data in advocacy work. Only four respondents noted using either internally or externally conducted research in public education campaigns. Of those 38.5 percent who engaged in research, many described it as very important and noted that when they could provide high-quality information policymakers reached out to them rather than the advocates needing to seek out the policymakers.

A scientific association described such a situation:

> Staff would call us and ask what our issues were and ask for feedback on different proposals and so it was a give and take kind of work environment on the different proposals: what was our reaction to the administration's proposal, what was our reaction to the House proposal, the Senate proposal, and in the end when they reached a compromise, what was our reaction to the final compromise. I should say I was approached, I didn't have to do a lot of outreach. They were asking us at that time for our input; they were reaching out to an expert for advice.

Other advocates who did not have the same level of organizational expertise sought out data and reports produced by other organizations. As a bill sponsor's staffer on the stock option expensing issue noted: "Also we saw that one of the analyst groups did a study that was really supportive of expensing so we contacted them and got their survey. So we keep our eyes out for that sort of thing and if we see something that is supportive of our position we get it and it becomes part of our stockpile of ammo, our support."

Lobbyists in Brussels similarly described the importance of such "ammo." A humanitarian NGO active on the child trafficking issue responded to the research question by saying:

We don't go without it as a rule. We go by the policy "first walk, then talk"; that is, we don't make advocacy until we have a broad, deep, and solid understanding of an issue. And that is our added value as an NGO—maybe some can talk better, but we base our advocacy on concrete experiences in the field, four and five years of research, gathering information from our field offices, compiling databases of trafficked children—this is their name, this is where they came from, this is where they were sent, this is when—very detailed work goes into our reports and then our advocacy.

While the majority of EU lobbyists reported using in-house or external research in their lobbying, 67 and 65 percent, respectively, others made the case for not taking facts and figures as part of their advocacy material. Some advocates argued that facts and figures are simply too burdensome for the quick policy meetings lobbyists get with policymakers: "We don't take statistics too much, officials are already inundated with paper, from their own administration and from the outside; they don't want more paper. Of the so-called facts and figures—we try to bring facts—this will be positive or negative for the industry. You can't take numbers on jobs created or lost—how do you calculate that? We can say, from our practical expertise this is going to have this effect."

An American information technology lobbyist similarly argued for the need to refine the message: "Less is more when you go to the Hill so we boil it down to one-pagers, that's far more effective. I think that if we are going to do a hearing we do a lot more paper, a lot more background in the way of testimony. But when knocking on doors less is more." While some lobbyists downplay the importance of research, a simple majority in the United States, 51 percent, and a large majority in the European Union, 82 percent, reported using some type of research as part of their advocacy campaign. This finding finally quantifies the general observation in the EU literature that research is an important part of Brussels lobbying.

ALTERNATIVE LOBBYING ROUTES IN THE UNITED STATES AND THE EUROPEAN UNION

In addition to direct Washington and Brussels lobbying routes, organizations in both polities also have a few alternative routes available, although more so in the European Union. In the United States, advocates with representation in Washington can sometimes find representation through a larger national association. Of the American lobbyists interviewed, 9.4 percent mentioned promoting their positions on the issue at hand through a larger association; those doing so were institutions or corporations. By working through a trade association, if you are a singular entity, you can demonstrate that your interests are shared by a broader cross section of the sector or industry.

In addition, it could be damaging to a corporation's image, and thus bottom line, if it is seen as meddling in public affairs. As one corporation's lobbyist described: "We work through our trade associations a lot, we have a trade association go and take a lot of the positions for us, there's a million of them—the National Grain and Feed Association, the American Meat Institute—there are scads of trade associations in agriculture, but we'll go have the trade associations take the more difficult, dangerous public view, and behind the scenes we'll work individually with our core group of folks."

The reason most advocates did not report working through a trade association is that they themselves were a national association. However, some individual companies and institutions noted that there are some dangers working through a trade or professional association. Similar to the risk that a hired consultant might shirk responsibilities, so too could a trade association; noted one company lobbyist: "We're really reliant on ourselves, I mean you can't leave something that big to somebody else and hope it gets done, hope that they are doing the assignments that you all gave each other. I mean this is our priority, we take care of it. Even if I asked [the trade association] to do something I'd still follow up myself. You just do it."

The other route available to lobbyists in the United States is working through the fifty states. However, while working through the member states in the European Union is very common at 59 percent, it is relatively rare for national associations to work through the U.S. states to influence federal policy; only 11 percent of advocates mentioned some type of activity through the states. In talking about how to influence the critical undecided members of Congress, one environmental NGO described how it was working through state chapters across the country, "making sure that people from their states and districts are contacting them and saying this is a critical issue for me, and talking to them in their states and districts. Going to them and making sure that, if there are town meetings happening or other things going on, that people are there to say hey, this is really an important issue . . . and making sure that the press in their states have the best information that they can have, trying to generate local editorials and those kinds of things."

In the European Union multiple-route lobbying is more prevalent, as the literature on multilevel governance anticipates. Of course, the vast majority of lobbyists interviewed in Brussels, 98.8 percent, were active through an EU-level entity. The one organization that registers as not working through an EU association at the EU level was a national organization based in Brussels and working on its own. About five percent of EU advocates mentioned directly lobbying at the national level as well—either at the perm reps in Brussels or directly in the capitals—although many more left it to their national affiliates.

Fifty-nine percent of advocates interviewed in Brussels reported working through their national associations at the national level; in addition, 38 percent of interviewees said they also lobbied EU-level institutions through their national associations. Only a small percentage of lobbyists work through an international/global organization or at the subnational level. A construction industry representative described the importance of finding the right mix of EU-level and national-level action:

> Then we coordinated the lobbying of our national associations in the national governments; that is very necessary. If you just have action in Brussels and not in the member states you won't get anywhere, and if you just have action in the member states and not in Brussels, that won't work either. The Commission has to be convinced because they write the proposal but the member states have to be convinced when they vote on it in Council. However, you don't need ten organizations lobbying in the member states, you can have just two or three as long as they are saying the same thing; then when they sit down to the table in EcoFin, and no one knows what's going on but three of them do know about it, and they are all saying the same thing, and raising the same concerns, then you are in a good position.

A business association advocate also highlighted the point that lobbying only a subset of key national ministries can be an efficient strategy: "We don't have the capacity here to contact all the national ministries directly but we can identify when a certain member state really needs to be talked to and then I get on the phone to my members and brief them on the situation and get them to talk to their officials at the national level. And of course, I give them the hymn sheet too."

While many recognize the importance of communicating to the Council through the national route, advocates also note the difficulty of doing so successfully; this may be in part why roughly 40 percent of lobbyists did not use the national route. As one lobbyist described, "We leave the national route up to the members, it goes via members, we don't touch perm reps here in Brussels. . . . We *try* to coordinate our members, but we don't have any control; it is easier when we have a concrete proposal and can identify some key MEPs and then we can ask the relevant members to contact those MEPs with the same message. But that doesn't always work out." And another business advocate, lobbying on the Services Directive, echoed this argument, but with more frustration:

> We don't go to the perm reps, and it is very difficult and as a Euro-organization—we have a problem of control of our members at the national level, we can give them the position paper, but we have no control

over what they do at the national level. . . . And the member states have different views about this directive and some of them want their borders to remained closed, and sometimes my members are affected by that, and feel the same way as their national governments, so we have very little power to influence in the Council, and oftentimes our federations are not playing the European game.

In sum, we see a greater range of lobbying routes in the European Union than in the United States, as expected, and within the European Union, EU-level group action at the EU level and national group action at the national level are the predominant routes. When it comes to using research as part of an advocacy campaign, EU lobbyists are conducting and disseminating research at a much higher rate. This greater use of research in the European Union is likely in part because of the inability to use constituency-based arguments on nonelected policymakers and the great information needs of the EU institutions. EU and U.S. lobbyists are employing hired consultants at approximately the same rate, with about one-fourth of advocates interviewed in each polity indicating this is helpful to their advocacy strategy.

Finally EU lobbyists are organizing issue-specific events at a rate more than six times that of U.S. lobbyists; possibly related to lobby disclosure and ethics rules, this finding may bolster the fears of EU lobbyists of the Commission proposal to regulate lobbying in Brussels. If the tactical repertoire of U.S. lobbyists has been constrained by lobbying regulations, EU lobbyists may have cause for concern that their lobbying strategies could be affected by the suggested plans called for in March 2005 by Commissioner for Administrative Affairs and Anti-Fraud Siim Kallas for a European Transparency Initiative to put EU lobbyists under tighter scrutiny.

ISSUE AND INTEREST CHARACTERISTICS

Within each polity the nature of the issue and characteristics of the advocate are expected to influence inside tactic selection. Specifically, issues that are large in scope and high in salience should lead advocates to use more, and a broader range of, inside lobbying tactics. Similarly, affluent advocates should be expected to use a broader range of tactics. To assess these hypotheses an aggregated dependent variable of the number of inside lobby tactics used was regressed on scope, salience, and staff size (as an indicator of financial resources). Table 7.3 reports the results for both polities; the findings suggest that interest resources matter more in the United States, with only staff size registering as having a significant and positive effect on the number of inside lobbying tactics used. In the European Union issue context matters more, with issue salience emerging as significant and positive.

Table 7.3   OLS Regression on Aggregate Number
of Inside Lobbying Tactics

	United States			European Union		
	Coefficient	SE	Probability	Coefficient	SE	Probability
Scope	0.371	0.270	0.175	−0.472	0.409	0.252
Salience	0.016	0.012	0.211	0.309	0.096	0.002*
Staff	0.011	0.004	0.008*	0.012	0.022	0.592
Constant	3.565	0.451	0.000	7.753	0.702	0.000
N	65			82		
R^2	0.1523			0.1356		

*Significant at .05 level.

In the United States groups with more resources are able to engage in a larger number and a broader range of tactics compared to poorer members of the advocacy community. The group's resources appear to matter more than the nature of this issue when it comes to inside tactic selection. In the EU model resources matter less in determining inside lobbying strategy, as indicated by the insignificant model findings. However, the salience of an issue to the public drives the intensity of advocates' inside lobbying activity. As issues become the object of public attention, EU advocates use more and a broader range of tactics.

Regarding the other expectation related to resources—the existence of more resources does not appear to lead to more use of the more expensive tactics of fly-ins and site visits in the United States or the European Union. These tactics are used at a similar rate by organizations with small, medium, and large offices in both polities.

It may be the case that, when it comes to the day-to-day business of advocates, lobbyists have their routines. Tactical preferences may have developed due to institutional culture or habit and thus advocates are not as influenced by issue context when selecting their inside strategies. We do see some patterns: U.S. advocates are affected by their financial resources and EU advocates are responsive to the salience of the issue, but the patterns are not overwhelming. One factor they do clearly take into consideration, albeit somewhat obvious, is the policymaking procedure.

In both arenas policymaking procedure emerges as an important determinant of inside lobbying activity. In the United States lobbyists active on legislative issues report the highest use of Congress-targeted tactics; those active on regulatory issues report the highest use of agency-targeted tactics. If a lobbyist is engaged in a legislative fight, he or she maximizes every single congressionally targeted lobbying tactic—organizing personal meetings, sending letters, strategizing with staffers, drafting legislative language, testifying, mobilizing the grass tops and their organizational elites, bringing them up to the Hill, and flying members of Congress and their staff to the field.

The same unambiguous pattern is evident for regulatory lobbying: every agency-targeted tactic is used most on issues that follow a regulatory policy-making process. In much regulatory lobbying, lobbyists are restricted to the venues defined by the process. As one trade association explained, "Interesting, we did nothing with Congress on this. This was strictly an agency-type initiative. We didn't go back to Congress and say will you amend the law and take us out, which maybe wouldn't have been a bad idea but it wouldn't have happened, I don't think. But it wasn't a case of going to Congress and trying to have them put pressure on EPA."

In the European case similar patterns are evident, but the patterns are not as crisp as those found in the United States. In the case of social dialogue all lobbying is directed at the Commission; the facilitator of the social dialogue process and all of the actors active on such issues reported conducting and sharing original research during the process. Lobbying related to the monitoring of implementation of EU regulations is also mainly focused on the Commission, understandably as the Commission is the institution to notify if member states are failing to implement EU law in a timely manner.

Turning to codecision and consultation, as expected, all three institutions are approached the most via personal meetings during codecision policy-making. The Parliament is targeted less during consultation policymaking. Also expected, however, so too is the Council, which remains a central decision maker during consultation. Thus we see more evidence of the role of institutional design on inside tactic selection. When lobbyists are lobbying on an issue decided by the consultation process, they choose to target the more open EP (at 65 percent) than the more closed Council (at 29 percent). They target the EP over the Council even though the EP has less power in the consultation process.

A more nuanced analysis of the effect of issue and interest characteristics on inside lobbying tactics can be achieved with a series of logit models predicting a selection of the inside lobbying tactics in both polities. Rather than looking only at the aggregate level of inside lobbying, I regressed the decision to draft legislative language, hire a consultant, and use research in one's lobbying campaign on a dichotomous variable indicating if the actor was part of the business community (professional, trade or business association, individual corporation, multinational corporation, or PR, law, or consultancy firm all coded one; other types of organizations coded zero) as well as the three issue characteristics of scope, salience, and policymaking procedure (converted into a series of dichotomous variables for each polity). In table 7.4 we see the policymaking procedure in the United States to be significant in the decision to draft language and hire a consultant. If the lobbyist is active on a legislative issue, he or she is *more* likely to engage in language drafting and *less* likely to hire a consultant. This fits with the qualitative evidence that suggests advocates make more use of hired experts when working on technically complex regulatory issues. Also significant for deciding to hire outside help is whether the advocate is a representative of the business community. Industry lobbyists are more likely to hire additional hands when devising their advocacy strategies.

Finally, on the decision to conduct research, only a single issue-level variable registers as significant: issue scope. The larger the issue an advocate is working on the more likely he or she is to conduct original research or seek out research reports to use in the advocacy. These same models were run for the European Union but none of the independent variables emerged as significant predictors of the inside lobbying decisions to hire a consultant, engage in research, or draft legislative or regulatory language; therefore the tables are not presented here.

What this analysis suggests is that different inside lobbying tactics may be driven by different contextual and organizational characteristics. In the United States, issue scope may not determine the total number of inside lobbying tac-

Table 7.4   Logit Models Predicting a Selection
of U.S. Inside Lobbying Tactics

	Drafting		Consultant		Research	
	Coefficient/ SE	Probability	Coefficient/ SE	Probability	Coefficient/ SE	Probability
Business	−0.713	0.202	1.502	0.023	0.398	0.454
	0.560		0.659		0.532	
Scope	−0.056	0.835	0.017	0.958	0.595	0.026
	0.271		0.333		0.267	
Salience	0.004	0.703	−0.015	0.369	0.001	0.960
	0.012		0.017		0.012	
Procedure	1.331	0.066	−1.326	0.054	0.148	0.809
	0.724		0.687		0.613	
Constant	−1.285	0.117	−0.814	0.294	−0.911	0.205
	0.821		0.775		0.718	
N	65		65		65	
Psuedo-R	0.0684		0.1447		0.0634	

tics an advocate uses but it can influence the decision to engage in policy research. Financial resources may drive the rate of inside lobbying but they don't seem to determine whether an advocate will draft legislation on a given issue (business groups were not more likely to draft in the logit model). It is also clear that the models determining inside lobbying decisions in both arenas are different. Interest group factors—specifically resources—matter more in the United States; issue-level factors—specifically issue salience—matter more in the European Union.

CONCLUSION

It appears lobbyists may have their routines when it comes to the daily business of sending position papers, meeting with staffers, testifying before committees, or drafting language—inside lobbying decisions are not as strongly determined by issue context as some of the other stages of the advocacy process. This is interesting to note in light of the fact that inside lobbying is often the sole focus of interest group scholars. This emphasizes why it is so important to study the advocacy process in its entirety; if we focus on only one stage we may come to inaccurate conclusions about the effects of context on lobbying.

While inside lobbying appeared to be less determined by context compared to other stages, there is some responsiveness to issue and interest characteristics. U.S. advocates vary their inside lobbying intensity depending on their resource base, whereas EU advocates intensify their inside lobbying as issue salience rises. In addition, advocates in both polities are very much attuned to the policymaking process when making their inside lobbying decisions. They employ the tactics targeted at the institutions with jurisdiction on a debate.

Moreover, the more nuanced analysis demonstrated that different factors may be at work on the decision to use each inside lobbying tactic, at least in the United States. Issue scope affected whether advocates engaged in issue research to support their advocacy campaigns, but scope did not appear to influence decisions regarding drafting language or hiring consultants. Groups representing industry were more likely to hire outside consultants to aid in a lobbying fight, but group type did not influence research and drafting decisions.

Institutional design does appear to play a role in inside lobbying, with advocates in the United States targeting the more open and accountable Congress and less likely to approach executive agencies or the White House. The power of the European Commission drives advocates to concentrate their energy and attention on that institution. In addition in both polities policymaking procedures, which determine what institutions have jurisdiction on an issue, have a consistently significant impact on inside lobbying decisions.

Somewhat different models may explain European and American advocates' inside lobbying decisions, but it is also important to remember how similar U.S. and EU tactical repertoires are when it comes to lobbying policymakers. The belief that EU advocates are still in the developmental stage when it comes to direct lobbying should be put to rest. Advocates in both polities are engaging in exactly the same types of techniques, at similar levels of sophistication, to convey their positions to policymakers.

In addition, advocates in both arenas are continually faced with the potential for further regulation of their inside lobbying activities. Lobbying rules can regulate how much advocates spend on activities aimed at conveying their message to policymakers. The United States has a long history of increasingly strict lobbying regulations but many observers argue they still do not go far enough. Similarly in the European Union, the debate about regulating lobbyists has gone on for at least two decades, and many observers say much more could be done to control the undue influence of special interests.

NOTES

1. As opposed to outside lobbying, the term originates from references to "outside the Beltway," meaning outside the city of Washington, D.C., which is surrounded by a circular highway called the Beltway.

2. No issues in the random sample fall under the "cooperation" policymaking process; therefore it is not included in the tables.

8

Outside Lobbying Tactics

AS THE PREVIOUS chapters have demonstrated, the complex world of insider lobbying involves countless critical decisions about which methods to use to directly communicate to policymakers and which policymakers to target. Effective lobbying campaigns, however, are not always limited to actions within the Beltway or Brussels. Sometimes it is necessary to reach out to the public to indirectly influence the policymaking process. Indeed Schattschneider suggested that the outcome of every conflict is determined by the extent to which the audience becomes involved in it, or the "scope of its contagion." He argued that "those that are successful in getting the audience involved win" (1960, 4). Thus, expanding the scope of conflict by notifying and mobilizing citizens may make a drastic difference in the outcome of a political debate. With some notable exceptions (Kollman 1998; Goldstein 1999; Beyers 2004), few have studied the degree to which formal lobbying groups engage in outside lobbying—tactics aimed at actively mobilizing the citizenry—or how factors at the institutional, issue, and interest group levels influence the decision by lobbyists to go public.

Outside lobbying is the point at which inside lobbying and policymaking intersect with social movements, public opinion, and citizen engagement. The first section highlights the expectations regarding the influence of institutions, issues, and interest group factors on the decision to use outside lobbying. Two factors likely influence the level of outside lobbying: electoral accountability and the presence of a media system. Outside lobbying is not always an optimal strategy or even feasible; issue and interest characteristics are fundamentally important in determining whether a given advocate uses outside lobbying tactics on a given policy debate. The second half of this chapter presents data and empirical findings; and the effects of institutional, issue, and interest group characteristics on the use of seven outside lobbying techniques are laid out, followed by a multivariate analysis to study the relative effects of the various factors.

INTEREST GROUPS AS INSTIGATORS

The terms "lobbyist" and "special interests" are often met with a less than warm reception on both sides of the Atlantic. Today interest groups are seen as a force derailing democracy from its proper course, packing policy with special interest exceptions at the expense of the common good. However, further thinking reminds us that the interest group community includes the very groups that scholars of social capital championed as vehicles of citizen engagement in politics—groups engaged in environmental, women's, and civil rights, as well as senior, antiglobalization, antipoverty, labor, community, recreational, and patient issues, among others. This tendency to overlook the positive side of lobbying communities may stem from the propensity of the interest group literature to look inside and focus on direct lobbying tactics.

Interest groups play a critical role in modern democracies by acting as watchdogs. By monitoring policy developments and notifying and mobilizing inattentive publics when policymakers act contrary to certain constituencies, interest groups do the investigative work for citizens who don't have the time to follow policy development on a daily basis. Arnold refers to groups acting in this regard as "instigators": "The availability of an *instigator* to help reveal citizens' stakes in an outcome also affects the probability that an individual [citizen] will notice a specific cost or benefit" of a policy proposal (1990, 30). He notes that instigators can be political candidates of the opposition monitoring the behaviour of policymakers in power with an eye toward unseating them in the next election, or they can be interest groups monitoring the daily policymaking process.

If interest groups see policymaking decisions they disagree with, they have an incentive to expand the scope of conflict by involving the offending policymaker's constituents (if that public would be in line with the interest group). For citizen groups this is almost always a possibility, but for trade, professional, and even individual corporations it is also a possibility to expand the scope of conflict in instances in which the public shares the goals of the organized interests (see Goldstein 1999). Through outside lobbying tactics—mobilizing letter-writing campaigns, media work, public advertising campaigns in print, radio, and TV media outlets or organizing grass-roots meetings, demonstrations, and other outreach programs—organized interests of all types can foster citizen engagement.

Thus citizens need not follow policy developments on every proposal, but if organized interests are monitoring the halls of government and notifying their constituents and various publics, citizens can become engaged on those issues that are most important to them. In short, interest groups often serve as instigators through the use of outside lobbying—playing Socrates' proverbial gadfly to the sleeping mule that is the public. The degree to which interest groups perform their role as mobilizers varies.

Previous literature on EU lobbying has suggested advocates are generally not employing tactics that lead to outside-Brussels mobilization (Greenwood 1997, 2002; Pedler and Van Schendelen 1994; Van Schendelen 1993; Pedler 2002; Bouwen 2002; Rucht 2001; Watson and Shackleton 2003). However, little empirical research has been done to systematically measure this general observation, nor to assess the determinants of the phenomena when they do go public. Literature on the lobbying community in the United States has empirically documented the use of outside tactics as well as some of its determinants (Schlozman and Tierney 1986; Baumgartner and Leech 1998; Kollman 1998; Goldstein 1999; Gerber 1999), but without a comparative framework we are unable to discern the role of institutional structure in the outside lobbying process.

Thus, the main questions are these: Are U.S. and EU interest groups fostering citizen engagement through outside lobbying? And what factors lead to public mobilization by interest groups? These in turn lead to many other more specific inquiries: Do some types of groups mobilize the public more than others? Do lobbyists on certain issues exhibit a higher degree of outside tactic usage? How do advocates in the two arenas compare—do we see more or less citizen mobilization by interest groups?

FACTORS INFLUENCING THE DECISION TO MOBILIZE THE PUBLIC

I proceed from the argument laid out above, that interest groups foster civic engagement through outside lobbying tactics, techniques aimed at mobilizing the public to influence the policymaking process. If we assume that civic engagement is desirable and that organized interests can foster it through their outside lobbying campaigns, the task then becomes determining what influences lobbyists' decisions to go outside.

Institutions

There are two important institutional differences: the method of selecting officials and the presence of a broad-reaching media system. Each is discussed in turn, followed by how scholars have suggested they should influence the use of outside lobbying, and the expectations related to each factor.

First, there is the democratic accountability of policymakers—the selection process. The democratic accountability of an institution will influence the use of outside lobbying, which is designed to evoke the will of the people and tap the fear of policymakers accountable to those citizens. Thus lobbyists are more likely to employ outside tactics if they are active in an arena where the officials are driven by the reelection motive. The expectation is that outside lobbying tactics such as grassroots letter-writing campaigns, advertising, press releases, press conferences, and protest activity should be more prevalent when lobbying is done in a political system that is highly democratically accountable, such as the United States.

Second, many observers of EU politics have noted the lack of a pan-EU media, or what some have termed a European Public Space. With twenty-three official languages in the European Union, and the lack of any widespread EU newspaper or television channel, there is no simple way to relay information about the European Union to the people; it has to be funnelled through the national outlets, which vary in their interest and their spin on EU affairs.

However, not all outside lobbying tactics should be suppressed by the lack of a media machine—specifically mobilizing letter-writing campaigns of organizational members and the mass public should still be possible. These two tactics can be coordinated at the EU level, with mobilization of the people carried out by the national associations. Neither requires complex media campaigns and both would foster citizen engagement aimed at influencing policymakers.

In sum, the democratic accountability of officials and the presence of a broad media system likely influence whether outside lobbying is employed. Knowing the institutional system within which an advocate is lobbying, however, is not enough; in addition we must consider the characteristics of the issue at hand as well as the type of advocate and its resource set. These factors are discussed next.

Issues

The second source of variation that influences the use of outside lobbying is at the issue level. The first variable of interest is the scope or size of the proposed policy, the magnitude of the impact on individuals (Baumgartner and Leech 2001; Browne 1995). The larger the issue, and the bigger its impact on citizens, the more likely an organization might attempt to mobilize the masses. Second is the salience of the issue to the mass public (Kollman 1998). Clearly, the more salient an issue is to the people—the more they are engaged on the topic and following its developments—the more likely an advocate will go outside and capitalize on that attention.

Third, the presence of a focusing event is an important factor influencing the possibility to mobilize the public (Kingdon 1995). If a crisis has occurred related to the policy, this event can crystallize the need for policy action and create a concrete example with which to mobilize people. The presence of a focusing event should increase the likelihood that an organization will engage in outside lobbying.

Fourth, as issues increase in conflict an increase in outside lobbying should occur (Salisbury et al. 1987). A high-conflict issue may compel one side of the debate to go public—those who want to expand the scope of conflict (Schattschneider 1960). This in turn can lead to more coverage—the media tend to cover controversy; it gets ratings. While the opposition may not like the coverage, once the scope of conflict is expanded, they will likely also have to go public to combat the opposing side's outside lobbying communications. Finally, the history of the issue is important. New issues have more room for manipulation of the dimensions of debate and alliance and opposition patterns, compared to older reoccurring issues (McKissick 1995). A new hot issue may be used by advocates to spark the interest of the people, thus making outside lobbying a good tactical option.

It should be noted that another issue characteristic often mentioned in the ability to use an outside lobbying strategy is complexity. Issues related to problems that are arcane or difficult to understand are more difficult to refine into a sound bite that the media can pick up. As one U.S. advocate described, "We didn't do any media, it was too hard of an issue and too complicated of an issue to actually break down into sound bites. I think if we had done anything like that it probably would have made the situation worse because you would have gotten a story printed in one of the major papers that wouldn't give all the necessary details."

However, the perceived complexity of an issue is very much tied up with framing and issue definition and an advocate's position on an issue. As another noted on a different issue: ". . . the problem is that the other side, the opposition, have these handy little sound bites that are often completely wrong but it's much easier when you say 'this thing lets terrorists in the country' and everybody goes 'oh well that's horrible' and then when you say 'well actually that's not true and these people have this visa' and you have to explain the whole process, it's a much harder sound bite to sell." While one version of their position may be harder to sell, a different conceptualization might be easier, for example, something like "this country was built by immigrants, so terrorist regulations should not prohibit legitimate immigration." Thus, the complexity of an issue is very much determined by how lobbyists can frame the issue, rendering it quite impossible to objectively code whether an issue is complex. This aspect of the discussion is therefore not included in this analysis.

Interests

The third level of analysis provides the final set of independent variables that influence the use of outside lobbying tactics. Organizational characteristics also have an impact on the decision of advocacy organizations to go public (Schlozman and Tierney 1986; Dür 2005). First, the type of organization, and thus its goals or purposes, determine whether the entity can engage in outside lobbying (Clark and Wilson 1961; Beyers 2002). For example a sectoral association of chemical manufacturers might be much less comfortable with their Washington or Brussels representative organizing a media blitz than an association of green activists. Kriesi, Jochuma, and Tresch note that the number and type of interests engaging in political debates have grown: "The struggle for the attention of the public includes elected political decision makers, but also an increasing number of collective political actors" (2005, 6). They distinguish between state actors, political parties, interest groups, and social movement organizations.

Another common distinction is between civil society and industry interests, while others divide the community by diffuse versus concentrated interests (Schneider and Baltz 2003; Pollack 1997). My coding of actor type is a bit more detailed, in an effort to identify differences between different types of interest groups. The general expectation is that citizen groups will be more likely to go public while organizations representing industry will be less likely to do so, but evidence on the full range of actor types is presented.

Second, the level of financial resources is a major determinant of outside lobbying. It plays a critical role in the type and number of outside lobbying tactics an organization can engage in (McCarthy and Zald 1978; Schlozman and Tierney 1986). Staff size is a good indicator of the level of financial resources an advocate controls; establishing a capital office (Brussels or Washington) and staffing it is an expensive undertaking. The more financial resources an organization controls, the more likely it should be to engage in outside lobbying tactics.

The size, type, and spread of an organization's membership is also an important determinant of its tactic options (Bacheller 1977; Kollman 1998). If an actor has a broad membership it is much easier and more likely effective at public mobilization than an organization composed of only a few hundred individuals; and thus it is expected to engage in outside lobbying at a higher rate. Finally, it is also important to consider how the group is organized, for this also affects lobbying strategies (Marks and McAdam 1996). If an advocate has a network of membership organizations in place in the states or member states, it should be much more likely to attempt to mobilize the masses than an interest with no member organizations such as a corporation or lobbying firm. In the European Union this is coded as whether the organization's structure is federated, direct membership, mixed membership, or no membership. In the United States it is coded as a dichotomous variable if the organization maintains local, state, or regional subunits.

In sum, a range of interest group-specific variables including monetary and membership resources as well as group type and organizational structure can be expected to affect the decision to go outside. Institutional, issue-specific, and interest group factors are all critical pieces of the advocacy puzzle and thus each is measured and analyzed so that a complete image of influences on outside lobbying can be constructed.

EMPIRICAL FINDINGS

Each interview transcript is coded (0–not mentioned; 1–mentioned) as to whether the advocate mentioned using a range of outside tactics in its advocacy strategy including: (a) grassroots mobilization of the organization's membership (contacting members, encouraging them to write, e-mail, call, attend town meetings, or otherwise communicate with elected representatives); (b) grassroots mobilization of the mass public; (c) media usage (issuing press releases, organizing press conferences, talking with the press, conducting interviews); (d) issue advertisements; (e) public education campaigns/public relations (coordinating large-scale public relations strategy including multiple routes to communicate to the public); (f) protest, demonstration, or rally; and (g) op-ed or editorial (writing op-eds, encouraging elite organization members or other experts to write op-eds). These are the strategies that organizations can use to influence policymaking and simultaneously promote civic engagement. As described in chapter 3, issue and interest group variables were coded from publicly available sources and research on the cases.

Institutions

As expected there is a marked difference in the use of outside lobbying in the United States and the European Union. Every outside lobbying tactic is used more by lobbyists in the United States than the European Union, as shown in table 8.1. Quite notable is the difference between grassroots mobilization of

Table 8.1   Outside Tactics by Institutional System

	United States		Europe	
	Frequency	Percent	Frequency	Percent
Grassroots – Organizational	16	25	1	1
Grassroots – Mass Public	3	5	1	1
Media	26	40	19	23
Issue Ads	4	6	2	2
Public Education/PR	5	8	3	4
Protest/Rally	1	2	1	1
Op-ed/Editorial	9	14	2	2

Note: Advocates could use more than one tactic.

organizational membership—at 25 percent in the United States but only 1 percent in the European Union—and also between media usage—40 percent in the United States versus 23 percent in the European Union.

A summary variable, an additive index of the total number of outside lobbying tactics used by each advocate, was calculated to look at the results in a slightly different way. Only 51 percent of advocates in the United States reported not engaging in any outside lobbying activity, whereas in the European Union outside lobbying was not employed at all by 76 percent of lobbyists. In addition, only six out of eighty-two EU advocates pursued more than one outside lobbying tactic, while combined strategies were much more prevalent in the United States, at 23 percent.

While the quantitative evidence is striking, the numbers alone cannot convey the difference in intensity of outside lobbying between the two polities. Advocates in both arenas may be coded as using a media strategy, but for the American advocate this may be a concerted media effort, whereas in the European Union it is a simple press release. In many instances media usage in the United States is a full-fledged campaign, as one lobbyist active on the debate over antiterrorism regulations explained: "We were constantly commenting on these issues in the media, speaking personally I probably gave a dozen newspaper interviews on this particular subject and half-a-dozen to a dozen radio interviews . . . Also we've had editorials published on the topic. We relied pretty heavily on advancing our agenda through the media."

A similarly aggressive media campaign was launched on the cloning prohibition case, as a professional association lobbyist described: "We've had a very aggressive media strategy both as part of the coalition and as individual organizations . . . I've done talk radio all over the country, I've done CNN a couple of times and we have a very strong relationship with a half dozen or so leading national reporters covering the issue . . . And you know we did an op-ed campaign, and we did paid advertising, we did a lot of talk show appearances, everybody from me to Christopher Reeve, and anybody in between."

Media are often an important part of an advocacy strategy in the United States and this is facilitated by the presence of a vigorous media community in Washington. In the European Union media-intensive tactics are more difficult to employ. A humanitarian organization active on the trafficking in children case explained that the Brussels press corps is often only covering the narrow topic of what dossiers are up for a vote: "We haven't done any press, Brussels media is interested in what's on the legislative agenda so there is not much interest in this, but that is just a fact of what Brussels news covers, not about if the issue is interesting—they just follow the legislative agenda and there hasn't been much legislative action on this."

While the presence or absence of an extensive media system is important, electoral accountability also plays a role. The electoral connection was quite apparent in a number of discussions with American lobbyists. One citizen group advocate active on the TANF reauthorization explained the importance of the constituency link:

What I do is to go to my constituency and say here's what you need to be telling them [their representatives]. They need to hear from you. It's important that I go and talk to them . . . but until they hear from you, people who are actually out there, living there, breathing this, eating and sleeping it every day of your life, they need to hear from you to better understand and to really bring home the impact of what's happening at the state level."

A trade association described a similar online system to promote citizen engagement, as did a number of other lobbyists interviewed: "We've used our website, on it you can write your member—we call it Making Waves—it is through Capitol Advantage, a lot of associations use them, but if you go there you can click on the Recreational Marine Employment Act and here we explain what the issue is, and you can even tell a friend, and you can compose a letter and the letter is written for you and you can edit it and then you can either mail it or e-mail it to your member of Congress."

A professional association active on the math and science education debate echoed the point that mobilizing constituents matters:

One of the most valuable lobbying tools we have is our legislative action network. . . . Five or six times a year we will send out an action alert to 7,000 of our members saying Congress is about to vote on this math and science education bill, here's the background, here's our position, here are the key players, please go to our website, type in your zip code, read more about the issue, and if you support our position then send an e-mail to your member of Congress. . . . What we do know is that all those members of Congress do listen to constituents. . . . So that's grass roots, getting your wide membership involved in the process, getting them to weigh in.

The level of constituent mobilization found among U.S. advocates is markedly absent in the EU arena. Thus, we see support of both parallel hypotheses—media presence and electoral accountability—predicting less outside lobbying in the European Union. However, the two tactics of grass-roots mobilization of organizational members and the mass public allow us to parse out the effects to some degree. That is, the two grassroots mobilization tactics do not require a broad-based media system. Both tactics could be accomplished by EU organizations encouraging citizens either directly or through their national associations to write, e-mail, fax, or call policymakers. Both of these tactics being used to a much smaller degree in the European Union suggests that the first institutional characteristic—the democratic accountability of the institutions—is also at play and that the lack of media tools is not the only explanation for limited use of outside lobbying.

Issues

In order to see how the use of outside tactics varies by issue characteristics, each of the seven dichotomous outside lobbying variables was tabulated by scope, conflict, the presence of a focusing event, the recurring/new nature of the issue, and salience. Table 8.2 reports a subset of the results for the U.S. system. The table shows, for example, that 25 percent of all groups used grassroots tactics associated with their own members. The first part of the table shows that only 13 percent of advocates involved in small-sector issues used the tactic but this rose to 30 percent for advocates active on systemwide issues. The last column shows the number of observations on which each of the individual sets of percentages is calculated.

There is a clear upward trend for issue scope with regard to grassroots mobilization of the membership, grassroots mobilization of the mass public, and media usage. As the issue increases in size each of these outside lobbying tactics is used by a larger percentage of advocates. There are no discernable patterns in advertising, public relations, protests, or op-ed writing.

For the issue characteristic of conflict, as issues exhibit higher levels of conflict, the outside lobbying tactics of grassroots mobilization of the masses, media use, protest, public relations, and op-ed writing all increase in usage. Only advertising and member mobilization do not exhibit any clear patterns. It is understandable that we see more outside lobbying as conflict increases. As one side of the debate gets coverage, the other side responds in kind. As one citizen group explained, "I don't want to say most importantly, but very important was also getting this information out to the media, because this issue had not been debated in a really comprehensive way, in over ten years . . . and there was a need to really rebut the industry's arguments and help people in the media and policymakers and the public kind of see an alternative point of view."

There is less evidence of a clear pattern for the presence of a focusing event; only two tactics trend in the hypothesized direction: media usage and op-ed writing (shifting from 33 percent to 55 percent and 11 percent to 20 percent, respectively, as we move from an issue with no event to an issue with a related focusing event). All the other tactics exhibit no pattern or, as in the case of mobilization of the grassroots, suggest the opposite direction: this type of outside lobbying happens more often on issues that have no focusing event. Similarly for the variable of issue history—whether the issue is a new topic or an older reoccurring issue—the evidence does not support the hypothesized

Table 8.2 Advocates Using Outside Tactics by Issue Characteristics in the United States (percent)

Scope	Grassroots		Media	Ads	PR	Protest	Op-ed	N
	Members	Public						
Small sector	13	4	30	4	4	0	13	23
Large sector	27	5	46	14	14	0	18	22
Multiple sectors	40	10	20	0	10	10	10	10
Systemwide	30	0	70	0	0	0	10	10

Conflict	Grassroots		Media	Ads	PR	Protest	Op-ed	N
	Members	Public						
None	19	5	33	0	0	0	5	21
Multiple perspectives	33	0	33	33	0	0	0	3
Opposing	27	5	44	7	12	2	20	41

Salience	Grassroots		Media	Ads	PR	Protest	Op-ed	N
	Members	Public						
0 stories	27	7	23	7	7	0	7	30
1–5 stories	14	0	36	0	0	0	7	14
6–50 stories	3	9	55	9	18	9	27	11
51 or more stories	20	0	80	10	10	0	30	10
Average total percent	25	5	40	6	8	2	14	

direction. Save for the slightly higher usage of media outreach on new issues, the data would suggest the opposite is in fact the case: the older the issue the more likely outside lobbying—with higher percentages of advocates using every other tactic when the issue is older.

Regarding salience, the hypothesized direction is exhibited for every outside lobbying tactic: the more salient the issue is to the mass public, the more advocates are engaging in outside lobbying techniques. It is extremely difficult to parse out the causation here but the fact that letter-writing campaigns among the public, grassroots mobilization of the membership, and protest activities are all also trending upward, in addition to the specifically media-oriented tactics, suggests high salience correlates with outside lobbying by advocates.

Now we turn to the same issue analysis in the EU system. As in the U.S. arena, use of outside lobbying tactics by advocates is related to some of the five issue characteristics of interest. Results are reported in table 8.3. In some cases, due to the much lower prevalence of outside lobbying in the European Union, patterns are difficult to discern.

In the EU case we see essentially no pattern between issue scope and the use of any of the seven outside tactics. For issue conflict there is generally an upward trend from zero for six of the seven tactics, with the exception of media outreach, which trends upward but with no cases registering in the middle category of "multiple but not conflicting viewpoints." For the variable of the occurrence of a focusing event, the majority of the cells display very small percentages; however, the two tactics with a more significant level of use confirm the hypothesized direction: As in the United States, media outreach and op-ed writing tactics are employed more on issues that have had some type of attention-grabbing event related to them (shifting from 21 percent to 75 percent for media and 1 percent to 25 percent for op-ed). The variable of issue history similarly trends in the expected direction for media outreach and op-ed writing but in the opposite direction for the other five tactics.

Finally, to look at the role of salience on outside lobbying in the European Union, all seven outside lobbying tactics trend upward the more salient the issue. When the public is not interested in an issue it is difficult for advocates to engage the media. As one trade association lobbying against the PEI packaging and packaging waste case noted: "We don't use the media much, our targets are the institutions, maybe sometimes the *European Voice*, but the media isn't interested in packaging waste, and if you went to your average Joe on the street, and tried to talk with him about packaging and packaging waste—good luck!"

In sum, we see support for the first two hypotheses that lobbyists active on larger issues and highly conflictual issues are more likely to employ outside lobbying tactics—working to engage the citizens in the policymaking process.

Table 8.3 Advocates Using Outside Tactics by Issue Characteristics in the European Union (percent)

Scope	Grassroots		Media	Ads	PR	Protest	Op-ed	N
	Members	Public						
Small sector	0	0	13	4	0	0	0	24
Large sector	4	4	39	4	9	0	9	23
Multiple sectors	0	0	21	0	5	0	0	19
Systemwide	0	0	19	0	0	6	0	16

Conflict	Grassroots		Media	Ads	PR	Protest	Op-ed	N
	Members	Public						
None	0	0	19	0	0	0	0	16
Multiple perspectives	0	0	0	0	0	0	0	7
Opposing	2	2	27	3	5	2	3	59

Salience	Grassroots		Media	Ads	PR	Protest	Op-ed	N
	Members	Public						
0 stories	0	0	9	3	0	0	0	32
1–2 stories	5	5	35	5	5	0	5	20
3 or more stories	0	0	30	0	7	3	3	30
Average total percent	1	1	23	2	4	1	2	

Support for the hypotheses regarding the second two issue characteristics is more mixed, suggesting that knowing the issue's history and whether a focusing event occurred may not be quite enough to predict lobbying strategies. Finally, there is evidence supporting the hypothesis that there will be more outside lobbying on more salient issues, although there is likely a positive feedback process at play.

Interests

The final level of independent variables that should have an effect on the use of outside lobbying is organizational characteristics. As readers of the literature would expect, in the United States citizen groups are much more inclined to employ outside lobbying tactics: they use them to a greater extent than the average on every tactic except placing issue advertisements (and protests, but only one advocate reported employing a protest strategy out of the sixty-five respondents). They are the only type of actor mobilizing the mass public (22 percent) other than trade associations, of which only 8 percent reported doing so. Professional associations are also large users of outside strategies, exhibiting higher-than-average use of five of the seven outside lobbying strategies. This category of actors is especially inclined to use grassroots mobilization of the membership with 57 percent of professional associations reporting that they used this tactic on the issue on which they were interviewed.

Also interesting to note is what types of actors are dominating certain tactics: issue advertisements are used by only 6.2 percent of actors on average, but only professional associations and corporations engage in this activity; 43 percent of professional organizations are advertising related to their policy fights and 14 percent of corporations. Advertising requires a significant amount of resources to design, produce, and air. An environmental advocate described the blitz advertising campaign being financed by industry in the CAFE debate: "A big part of their ad campaign, before the vote in Congress this past year, was to have ads running in rural America saying Congress is going to take away your pickup truck and you're going to be hauling hay in the back of a little Pinto."

All the think tanks reported pursuing media strategies and a third also reported engaging in public relations campaigns and writing editorials. Multinational corporations were not engaging in any form of outside lobbying. One company lobbyist described how they try to stay out of the media: "We generally stay behind the scenes, we are not one to go grab a microphone or a spotlight very often, we will call people, rather than go see them, we are a company that draws a lot of criticism because we are so big. . . . So we basically keep to ourselves, sort of lurk in the shadows and try not to put our fingerprints on anything."

Regarding the interest group characteristic of staff, the data do not clearly support the hypothesized relationship.[1] Larger staff sizes seem to be related to a higher use of outside lobbying tactics only in the case of media, where 43 percent of small offices reported media tactics, 50 percent of medium-sized offices, and 57 percent of large offices. For both types of grassroots mobilization and protest, it appears some threshold of staff resources needs to be crossed to engage in these outside tactics, but that the largest offices are not going public as much as mid-range ones. This finding might not be as surprising as it seems at first, for it is the well-heeled lobbying firms, corporations, and business associations that have the well-staffed offices, the very types of advocates unlikely to engage in large public mobilization campaigns. Thus it appears, when you don't have the money and inside-the-beltway staff to engage in incessant direct lobbying, you rely on the masses and mass membership to communicate your message to lawmakers. However, you need enough staff to put into motion the outside strategy.

Organizational structure seems to have a clear influence in the decision to go outside or not. Advocates with subunits at the regional, state, or local level use outside lobbying strategies at a higher rate than groups with no local units. This is true for every outside lobbying tactic except op-ed writing, which is often done by expert members or Washington staff. This finding follows logic, for it is easier to mobilize the members, citizens in the communities, coverage in local papers, public education campaigns, and protests if you have established offices already active in the field. This was exemplified by one of the environmental organizations interviewed; as its lobbyist explained: "We are the largest grassroots environmental organization in the country, we have about 750,000 members, and the real strength of our organization is the ability to mobilize people across the country, so we often help in the release of other organizations' reports because they don't have that field staff, they don't have the regional offices, and the chapter office in every state and volunteers that can put on a press conference in just about any city you would want."

To assess the relationship between membership size and outside lobbying, it was necessary to distinguish between individual members and organizational members—be they organizations, corporations. or institutions.[2] The larger the individual membership the higher the percentage of outside lobbying usage—and that is true for every lobbying tactic. A similar pattern also holds for corporate membership; the more members the more outside lobbying, but only for the tactics of grassroots mobilization of organizational members, grassroots mobilization of the public, and media use. The other four tactics are not used by organizations with corporate or institutional members, regardless of how large the membership.

Turning to the European Union and investigating the relationship between group type and outside lobbying, a pattern similar to that in the United States emerges: domination by the citizen groups. It is they who use the majority of outside lobbying tactics more than the average of all groups. In addition, they are the only category of actors mobilizing the mass public. Second to citizen groups are trade associations, using four of the seven outside tactics at a higher-than-average rate. As in the United States it is the industry associations that are the only category of actors using advertising. A number of actor categories reported using no outside tactics: professional associations, business groups, lobbying firms, and governmental actors. While the governmental actors are unlikely to mobilize letter-writing campaigns or protest events, tactics they do engage in are media, advertising, public relations, and op-eds.

When it comes to the relationship between staff and outside lobbying, the opposite of the hypothesized relationship is exhibited, with more outside lobbying being done by smaller and mid-range offices. Again, as in the United States, this makes sense—it is the well-heeled offices that can engage in aggressive inside lobbying strategies; they do not need to resort to outside mobilization.

Again, as expected, organizational structure has a clear relationship to outside lobbying. Organizations without subunits in the member states use only one type of outside lobbying—media—and they do so at a level lower than the average. It is the organizations that have a federated structure, composed of member associations, that exhibit higher-than-average outside lobbying on every type of tactic. These types of umbrella organizations can spread the message and call for action through their member associations down to the individual members.

The one organization that reported mobilizing the masses and membership described its strategy on the live animal transport debate: "So we try to coordinate with our member associations, and get the media done at the same time, so we did that on this issue. Citizens write to their MPs and to their MEPs. MEPs say that animal welfare is the largest number of letters they get, that is, the most letters they get about one topic is on animal welfare. People care about this, people care about animals and they write."

The European Union differs from the United States in that there are few mass membership organizations. Only one organization that fell into my sample had direct individual members, of which there were only ninety-one. This organization was not pursuing any outside lobbying tactics. Thus, for the EU arena, the membership analysis is limited to organizations with institutional members, which could be associations, corporations, or institutions.[3] In the EU arena, differing from the U.S. findings, it is the mid-range category of advocates—those with members but not a large number of members who employ outside lobbying tactics at a higher rate.

In sum, the findings fit with previous suggestions by political observers— it is the citizen groups, and those with a weak insider presence that resort to outside lobbying. In addition, organizational composition plays a role. Those groups that have local offices in the field are better able to engage in outside lobbying and thus draw the public into the policy debates in the capitals. In the United States, organizations with more members, whether individual or institutional, are using outside lobbying at a higher rate while in the European Union, it is the groups with medium-sized institutional membership.

CONCLUSION

The data presented in this chapter show that the political context combines with individual interest group characteristics to determine whether a lobbyist will pursue an outside lobbying campaign. Knowing any single factor is not enough to predict the use of outside lobbying tactics; it is the melding of factors from all three levels that influences the ultimate tactical strategy.

The findings show that civil society groups are most likely to use outside lobbying, and members of the business community less inclined. Small and medium staff sizes also suggest an outside approach. In the United States a large membership base further suggests more outside lobbying, while in the European Union it is the mid-range groups that are pursing outside tactics, not the largest membership organizations. In both polities we see that an established on-the-ground network of local and regional offices facilitates going public.

At the issue level, evidence from both arenas supports the hypotheses that more outside lobbying is exhibited on issues that are high in conflict and salience. In the United States outside lobbying is also more common on issues that are large in scope, while the opposite relationship is found in the European Union. A clear pattern was lacking when it came to the history of the issue and whether a focusing event was linked to the issue by a policy entrepreneur.

It is clear from comparing the EU and U.S. findings that EU advocates are not mobilizing European citizens as much as they might be. The institutional structure plays a large role in explaining the lack of outside lobbying. And the requirements of the various outside lobbying tactics—some requiring a media system, and some not—have allowed us to confirm both institutional factors are likely at play: the presence of a media system and the selection of officials. Even if the constellation of organizational and issue characteristics are those that would suggest high use of outside lobbying, in the EU such an advocate is still unlikely to mobilize the masses and foster citizen engagement. One reason we may be seeing less outside lobbying activity in the European Union at the EU level is that these types of tactics are being left to the national associations to carry out at the national level. Kriesi, Jochuma, and Tresch's (2005) study provides evidence for this.

Institutional reforms could bring about a change in that tendency, which would open the door for more citizen involvement via outside lobbying. First, the lack of a pan-EU media machine may be changing. With the rise of the blogosphere and other online papers, it may be more and more possible to bypass the slow-moving traditional forms of media and spread a pan-EU message through the Internet and mass e-mails. Margot Wallström, commissioner for communication, called for this in June 2005 following the constitutional crisis, saying: "Innovative steps must be taken to create cross-border public space for debate at the European level. This might include translation facilities, venues for exchanging articles, and exchange programs for journalists" (June 21, 2005, *International Herald Tribune*). While the *European Voice, Euractiv, and EU-Observer* do not have much readership outside of Brussels, a new journal available electronically is seeking pan-EU readership and working to build such a cross-border public space—*Europe's World*. This new Europe-wide policy journal is planning to reach two hundred thousand people across Europe and beyond.

Many independent blogs have been surfacing in the past few years. It is a very dynamic and fluid community; blogs popular one month may disappear the next, replaced by a new EU-watcher that has come on the scene with insightful interpretations of current events. As those familiar with the blogosphere are aware, bloggers link to other blogs they frequent and suggest others to visit. High on such lists are: A Fistful of Euros, which provides news and witty commentary on the European Union and member states; Euroblog, providing a northern perspective, an English-language commentary on EU issues coming out of Sweden; Europhobia, EU commentary from a reformed Eurosceptic; and A. European, featuring less neutral news and more political position taking, clearly supporting the 'Yes' campaign for the EU Constitution—a clear Euro-federalist. A number of portals or networks also exist that bring together EU journalists and include Euro-Correspondent, a network of freelance journalists writing mainly on European and EU affairs, and Eurozine, a network of fifty European cultural journals. Eurozine's netzine posts articles from member journals as well as translations of those articles.[4] Through these forums EU citizens both inside and outside Brussels are sharing information, interpreting current EU events in real time, commenting on each other's viewpoints, and developing new perspectives that are the result of pan-EU dialogue.

In September 2005 the EP decided to join this technological revolution, launching a newly revised website advertised as "457 million citizens at one address." The restructured website is designed to be user friendly and "aimed primarily at the citizens of the European Union." At the launch of the new site EP President Josep Borrell Fontelles noted:

> By nature, Europe is a vast and extremely complex subject. However, this does not mean that it is impossible to help people to understand Europe,

its workings and its issues. This is an important task. It is difficult, but it is expected of us. Everyone could see the scale of the debates surrounding the draft constitution in the member states. This demonstrated that people are interested in Europe and want to understand it. Because it represents Europe's citizens, the EP has a duty to encourage this interest in Europe by providing access to all the views expressed within it" (EP 2005). The EP is taking steps, as are individual policymakers like MEP Richard Corbett and Commissioner Margaret Wallström who have their own blogs, to create forums for information exchange with EU citizens and to promote the construction of an EU public space and possibly an EU demos.

If the pan-EU media space develops, we may begin to see more outside lobbying in the European Union, but orchestrated through virtual news outlets rather than traditional print periodicals. However, as the data show, even the two outside lobbying tactics that do not require a pan-EU media system—mobilization of members and the mass public to produce grass-roots communications—are also less prevalent in the European Union, which suggests that democratic responsiveness of policymakers is also very much at play. Thus, changes in the democratic accountability of the primary political institutions seem to be required to impose a reelection concern on policymakers, making them more responsive to communications from the citizenry.

NOTES

1. This analysis is run on an N of 46 rather than 65 because it excludes congressional advocates.

2. Twenty actors are excluded from this analysis because they are governmental actors and the concept of membership is not applicable.

3. Five actors are excluded from this analysis because they are governmental actors and the concept of membership is not applicable.

4. A Fistful of Euros (http://fistfulofeuros.net/); Euroblog (www.karlsson.at/euroblog.htm); Europhobia (http://europhobia.blogspot.com/); A. European (www.aeuropean.org/); Euro-Correspondent (www.euro-correspondent.com); Eurozine (www.eurozine.com/); MEP Corbett Blog (www.corbett-euro.demon.co.uk/blog/); Wallström Blog (http://weblog.jrc.cec.eu.int/page/wallstrom)

9

Networking and Coalitions

ONE OFTEN-CITED adage about lobbying is "It's all about who you know." While that might not be the *entire* story, as the previous chapters have shown, it is clear that knowing the right people—talking with them, sharing information with them—are important determinants of lobbying behavior. Talking matters; communication is paramount. Indeed, an introverted lobbyist would not likely go far in either Washington or Brussels.

Nearly every scholarly work on lobbying mentions networking of one type or another (especially Heclo 1978; Sabatier 1988; Salisbury et al. 1987). Lobbyists share tidbits of information during hearing recesses, they forward e-mails with talking points, they hold conference calls getting like-minded interests up to speed on policymaking developments, they organize meetings to develop common positions, and they send joint letters to policymakers, place joint ads in newspapers, and appoint or hire secretariats to coordinate their activities. All of these activities can be referred to as networking, alliance building, or coalition activity.

Networking ranges on a continuum from very informal and loose, composed of occasional information sharing, to highly coordinated enterprises with logos, letterhead, and secretariats. Almost without exception, all lobbyists engage in some degree of networking, although not all advocates pursue more formalized coalition action. What determines the level of coordination of like-minded advocates? When are informal discussions in the lobbies of hearings sufficient and when are ad hoc issue coalitions required?

This chapter presents data on the informal and formal coalition activity of advocates in both polities. The existing body of literature suggests that informal coalition activity, or networking, is nearly incessant. In fact, this is what was found. Because there is nearly no variation—almost every advocate in both polities reported engaging in this behavior—extensive theorizing on this point is unnecessary. In addition, empirical evidence does not convey much; thus, more qualitative evidence is presented on this point. The extant literature on more formal ad hoc issue coalitions has established that there is indeed variation on the formation of and activity in coalitions; empirical evidence is therefore presented on this type of coalition activity.

PREVIOUS RESEARCH ON INTEREST GROUPS IN COALITION

As mentioned, networking is ubiquitous. Lobbyists need information on policy proposals, intelligence on policy developments, and knowledge of the positions of other advocates active on a policy debate. Much of this knowledge can be gathered from simply talking with other lobbyists, and thus some level of networking is expected on every issue.

But the question remains: why move beyond networking to build more formal ad hoc issue coalitions? By ad hoc issue coalitions I mean a very specific type of coalition of groups—one that forms for a single discrete issue fight. Pijnenburg (1998) notes that ad hoc issue coalitions are characterized by low levels of formalization (compared to formal interest group organizations) and high levels of autonomy for the coalition's members. They are established in the short to medium term for the duration of a single legislative or regulatory debate. While some issue coalitions may last longer, they remain a coalition of autonomous groups; they do not establish their own direct membership or organizational structure. There are usually a coalition leader organizing the efforts of the members, regular meetings of the coalition members, joint lobbying actions such as joint letters, advertisements, or press conferences, and very often an official name for the coalition and even letterhead and a secretariat acting as the headquarters of the coalition (Berry 1989). Ad hoc coalitions are most often composed of different types of groups or associations representing different sets of interests.

Groups could choose to work alone, or through their federation, or through a hired lobbyist but the ad hoc advocacy coalition offers unique advantages. From the literature it is clear that coalitions can be beneficial to interest groups in a political fight in two ways: (a) The coalition can signal to policymakers that a policy position has the support of a large and varied group of interests, and (b) the coalition can provide a framework for more efficient use of resources.

Scholars from Mayhew (1974) to Kingdon (1995) to Esterling (2005) have suggested that policymakers look for signs that a policy proposal has broad support. In political systems where policymakers are elected, they will want to know whether a vote in favor of a provision could prove later to be detrimental to them in an election. If a large majority of the public is opposed to a proposal supported by a policymaker, he or she could pay for it in the next election (Mayhew 1974; Arnold 1990). Thus coalitions can signal to policymakers where the bulk of support lies. Coalitions can also indicate that advocates have worked out differences among themselves before approaching government officials and thus their final position is one that can be supported by a majority of the legislature and the public (Heclo 1978; Hula 1995, 1999). A coalition can thus garner more political support for a policy position by demonstrating that a large set of interests already supports the position.

From a resource efficiency standpoint, coalitions have the potential to pool the resources of their members, and thus coalition activity could be more economical. As Hojnacki notes, "Almost all discussions of interest group coalitions refer to resource sharing as a benefit of coalition advocacy (Berry 1977, 1989; DeGregorio and Rossotti 1995; Hula 1995; Ornstein and Elder 1978; Schlozman and Tierney 1986)" (Hojnacki 1998, 439). Some tactics like running issue advertisements can be very expensive, but if everyone in the coalition contributes some funds it lightens the burden on any one advocate. Moreover, if coalition members divide up the lobbying work among themselves they can more efficiently use the resources of the collective in a given policy fight. In addition, joining a coalition can be a relatively low-cost tactic and a rational lobbyist may incorporate this one tool along with many others in an advocacy strategy (Coen 1997; Pijnenburg 1998).

Because coalitions send cues to policymakers about the desirability of a policy option and because they pool scarce resources, advocates have an incentive to join them. However there are also costs associated with coalition membership; some money and time need to be devoted to the coalition and a group may need to modify its position on an issue to be in line with the coalition position. In addition, groups in crowded advocacy communities have an incentive to differentiate themselves from other interest groups in order to attract membership (Browne 1995). In short, there are also forces pushing groups to work alone. Thus we would expect groups to join coalitions in instances where there is a greater need than usual to signal to leaders the breadth of support for a position and a greater need to pool resources.

A few studies have considered why advocates join coalitions. Hula's (1999) work lays out a range of resource incentives that coalitions present to potential members—the traditional monetary resources, but also informational resources and political contact resources. He argues that resource sharing is an incentive that attracts members to a coalition even though they may need to modify their position to be included in the coalition. Pijnenburg's (1998) exploratory case study in the European Union leads him to similar conclusions about the importance of resource incentives, specifically the provision of insider information and how the insider status of some coalition members can be shared with other members. He also notes that coalitions provide an alternative lobbying route when disagreements divide traditional permanent associations or Euro-federations. This is in line with other research that has found the behavior of other actors in the advocacy community to be a major determinant of coalition membership.

Hojnacki (1997) models the decision to join a coalition as a cost-benefit analysis. Her evidence shows that U.S. groups will not join a coalition when the costs of joining the coalition outweigh the potential benefits that the coalition might provide. Specifically groups will join when they perceive other groups in the coalition as pivotal to the success of the policy fight or when they perceive a strong opposition to their position. Coen's (2004) work also highlights the importance of other actors in the advocacy community as well as institutional pressures when considering the rise of ad hoc coalitions in the European Union's environmental domain in the 1990s. He notes that competition among groups for sought-after access to restricted policy forums drove business interests to ally and even modify their positions to gain entrance.

INSTITUTIONS, ISSUES, AND INTERESTS: FACTORS INFLUENCING THE DECISION TO JOIN AN ADVOCACY COALITION

As the preceding section has shown, previous studies of ad hoc issue coalitions have considered the importance of a number of issue characteristics (i.e., conflict, importance of issue, position of other actors on an issue) and some interest group characteristics (i.e., resources, issue positions) on coalition membership, but there has been little research on the effect of institutional design on coalition formation. This omission is understandable since most studies of coalition activity are restricted to a single political system.

At the institutional level I hypothesize that the democratic accountability of policymakers is a key institutional factor when we seek to understand the decision to join a coalition. As discussed above, ad hoc issue coalitions have two advantages: they pool resources and they signal to policymakers the breadth of support for a policy position. All things being equal, advocates should have some base level of attraction to coalitions because they efficiently pool resources, but that attraction should increase in political systems where policymakers are highly attuned to cues about public support for policy proposals, as they are when they are directly elected. When policymakers are directly accountable to their constituents they should be more susceptible to claims about the broad support of interests for a specific proposal. Thus, we should expect more ad hoc issue coalitions to form in the United States than in the European Union.

There are of course other system differences that could account for differences in the prevalence of coalitions in the two systems. First, the EU system is characterized by multilevel governance. It could be that while ad hoc issue coalitions may not form at the EU level (the focus of this study) they may be forming in the member-state capitals. National-level lobbying remains a significant focus of European interests (Kohler-Koch 1994; Beyers 2002; Imig and Tarrow 2001). Second, EU groups may have fewer resources to devote to an ad hoc coalition. While Brussels has long been making important public policy, some industries, sectors, and interests still find it difficult to encourage their national organizations to contribute significant amounts of funding to the EU level. Some Eurogroups may simply not have the resources at their disposal to pass up to another level of organization. Third, there could be a difference in the composition of the interest group communities in the United States and the European Union—with the United States having many more, smaller specialized groups and the European Union having more large, encompassing umbrella organizations. The smaller specialized groups in the United States would have more reason to ban together than would larger Euro-federations of national associations. To parse out which of these factors, or combinations thereof, are most likely at play, I will rely on qualitative data from in-depth interviews in addition to quantitative data.

Issues and Interests

The characteristics of the issue at hand should also determine whether a coalition is established on a given policy debate. First, highly conflictual issues may more likely lead to coalition formation because conflict gives groups an incentive to band together to face a common threat (Gais and Walker 1991; Hojnacki 1997; Whitford 2003). Advocates need to signal to policymakers the strength of their position relative to their competitors. Thus, it is expected that the higher the conflict among actors on the issue, the higher the probability of coalition membership. Second, highly salient issues are also expected to lead to coalition formation because these types of issues require advocates to demonstrate a broad base of support. In addition, issues that are the object of a great deal of public attention may require advocates to engage in more costly tactics such as issue advertisements or publicity-raising events, making pooling resources even more attractive.

Third, the scope should play a role. Larger-scope issues that affect large portions of the population can be costly since advocates may need to convey their position to the affected public. In addition, large-scope issues, which will have significant implications for large sections of the electorate, should drive groups to signal their strength to policymakers through allying in a coalition. Thus, the expectation is that the larger the scope of the issue, the higher the probability of coalition membership.

Some authors have suggested some types of organizations are less likely to engage in coalition activity than other types of advocates. Clark and Wilson

(1961) suggest that cooperation is more likely among utilitarian groups and less likely among purposive groups, largely because the latter are more restricted in their activities due to incentive systems (ibid., 162). The idea here is that the added benefit of signaling and resource pooling does not outweigh the ideological cost of potentially having to modify one's position to fit with the coalition. Thus actor type should play a role in the decision to join a coalition, with the expectation that ideological citizen groups should be less likely to align.

Organizational resources should also play a role in the decision to work through a coalition. Resource mobilization theorists emphasize the importance of resources in interest group mobilization and advocacy efforts (McCarthy and Zald 1978; Cress and Snow 1998). In order to mobilize for a policy debate, resource-poor groups need to identify resource sources and spend conservatively. Since coalitions pool resources, coalition activity could stretch scarce resources. Wealthy advocates on the other hand, such as trade associations and corporations, do not face the same type of hurdles to mobilize. As an issue rises on their agenda, resource-rich advocates can more easily mobilize for the debate without having to rely on like-minded interests. Indeed this may be the cause for Caldeira and Wright's findings in their study of *amici curiae* activity, which showed public firms and peak trade or professional associations to be less likely to work in coalition (1990, 799). I use staff size as a proxy for resources and test whether organizational resources influence the decision to join a formal coalition. Since coalitions pool resources, the expectation is that resource-poor groups will be more likely to join coalitions.

EMPIRICAL FINDINGS

Advocates were asked what other organizations or actors they were talking to or working with, as well as who else was involved on the issue. This was used to code whether the advocates were members of any ad hoc issue coalitions, what the coalitions were, and whether any other coalitions were engaged in the policy debate. Establishing formal coalitions requires a different level of commitment and coordination than networking. The findings suggest that the political context and the characteristics of the actors themselves play a role in the decision to join an issue coalition.

Institutions

As expected more ad hoc issue coalitions were formed in the United States than the European Union. Across the sample of twenty-one U.S. issues a total of twenty-two ad hoc issue coalitions were established. In the European Union, only five coalitions were formed across twenty-six issues. Some issues prompted multiple coalitions to form, such as with the Transportation Reauthorization issue in the United States, where seven ad hoc issue coalitions formed or the packaging and packaging waste issue in the European Union, which mobilized two coalitions. Looking at the number of issues in the United States and the European Union on which one or more coalitions formed shows 57 percent of U.S. issues with coalition activity while only 15 percent of EU issues exhibit coalition activity, as seen in figure 9.1A.

Looking at this at the advocate level, in the United States nineteen of the sixty-five advocates interviewed, or 29 percent, joined ad hoc coalitions established on the issue at hand. In the European Union, only eight of eighty-two advocates, or 9.8 percent of advocates, reported joining an ad hoc issue coalition, as seen in figure 9.1B.

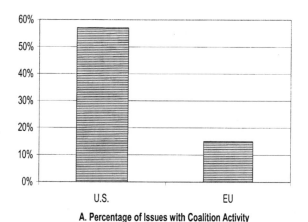

A. Percentage of Issues with Coalition Activity

B. Percentage of Advocates in a Coalition

Figure 9.1   Coalition Activity in the United States and the European Union

The majority of issues in the United States have coalitions organizing on them, while coalition activity in the European Union is quite rare. However, not every advocate in the United States is opting to work through coalitions on every issue; 70 percent of U.S. advocates are not joining coalitions on some issues. The nearly ubiquitous nature of coalitions across the twenty-two issues in the U. S. sample suggests that a leader often forms a coalition, making the lobbying route available to advocates active on the issue. Whether the coalition then becomes one of the most important actors, or whether prominent advocates work through it appears to be a different story. The data make clear that, at either the issue or individual level, the rate of coalition activity remains much higher in the United States than the European Union.

One explanation for this may be that many advocates in the United States sign on to coalitions only in name but do not actually allocate much in the way of resources toward the coalition. This type of nonactive coalition participation has been documented by previous authors (Hula 1995; Hojnacki 1998; Heaney 2004). While it is true that a wide range of engagement can be found among coalition members, each of the nineteen American advocates who indicated involvement in this sample was a highly active member or a leader of a coalition. All were attending meetings and coalition Hill visits, sharing information, and contributing to coalition position development. None described a situation in which the contribution was in name only.

Similarly in the European Union those few advocates who mentioned coalition activity were highly engaged. This is likely due to the selection process used in this research—the identifying advocates named an issue they were working on and thus contributing some level of resources to; advocates identified in the snowball portion of the sample were those who were major players on the issue. Thus, actors who were only marginally interested in the issues—those that would presumably be a coalition member in name only—are not included in the sample. The findings here coupled with previous research in the United States suggest that if the sample were broadened we would find even more actors in the United States reporting some level of coalition activity.

In the United States the coalitions that formed were largely short term, coalescing for a battle on a single legislative initiative. Examples include the Basic Education Coalition, the Coalition for Vehicle Choice to combat rising CAFE standards, and the Water Infrastructure Network and the opposing H_2O Coalition on the water infrastructure financing case. The Coalition for the Advancement of Medical Research coalesced to promote stem cell research in the debate on a ban on human cloning but also worked on other noncloning issues.

The simple differences between coalition activity in the United States and the European Union are not enough to determine whether electoral accountability is driving the difference or whether another factor explains these system-level differences. However, the hypothesis that advocates active in a system with greater electoral accountability will be more likely to work through coalitions does find qualitative support in addition to the quantitative evidence presented.

In the United States a number of lobbyists active in coalitions describe the attempt to convey the breadth of support for their positions. A company lobbyist on the CAFE debate described a coalition: "The Coalition for Vehicle Choice is a very broad group—there are auto companies in it, the suppliers are in it, the dealers are in it, but it also includes some of the safety organizations that are concerned about highway safety and some consumer groups like the Snowmobile Association; the recreation industry has been involved in this as well. So we've tried to be as creative and broad—reaching out to other groups—as we could be."

Similarly, a trade association lobbyist on the marine employment issue tried to convey the breadth of the coalition she was leading: "We have more than one hundred people in the coalition, all different types of people, the marine-related people, people from the insurance industry—we thought they would have a problem with it, but they've actually joined the coalition." A member of the Water Infrastructure Network (WIN) coalition on the water infrastructure case stressed the support it had behind its position:

> We were one of the charter members of the WIN coalition. . . . First thing, we tried to organize everybody who had a stake, that meant the state regulatory bodies, the organizations of actual utility companies, public and private, all the people involved in the design and construction of utilities. . . . In addition, we have people who are designers, people in construction, the people who actually build the facilities. So we represent a broad cross-section of the engineering community. We also have all the suppliers, the vendors—the pipe manufacturers, the people who make the equipment. So it's a very broad coalition.

In addition to conveying the sheer size of support, it can be equally important to convey to elected policymakers that different types of organized interests are on board. Some have referred to coalitions with traditionally opposing interests allying on a certain issue as "strange bedfellow coalitions." These are instances such as the extreme left and the extreme right agreeing on free speech issues, or leftist human rights groups and conservative religious groups agreeing on foreign policy proposals against oppressive regimes. In the U.S. sample, strange bedfellow coalitions could be found between business and the environmental community. Advocates active on such coalitions emphasized the power of such alliances. A trade association lobbyist on the wind energy tax credit case explained: "That's good when you can get disparate parties signing on to a letter; a member of Congress sees a letter and it's signed by the Chamber of Commerce and the Sierra Club, how often do you see that?"

The aim then is to build as big and as broad a coalition as possible. In this way advocates can signal to elected policymakers that a large majority of the electorate will likely support them, if they support this proposal. This electoral signaling in effect says to elected officials: vote for this without concern for negative political consequences. There is also evidence that pooling resources becomes part of the decision. While coalitions are in part about sending signals to policymakers, they are also about resource efficiency. A citizen organization active on the issue of disability rights in the welfare program described how CCD members tried to stretch their resources by divvying up meetings with members of Congress. A member of the basic education coalition painted a similar picture of trying to magnify the impact of coalition members. She explained how coalition members pooled resources to finance a trip for members of Congress to visit education projects in developing countries. Thus in the United States while we see strong evidence that coalition building is about sending a big and broad message to elected officials, stretching resources is also a goal.

In the European Union the few actors reporting coalition activity focused more on resource sharing, rather than conveying the sheer breadth of support. As one member of the coalition on the CCD explained, the aim was to share information and work out the details of their position before they approached policymakers: "We set up last year the EBIC—the European Banking Industry Committee—and that has as members ourselves, the European Banking Federation, the European Savings Bank Group, and some others; it is a kind of platform, the aim is to find our convergences, and once we do the outcome is the drafting of letters to the Commission to the EP."

Similarly, a trade association active on the packaging environment indicator in the Packaging and Packaging Waste Directive described how the coalition's goal was to work out technical details: "We are really, I don't want to say the authority, but the major player when it comes to packaging. Now each of the major sectors or materials also has its own organization; beverage has its own; plastic, paper, and each has its own subsection dealing with packaging and some resource devoted to that. We work in coalition with them. . . . So in those we exchange ideas, make sure we are all singing from the same hymn sheet."

Finally, a member of the coalition on solvent producers and users on the Clean Air for Europe issue emphasized that coalitions are more about hashing out the details and exchanging information than sending a political message. He noted that they met sixteen times a year to debate the current problems and decide on a common position.

In further evidence of the resource pooling—and not political signaling—aim of coordinated activity in the European Union, advocates reported high levels of networking. Although they may not have needed to convey the magnitude of their support, and thus did not need to establish an ad hoc issue coalition, advocates active on the CAFE, REACH, data retention, and animal transport debates all engaged in highly organized networking. A trade association on the data retention issue explained: "We decided to work closely with the other E-associations, so EUROISPA, GSM Europe, ECTA—the smaller telecoms companies, we did a lot of lobbying, we wrote letters, we did a lot of information gathering and sharing." The coordination of industry on the CAFE debate was nearly surgical in its precision, organized at the top by the pan-EU business association UNICE. Each of the lobbyists described divvying up tasks, sharing information, and working in synchronization. One trade association explained:

> I can't possibly attend all the meetings, but we are always represented by UNICE, there is always one member of the working group at the meetings and then they share that and we circulate documents around. UNICE has a small working group set up on CAFE and it meets fairly often, once a month, and so we stay up to date that way. . . . And UNICE is sending a letter to all the commissioners, and we divide it up in the working group, so electricity has good contacts with DG Energy and so they will work on them, and we will talk with Enterprise, and it goes like that.

If the aim was to signal to policymakers the breadth of their support it may have made sense to form an official ad hoc issue coalition with a catchy name and send out countless letters advertising their large and diverse membership. As it was, their aim was resource efficiency and they therefore organized their work and resource pooling behind the scenes.

Highly professional networking is not reserved for industry alone. An environmental organization active on REACH described how the green EU groups worked to coordinate their activities: "We all try to coordinate as much as possible so as to not step on each other's toes and also to enhance our work because each can do a different part. Also, each likely only has one person working on this, so that isn't that many people really, and they also have other issues they have to cover; compared to CEFIC, they have like 140 people here spending about 100 percent of their time on REACH."

While policymakers in the EU may be less responsive to coalition communications because of their limited electoral accountability, one alternative explanation—that the advocacy communities in the United States and the European Union are composed of different types of actors, more specialized in the United States, broader in the European Union—also finds some support. Since EU umbrella organizations are alliances of national associations, they already represent a number of organizations and thus don't find it necessary to ally with other interest groups. As one industry lobbyist succinctly put it: "We are the entire industry, so we don't really work with any other organizations." A trade association active on the REACH debate conveyed a similar logic: "Since we are an umbrella organization of fifty national and sectoral associations, we are in a way a coalition."

It is difficult to discount the other two alternative hypotheses regarding multilevel governance and resource scarcity in the EU, but no evidence for them emerged from advocates' discussions of their coalition activity. I did ask advocates if they were also pursuing the national route as part of the larger project from which these data stem and none of the eighty-two lobbyists mentioned an ad hoc issue coalition was established in any of the member states. A larger study that would specifically collect data on coalition activity at both the national and European levels would be needed to accurately assess whether this factor plays a role in lack of coalition formation in Brussels. Many actors in the European Union did mention lack of funds, and the inability of their constituent members to see the importance of contributing money for representation in Brussels, but much the same complaints could be heard from the U.S. lobbyists. Even the largest lobbies consistently feel their industry, sector, or membership does not invest enough in their government relations activity. Moreover, while the lobbying industry as a whole may be better funded in the United States, this should perhaps lead to more coalition activity in the European Union rather than less. Coalitions do not necessarily require dues from the members; they can also be more of a work-sharing framework to erase redundancies. If there is a set of interest groups that share the same goal on an individual issue and are resource poor, they could coordinate their efforts—divvying up MEPs to visit and tactics to pursue. Net lack of resources in the European Union therefore does not seem to be the strongest explanation for the lack of coalition activity in the European Union. I look at the role of resources more directly within the United States and the European Union under the interest group characteristics section below.

In sum, we see evidence that the democratic institutional design of a polity plays a role in coalition activity. Coalitions in any polity offer the potential to pool resources and thus there is an incentive to forge coalitions. However, there is an added incentive to forge coalitions in systems in which policymakers are accountable to the public in direct elections, since those officials need to ensure the votes they take on individual policy proposals are supported by large portions of the electorate. Ad hoc issue coalitions convey to elected officials the size and breadth of support for a proposal; and this may drive more coalition activity in the United States than the European Union.

Issues

The institutional structure within which an advocate is working is not, of course, the only consideration when deciding to join an issue coalition. As discussed in the theoretical section, previous scholarship has suggested that issues characterized by high conflict may lead advocates to band together. The findings show that indeed this is the case in the European Union, where the highest percentage of advocates joining coalitions are doing so on issues that have opposing perspectives fighting against each other. In the United States, however, the data are more ambiguous. Table 9.1 suggests advocates are most likely to join coalitions on issues that have a number of different perspectives, but not necessarily in direct opposition to each other. These are issues about which camps of advocates are promoting different ways to solve a political problem. It is important however to not overinterpret the finding since the number of observations is rather small for this category. Issues characterized by no conflict differ from cases with numerous perspectives or directly opposing perspectives. On issues with some level of conflict or intense conflict, advocates have an incentive to band together.

Table 9.1 Coalition Membership by Issue Characteristics in the United States and the European Union

	United States			European Union	
	Frequency	%		Frequency	%
Conflict					
None	6	29	None	1	6
Multiple P	2	67	Multiple P	0	0
Opposing	11	27	Opposing	7	12
Scope					
Small sector	5	22	Small sector	2	8
Large sector	7	32	Large sector	4	17
Multiple sectors	3	30	Multiple sectors	1	5
Systemwide	4	40	Systemwide	1	6
Salience					
0 stories	10	33	0 stories	3	9
1–5 stories	6	43	1–2 stories	4	20
6–50 stories	1	9	3 or more stories	1	3
51 or more stories	2	20			
Total	19	29		8	10

Regarding issue scope, there is a clear pattern among advocates in the United States; as the scope of their issue increases, they are more likely to join a coalition. Twenty-two percent of advocates that join coalitions are active on issues that will impact only a small sector, and 32 and 30 percent of joining advocates are active on those impacting large and multiple sectors, while 40 percent of advocates that decide to ally do so on the largest-scope issues with systemwide ramifications. There is no clear relationship in the EU system between issue scope and coalition activity.

The other hypothesized relationship—that increasing salience will lead to coalition membership—is also supported by the data but the effect requires only that there be some level of coverage of the issue in the news, there needn't be hundreds of stories. In both the United States and the European Union, coalition membership is most likely when there is some level (even low) of news coverage of the issue. The findings suggest that conflict and salience do play a role in the decision to join a coalition, while issue scope is influential only in the United States. However, factors at the advocate level also play a role.

Interests

The expectations about organizational resources are not borne out in the findings, as presented in table 9.2. It is not the poorest organizations that need to pool resources and join coalitions, but rather the wealthier organizations that are engaging in this lobbying strategy.[1] This may be because resource-poor organizations do not feel they can spare funding to donate it to a coalition of organizations, or because coalition membership is more cost-intensive than scholars have realized—in time, money, and labor. The effort and energy expended hashing out a common position that is accepted by all coalition members could be saved if an organization decided to go it alone and were thus able to make the final call on all advocacy decisions.

Turning to the second interest group-level factor that was hypothesized to play a role in coalition membership, the type of actor does influence whether the advocate chooses to go it alone or band together with like-minded actors. The findings differ from expectations of Clark and Wilson (1961) that ideological groups may be constrained from working with other organizations. In the United States citizen groups are the most likely to engage in coalition activities, with 50 percent of citizen group advocates reporting coalition activity compared to the average of 29 percent. The next most likely are trade associations, with 42 percent reporting joining ad hoc coalitions. In the European Union trade associations are the advocate type most commonly active in coalitions. However, citizen groups are the second most likely to engage in coalition activity and they are the only other actor type that reported doing so. Taken together, these findings suggest citizen groups in both the United

Table 9.2   Coalition Membership by Interest Characteristics in the
United States and the European Union (percent)

	United States			European Union	
	Frequency	%		Frequency	%
Staff					
1–5	4	29	1–5	1	3
6–20	8	44	6–20	6	16
21 or more	7	50	21 or more	1	7
Total	19	41		8	10
Type					
Citizen	5	50	Citizen	1	6
Foundation	3	38	Foundation	0	0
Trade	8	42	Trade	7	15
Corporations*	3	33	Hired firms*	0	0
Government	0	0	Government	0	0
Total	19	29		8	10

*The U.S. sample included a number of individual corporations but no hired lobby firms; thus "Corporations" is listed. The EU sample included a number of hired lobbying firms but only four individual corporations; thus "Hired Firms" is listed and the corporations are included in "Trade."

States and the European Union have a tendency to ally, but that they must have some level of resources to foot the bill that coalition activity requires.

A multivariate analysis was also run to examine the relative influence of issue and interest group factors in the two polities. A logit model showed the issue-level factors to be significant, while the interest group-level factors were not, controlling for the nature of the issue. However the models were not very robust, with coefficient estimates changing with slight model adjustments. Due to the instability of the coefficients, the multivariate analysis is not presented here.

CONCLUSION

Understanding the decision to join a coalition requires contextual and interest group information. The institutional design of the system in which an advocate is operating is critical. Will policymakers respond to lobbying tactics aimed at signalling the support of large swaths of the electorate? If not, is there much sense in putting resources into coalition building and coordinating? The data gathered from lobbyists in the United States and the European Union suggest the answer is no. The democratic accountability of policymakers appears to play a role in the decision to form and join coalitions. However, we also saw evidence that the differences in the composition of the U.S. and EU advocacy communities may also affect the propensity of EU groups to align, since larger pan-European federations don't see the same benefits as smaller specialized U.S. groups.

Institutional explanations are only part of the story. Although coalition signals may be more useful in the United States, they still are not ubiquitous. Likewise, coalitions are not totally absent from the EU scene. Issue characteristics also play a role; U.S. advocates ally more often on issues with multiple viewpoints, with a larger societal impact and some level of salience. The same pattern is evident in the European Union. Finally, the characteristics of the advocates themselves determine whether they will work closely with other organizations in an ad hoc issue coalition. Different types of actors engage in coalition activity at varying levels. Importantly, citizen groups in both systems see an advantage in banding together and in the process showing their solidarity and pooling their resources. Finally, coalition membership requires some threshold of resources in both polities, with advocates supported by medium and large offices more likely to engage in coalition activity.

The data presented here on the influence of institutions, issues, and interests on coalition activity—the last stage of the advocacy process in which advocates make decisions about their lobbying strategy—have driven home the point: to understand lobbying we must look to the broader political context and the character of the advocate. At every stage so far—determining lobbying positions, formulating arguments, selecting targets, choosing inside and outside tactics, and deciding on coalition activity—it is the wider political environment that determines the lobbying strategies an advocate will pursue. The next chapter will look at the final stage of the advocacy process: whether advocates achieve lobbying success.

NOTE

1. Congressional advocates are left out of this analysis; thus it is run on an *N* of 46.

10

Lobbying Success

THE AIM OF lobbying is to influence public policy; thus it is natural as political scientists we would seek to study lobbyists' ability to achieve influence. As natural as it may seem, however, group scholars have not by and large studied lobbying influence. Instead they have tended to avoid it, finding it troubling to quantitatively measure the concept. In both the United States and the European Union scholars have focused on a whole host of lobbying-related phenomena—formation, organization, access, activity—but not influence. This is especially ironic because the question of influence seems to be the first thing that comes to mind when anyone considers lobbying in a transatlantic comparison: in which system are interest groups more influential?

There have been a number of reviews detailing the reasons why scholars have avoided the concept of interest group influence (Baumgartner and Leech 1998; De Bièvre and Dür 2007; Dür 2005). The range of factors that determine policy outcomes is vast and how they interact is complex, changing, and fluid (Kingdon 1995). Interest groups are only one element in the political mix of politicians, the public, and exogenous shocks. For all intents and purposes, it is impossible to determine whether an individual interest group or advocate was *the* deciding factor in a policy outcome. I argue that analyzing lobbying success—whether advocates achieve their goals or not at the conclusion of a policy debate—can help us move toward understanding lobbying influence.

IDENTIFYING INFLUENCE

Many system-level or macro factors play a role in the power of societal actors vis-à-vis governments, such as the structure of international negotiations, the freedom of markets, and the existence of war (De Bièvre and Dür 2007). In addition to these macro factors, when we focus on the interest group universe and the activity therein, additional factors affect the relative power of societal actors—that is, the power of one interest in the policymaking process compared to another—including collective action problems, mobilization bias, internal disputes within societal organizations, and the ability of groups to wield the second face of power: the ability to set the political agenda (Bachrach and Baratz 1962).

In an attempt to gain some leverage on the question of influence, this analysis is constrained to those societal actors that have mobilized and engaged with policymakers on issues high on the political agenda. Thus the analysis focuses on interest groups attempting to influence specific issues within the Washington and Brussels lobbying communities. There is still difficulty measuring influence in this constrained realm: even knowing groups' stated objectives and the policy outcomes that materialize, we still do not have enough information for a correct assessment of lobbying influence. If an interest group achieves some or all of what it wanted, can that really be attributed to its activities? Perhaps the majority of policymakers already wanted that outcome and were moving in that direction or perhaps public opinion had long been trending toward support for the policy. Alternatively it could have been the combined effect of large numbers of powerful interest groups pushing for a policy outcome that brought it about, and just happened to be in line with the advocate under investigation. To precisely identify the unique influence of a single actor is difficult.

Moreover, determining what would constitute influence is also problematic. If an interest group gets nothing, but prevented something worse has it succeeded? If it got some of what it wanted but not all, has it failed? When discussing interest group influence, we often slip into simplistic descriptions of policymaking outcomes that suggest zero-sum games, asking who won and who lost. However, non-zero-sum games—with some type of compromise emerging as the end result—should be expected. In policymaking multiple players can win (or lose).

Envision an immigration bill to regulate illegal immigration. The status quo situation allowing high numbers of illegal immigrants to flow across a polity's borders becomes untenable. Immigrant rights activists push for naturalization of five hundred thousand illegal immigrants a year with no penalties for coming forward to authorities and argue against harsh enforcement procedures. Anti-immigration activists push for strict border controls, increased raids by immigration officials, and mandatory deportation for all illegal aliens found; they fight hard against naturalizing illegal immigrants. The compromised outcome on the case is that three hundred thousand immigrants will be allowed to naturalize each year, but those that fail to come forward will be automatically deported and strict border controls and raids increase the probability of them being found. Both sides achieved some of their goals. Hundreds of thousands of immigrants who had no chance of becoming citizens will now be able to do so. At the same time, anti-immigrant rights activists gain crackdown measures aimed at capturing, prosecuting, and deporting illegal immigrants—enforcement mechanisms they did not have before. However, both sides also failed to achieve some of their goals. At first glace, it is difficult to assess who won—a zero-sum game is not the process format. When assessing interest group lobbying success we must consider what they sought and what they received, allowing room for degrees of success.

By comparing the objectives of interest groups—from their stated goals, triangulated with contextual issue information and interviews with other actors active on the issue—with final outcomes it is possible to assess lobbying success. It can be measured on an ordinal scale: achieved none of the objectives to achieved some objectives, to fully achieved all goals.

I refer to this as *lobbying success* to be precise and draw a distinction between this measure and the broader concept of interest group influence. Interest groups can wield influence through mobilization, agenda setting, electoral support of political candidates (in certain political systems), among others. Measuring lobbying success however and analyzing its determinants can provide us with a better understanding of one aspect of the influence process related to shaping public policy. This type of analysis can tell us who is winning and losing in the policymaking game. In addition, we can learn what contextual factors affect who wins, who loses, and who achieves compromised success.

Even if social scientists are never able to precisely pinpoint the true goals of advocates, never able to identify every possible factor driving influence and map out the exact model, we can still achieve a better understanding of the effect of lobbying on public policy through the method described here: drawing a random sample of issues, interviewing those involved on all sides, asking them what they were trying to make happen, and then seeing what occurred. Some might get lucky and see their goal achieved through no action of their own and some might do everything right but still not succeed through no fault of their own, but across many issues and hundreds of actors the noise will wash out and a signal will emerge—we will come to understand what factors on average lead to lobbying success, and which tend toward failure.

INSTITUTIONS, ISSUES, AND INTERESTS: THE FACTORS DETERMINING LOBBYING SUCCESS

Two aspects of institutional design are critical to understanding lobbying success. First, the degree of democratic accountability in a political system has an impact on the degree of lobbying success an advocate can achieve. Chapter 2 offered a number of alternative explanations for how this relationship might play out, especially when we consider the presence of money in elections.

First, advocates may be more influential in a system with direct elections—advocates can threaten to mobilize the electorate and therefore may have more sway over policymakers than advocates operating in a less democratically accountable system. The expectation then would be that U.S. advocates, in the aggregate, would be more successful than advocates in the European Union. The alternative is also feasible: interest groups are more influential in a system without direct elections, for they are the only external input into a political system lacking voters. If this logic is correct, EU interest groups, on average, would achieve more lobbying success than their U.S. counterparts.

In addition to these aggregate hypotheses about the relationship between electoral accountability and lobbying success, it is also possible to formulate more nuanced expectations regarding the influence of different types of actors. Within a system where policymakers are held accountable through direct elections, advocates representing citizen interests may be more successful than other types of actors, as it is citizen votes that policymakers need to win reelection. However, it is not only votes that count in many modern democracies—money also matters. Therefore an alternative hypothesis is plausible: In a system where policymakers are held accountable through direct elections, advocates who can provide funding to policymakers' campaigns will be more successful than other types of actors. These four expectations will be evaluated by considering lobbying success in the aggregate in the United States and the European Union, broken down by actor type.

The other institutional factor that should have an effect on lobbying success is the rules of the policymaking process, which influence the likelihood of policy change. As shown in chapter 4, the rules of the policymaking process influence the lobbying positions advocates assume. In systems where policy change is less likely, such as the United States, advocates opposing a proposal can work to kill the bill. In systems where policy change is more likely, or almost a given due to the rules of the policymaking process, advocates opposing a proposal will work to modify, as they do in the European Union. In addition, the rules of the policymaking process on proposal introduction in the United States and the European Union also differ. In the United States any member of Congress can propose a bill and therefore advocates push their ideas before any member who will listen. In the European Union, on the other hand, the Commission has the sole right of initiative and proposals need to be agreed upon by the entire college of commissioners. While it is true that advocates could suggest policy proposals to desk officers and mid-level Commission officials to push a policy idea, the proposal would need to clear many hurdles before emerging as an official policy proposal: a low-level desk officer would need to have the concept cleared by the head of department, who would need to have it cleared by the head of unit, who would need to have it cleared by the directorate general for the leadership of the DG, whose commisioner would then need to get the approval of the rest of the college of commission-ers—a much more arduous task than simply asking a member of Congress to propose a bill by dropping it in the hopper. This leads EU advocates to be less likely to promote new policy proposals than their American counterparts.

It is important to note that promoting a proposal, working to modify it, or blocking it are all different from being for or against the status quo. For example, you could be against the status quo and want to see policy change but decide your best bet to achieve a favorable policy is working within the confines of a proposed policy and trying to modify it to your preferences.

While the institutional structure pushes advocates to be more likely to pro-mote and block in the United States and more likely to modify in the Euro-pean Union, there is still a great deal of variation within the two systems. With advocates in both systems assuming all three positions, depending on their preferences and the characteristics of the issues, the question becomes: Are advocates in some positions more likely to be successful than others? The ex-pectation is that those promoting a proposal will be less successful than those working to modify or block a proposal because bringing about policy change is almost always more difficult in any political system.

The institutional context, however, is not the only consideration; issue-level factors are critical components in understanding when a civil society organiza-tion is likely to be successful in its lobbying activities. Advocates should be less likely to succeed in their lobbying goals the larger the scope of the issue, that is, issues having far-reaching policy implications (Browne 1995). Large-scope is-sues involve a larger number of vested interests and large portions of the gen-eral public, meaning policymakers dealing with a large-scope issue would not be well advised to follow the lead of a single narrow special interest.

This is related to another important contextual factor in determining lob-bying success: the presence of countervailing forces. Highly conflictual issues, with opposing forces battling it out, present a very different lobbying environ-ment than issues in which only one perspective is promoting its policymaking vision unopposed (Salisbury et al. 1987). Organizations are less likely to be suc-cessful in their lobbying goals if they are engaged on a highly conflictual issue than if they are active on an issue where they are up against no opposition.

Highly salient issues are hypothesized to exhibit a similar pattern—the more salient, the less successful individual advocates are in their lobbying. Regardless of the actual scope of the issue, if a topic is of interest to a large proportion of the public, policymakers should be less likely to take the advice of a single advocate. Even an issue like human cloning, which doesn't have a direct effect on a large number of people, still interests many citizens, forcing policymakers to take public opinion into consideration.

Whether a focusing event occurred on an issue can also play a role in the likelihood of lobbying success. Focusing events can alert policymakers and the public to a policy problem. However the effect of a focusing event on lobbying success depends on what perspective a group has on an issue and whether the event galvanized support in its favor. For example, in a debate about increased antiterrorism measures, a terrorist attack works in favor of proponents of more stringent antiterrorism laws and against advocates arguing for less expansive regulations. Thus whether a focusing event occurred on an issue and whether it was in an advocate's favor must both be taken into consideration when one investigates the relationship to lobbying success.

These issue characteristics combine to create either an environment in which an advocate is more likely to succeed—a situation where few other parties are involved or invested, allowing an advocate to advance his or her goals with little opposition—or an environment where success is less likely, a situation where large numbers of interests are also mobilized for the debate, some actors are actively fighting against them, and the public is scrutinizing the case as it unfolds.

The characteristics of the advocate itself can also play a role in the chances of lobbying success. First is the level of financial resources. Leaving aside for a moment the expectations regarding the relationship between democratic institutional design and group wealth, groups that are well-heeled are able to put more resources into each issue, engage in more tactics, and devote more staff power to the topic. Considering this, they should be more likely to succeed in their lobbying activities. Second is membership size. Larger groups convey some degree of legitimacy to policymakers and should be more likely to achieve lobbying success than organizations that cannot claim to represent a large group of citizens. Third is advocate type—whether a group represents the interests of citizens, professionals, industry, unions, or an individual corporation should play a role in lobbying success. As discussed in the institutional section, there are two alternative hypotheses regarding the relationship between group type and lobbying success in democratically accountable systems: citizen groups will be more influential than other types of actors and compared to less-accountable systems, or corporations and business groups will be more influential than other types of actors and compared to less accountable systems.

In additional to the permanent characteristics of the advocate, also important at the interest group level are the position of the advocate on that case and the tactics the advocate employs during the given lobbying campaign. On this first point, whether an advocate is pushing for the status quo or promoting a new policy that would change the current regulatory environment should have an impact on lobbying success. Due to institutional stickiness it is easier to stay still than move to a new policy equilibrium (Jones and Baumgartner 2005); thus advocates fighting for the status quo should be more likely to achieve their lobbying goals than those pushing for policy change.

Finally, nearly every advocate engages in some type of direct lobbying, although not all advocates engage in some of the more specialized lobbying techniques like hiring a consultant, working through a coalition, or employing outside lobbying. These additional techniques are expected to be helpful by lobbyists, as is suggested by previous research (consultancies: Lahusen 2002; coalitions: Hojnacki 1997, Hula 1999; outside lobbying: Kollman 1998, Kriesi et al. 2005) and thus the expectation is that those who use them should be more likely to achieve their lobbying goals.

EMPIRICAL ANALYSIS

The interviewed advocate's success forms the dependent variable of the analysis in this chapter. This was coded by considering objectives for the lobbying campaign, as described by the advocate in the interview and in the case research and comparing those objectives with the actual outcome of the issue at the end of the Congress in the U.S. case (roughly a year after the interviewing period) and roughly a year after the interviewing in the EU case (no official institutional time limit exists). The degree of success is measured: 0–did not achieve objective at all; 1–achieved some portion of objective; and 2–fully achieved objective. Some of the relationships between the factors at the institutional, issue, and interest group levels and lobbying success are explored through bivariate analyses, followed by a multivariate ordered logit analysis.

Institutions

Considering lobbying success in transatlantic comparison reveals that the two systems do not differ dramatically but tend toward different outcomes: EU policymaking leads to more compromise, with all parties achieving some level of success, while the U.S. policymaking system tends toward winner-take-all outcomes. We see support for the second hypothesized relationship: policymakers appear to be more responsive to the views of organized interests in the less electorally accountable system. European Union advocates in the aggregate are more likely to achieve some level of success (60 percent) than U.S. advocates (54 percent). Comparative aggregate levels of success, however, are not the most interesting pattern that emerges from this analysis.

In 28.6 percent of U.S. cases a compromise was reached, while in the EU that figure was 46.2 percent, a difference that is marginally significant in a difference of proportions test ($p = .11$, one tailed test). This pattern can also be seen at the advocate level; in the United States more advocates attained either all or nothing compared to their counterparts in the European Union. As seen in figure 10.1, more U.S. lobbyists, 23 percent, attained all of their lobbying goals compared to the EU figure of 17 percent ($p = .18$), and more U.S. lobbyists, 46 percent, attained none of their lobbying goals compared to those in

Europe where only 39 percent attained nothing ($p = 19$). While only 31 percent of U.S. lobbyists attained a compromised success, in the European Union
that figure was 44 percent ($p = .05$). On average, therefore, EU lobbyists are
more likely to attain lobbying success, but a compromised success—a type of
success that comes from policy resolutions where everyone wins, at least a little.

These numbers, along with advocates' descriptions of deliberations on these
issues, indicate that the European Union may result in outcomes that strike a
balance between competing advocates, leading to more interests seeing some
of their preferences incorporated into the final outcome. In the United States,
rather than drawing from all the vested interests engaged on a policy debate
and working toward a compromise, the system tends toward absolute victo-
ries for some and absolute losses for others. Thus, we do not see higher levels
of lobbying success in the United States compared to the European Union. In
fact, more advocates are not successful (46 percent) in the United States compared to the European Union (39 percent) and therefore the first hypothesis
is not supported.

There is evidence supporting the hypothesis related to the second aspect
of the institutional system—the rules surrounding the policymaking process
and the related likelihood of policy change. Lobbyists in the European Union,
working in a system where policy change is more likely, are more often attaining compromised successes. U.S. advocates, operating in an environment in
which policy change is less assured, attain clearer wins or losses.

When we look specifically at the level of lobbying success by the lobbying
position of advocates, we see additional evidence that institutional rules in-

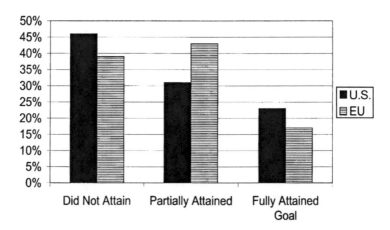

**Figure 10.1   Lobbying Success in the United States
and the European Union**

fluence lobbying success indirectly through lobbying positions. In the United States, of advocates promoting a policy proposal, the majority (56 percent) achieve none of their goals, while in the European Union only 32 percent of advocates promoting policy change achieve none of their goals. As you will recall from chapter 4, more advocates assume promoting positions in the United States (52 percent) than in the European Union (38 percent), and the data presented here show that those advocates assuming promoting positions in the United States are less likely to achieve their goals—presumably due to the lower probability of policy change in the United States.

Turning to blocking positions, of those advocates assuming blocking positions in the United States, 73 percent achieved all of their goals, 18 percent achieved some of their goals, and only 9 percent failed to accomplish any of their goals. The pattern is significantly weaker in the European Union, where advocates assuming blocking positions were roughly evenly divided across the three categories of lobbying success.

Thus we see evidence that institutional design affects lobbying success directly and indirectly. Directly we see more aggregate lobbying success in the European Union than the United States due to the ability of the system to arrive at compromised outcomes that allow more advocates to achieve some of their goals. Indirectly, we see evidence that institutional rules influence lobbying positions, which in turn influence an advocate's chances of lobbying success. Investigation of the alternative hypothesis related to democratic accountability—that reelection motives coupled with privately funded elections may lead to biased responsiveness in the United States—will be addressed during the interest-group level analysis of group type.

Before turning to issue-level factors, looking at some of the cases in more detail can clarify the difference in lobbying success patterns in the two systems. The EU CAFE issue is an example where the outcome resulted in compromised success—that is, advocates achieved some of their goals but not all— for both sides of the debate. CAFE was an issue where industry representatives arguing for regulatory moderation were pitted against environmental advocates fighting for tougher standards on emissions. In the end stricter regulations were approved that would help clean up Europe's air but the rules were not as far-reaching as initially proposed.

As the *Financial Times* reported on September 21, 2005: "Controversial plans to improve Europe's air quality have been diluted by the European Commission following protests from industry, reducing projected annual compliance costs from €12bn to €7.1bn. The proposal, expected to be approved by the EU executive today, aims to reduce the number of premature deaths caused by pollution in the European Union from 370,000 a year to 225,000 by 2020. It would introduce tougher controls on particulate matter, or fine dust, which accounts for most premature deaths.

Environmentalists won because they had been pushing for stricter controls on particulate matter emitted from plants, cars, and industry. Industry won because it succeeded in tempering the Commission's original proposals, paring back the €12bn price tag to €7.1bn. Granted, both sides released statements following the law's passage indicating they were displeased with the outcome. The European Environmental Bureau (EEB) released a statement saying that it was "very disappointed that the European Commission's Thematic Strategy on air pollution published today does not go far enough in improving Europe's air quality" (EEB press release, September 21, 2005). One of the leading industry trade associations also released a statement arguing that "the proposed ambition levels are not cost-effective since the levels set are in the steeply rising part of the cost curves where incremental costs outweigh incremental changes in air quality" (Eurelectric press release, December 2, 2005). While both groups may have left this debate unsatisfied, objectively they did both win . . . a little. Indeed, *Euractiv's* headline read: "Clean air strategy seeks balance between health and business concerns" (2005b).

Similar outcomes could be seen on the issue of alcohol advertising, where the alcoholic beverage industry and the alcohol-related harm advocacy groups saw a compromised outcome, as well as the case of live animal transportation, where both the meat traders and animal rights activists realized some of their goals but not all.

In the United States we see less compromise and more winner-take-all outcomes and the winners, more often than not, are industry representatives. The over-the-counter derivative case is one example. Advocates pushing for regulation of these financial instruments in the wake of the Enron scandal found their initiative crushed under heavy lobbying by the financial services industry. Similarly, advocates for stricter regulations of fuel economy—the CAFE case—found steady lobbying by auto manufacturers staved off any advancement toward their goals.

Another initiative coming off the heels of the Enron scandal was a push for stock option expensing. Advocates for stock option expensing argued that forcing publicly held companies to expense or include stock options in their financial reports would hold companies accountable for their stock option issuing and be more transparent for investors, ultimately preventing future scandals. These advocates also achieved none of their goals as the major Fortune 500 and tech companies blocked the proposal.

The winner-take-all scenarios are not always pro-industry. The case of modification of the Food Quality Protection Act concluded in favor of public health and the EPA. Industry representatives did not achieve their goals of changing the screening process for pesticides. Another case that saw citizen groups win the day was the issue of development aid for basic education, perhaps due in part to the lack of organized opposition. Advocates pushing for higher rates of funding for basic education in developing countries were over-whelmingly successful in their fight—while they could always hope for even higher levels of funding, the advocates pushing for this increase were extremely pleased with the result.

This finding of a higher rate of compromise in the European Union fits with the findings in chapter 4, which looked at the lobbying positions advocates in the United States and the European Union assume at the outset of a lobby-ing fight. U.S. advocates were more likely to try to kill a bill than EU advo-cates and were most likely to try to promote new proposals; EU advocates on the other hand were more likely than their U.S. counterparts to work to modify proposals and to assume this lobbying position than any other. These initial positions may explain in part why we see more compromise in the European Union, but more likely the institutional design of the systems leads to the dif-ferences in both lobbying positions and lobbying success.

In short, the United States and the European Union differ institutionally in the democratic accountability of policymakers and in the rules surround-ing the legislative process; these differences lead to different likelihoods of policy change—in the United States policy change is less likely, in the Euro-pean Union it is more likely. Policy change is nearly inevitable once the pro-cess begins in the European Union—advocates are forced to work to modify the proposal, and as the data presented here have shown, they often succeed. In the United States it is possible to kill proposals, and thus advocates who oppose something work to do so—if they achieve their goal, they wind up winners and the proponents of the proposal lose out.

Thus, institutional design emerges as a factor in understanding lobbying success. In the United States we see debates that more often play out result-ing in clear winners and losers. In the European Union we see the policy-making process lead more often to compromised conclusions allowing all sides to achieve some of their goals. However, these patterns are tendencies, not absolutes; differences between the two systems in levels of lobbying suc-cess are not massive. This finding suggests that other factors, such as issue and interest group characteristics, are needed to explain variation in lobby-ing success.

Issue Characteristics

The nature of the issue at hand plays a significant role in the likelihood that advocates will succeed or fail in their lobbying efforts. A number of aspects are considered here: the scope of the issue, the level of conflict on an issue, the presence of a focusing event on the case, and the salience of the issue.

In the United States, as expected, the size of the issue matters. Figure 10.2 shows that as issue scope increases the likelihood of fully attaining a goal de-

Chapter 10

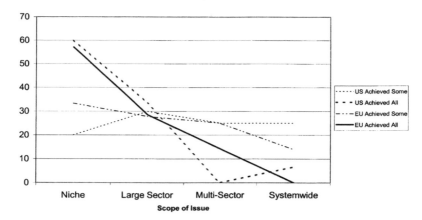

Figure 10.2   Relationship between Lobbying Success and Issue Scope

creases dramatically from 60 percent of advocates fully attaining their goal on niche issues, to 33 percent on larger-sector issues, and dropping to 7 percent for systemwide issues.

In the European Union the same pattern is evident. As the scope of the issue increases, the percentage of advocates fully attaining their goal steadily decreases: from 57 percent on niche issues to 28 percent on large-sector issues, to 14 percent on multiple-sector issues, and 0 percent on systemwide issues. In the European Union the pattern holds for compromise success as well. The percentage of advocates attaining some but not all of their goals decreases as the issue gets larger, steadily dropping from 33 percent on niche issues, to 28 percent to 25 percent and finally to 14 percent on the biggest issues. Thus, we see evidence that as issues get bigger and their outcomes will impact larger and larger sections of the population, the likelihood of lobbying success declines because policymakers need to take into account the full range of interests concerned about the outcome.

The likelihood of not attaining a goal increases as the conflict on an issue rises (table 10.1). A Pearson chi-square test shows the relationship to be significant at the .1 level in the United States and significant at the .01 level in the European Union. It is important to note the number of cases falling under the conflict category "multiple competing perspectives but not in direct opposition" is quite low in both polities; therefore I focus on the categories of "no opposition" and "direct opposition." In the United States 30 percent of advocates failed to attain any of their goals on issues with no conflict, but that figure more than doubled to 70 percent on issues with directly opposing camps. The expectation is also borne out on partially attaining goals: U.S. advocates are more likely to achieve only some of their goals as the conflict increases. A similar pattern is found in the European Union: while only 13

Table 10.1   Lobbying Success in the United States and
the European Union by Conflict

	No Opposition	Multiple Positions	Directly Opposing	N	Percent
United States					
Did not attain	30	0	70	30	46
Partially attained	25	15	60	20	31
Fully attained goal	47	0	53	15	23
Total N	21	3	41	65	100
European Union					
Did not attain	13	0	88	32	39
Partially attained	33	11	56	36	44
Fully attained goal	0	21	79	14	17
Total N	16	7	59	82	100

| | Lobbying Success | | | | | | | |
| | United States | | | | European Union | | | |
Conflict	None	Some	Full	N	None	Some	Full	N
No opposition	43	24	33	21	25	75	0	16
Multiple positions	0	100	0	3	0	57	43	7
Direct opposition	51	29	20	41	48	34	19	59
Total N	30	20	15	65	32	36	14	82
Total percent	46	31	23		39	44	17	

percent of EU advocates failed to attain their goals on no-conflict issues, that figure jumps 75 percentage points to 88 percent of advocates active on issues with direct opposition. Again this also holds for partial success: only 33 percent of advocates active on low-conflict issues did not achieve their goals, while 56 percent of those active on high-conflict issues did not reach their goals.

Examining the data a different way, by conflict type rather than lobbying success, we see additional support for the institutional hypothesis. Even when we hold conflict constant we see more winners and losers in the United States and more compromised successes in the European Union. Holding conflict constant at the low-conflict level, more U.S. advocates achieve none or all of their advocacy goals (43 percent and 33 percent) compared to EU advocates (25 percent and 0 percent) while more EU advocates achieve compromised success, 75 percent compared to their U.S. counterparts, at 24 percent. Similarly, holding conflict constant at the high-conflict level, slightly more U.S. advocates (51 percent and 20 percent) are failing to achieve or fully achieve their goals than advocates in the European Union (48 percent and 19 percent), while again more EU advocates are achieving compromised successes, 34 percent compared to 29 percent of U.S. advocates.

At times high conflict and large scope coincide, but other variations are a small-scope issue with two staunchly opposed groups, or a policy proposal with massive reach on which everyone agrees. The important point is that the constellation of actors engaged on an issue, and their positions on the debate, have a fundamental impact on the probability of an advocate achieving lobbying goals.

The relationship between salience and lobbying successes in the United States is not immediately apparent in table 10.2, but the Pearson chi-square demonstrates that the two are related, significant at the .01 level. As the salience of an issue to the public increases, the percentage of advocates fully attaining their goal decreases, but for the other levels of lobbying success there is no pattern or it is the reverse of the hypothesized direction. In the European Union, however, the hypothesized pattern emerges, demonstrated by the Pearson chi-square test significant at the .001 level. As salience increases, the

Table 10.2   Lobbying Success in the United States
and the European Union by Salience (percents)

	United States					
	0 stories	1–5 stories	6–50 stories	51 or more stories	N	Percent
Did not attain	63	17	10	10	30	46
Partially attained	25	15	25	35	20	31
Fully attained goal	40	40	20	0	15	23
Total N	30	14	11	10	65	100

	European Union				
	0 stories	1–2 stories	3 or more stories	N	Percent
Did not attain	16	22	63	32	39
Partially attained	50	25	25	36	44
Fully attained goal	64	29	7	14	17
Total N	32	20	30	82	100

percentage of EU advocates fully attaining their goals or partially attaining their goals steadily decreases while the percentage of those attaining nothing steadily increases.

Again, cutting the data the other way, holding salience constant we see additional support for the institutional hypothesis. Comparing salience levels is somewhat difficult because there is such a higher level of coverage of U.S. issues in the U.S. news than there is of EU issues in the European leading papers. However, holding salience constant at the no-coverage level, we see U.S. advocates are more likely to achieve none or all of their goals (63 percent and 20 percent) compared to EU advocates (16 percent and 28 percent), while more EU advocates achieve a compromised success (56 percent compared to only 17 percent of U.S. advocates) on nonsalient issues. Holding salience constant at the low-coverage level of one to five stories in the United States and one to two stories in the European Union, we see the same pattern: more advocates winning all or losing all in the United States (36 percent and 43 percent) compared to those in the European Union (35 percent and 20 percent), while 45 percent of EU advocates achieve some of their goals through compromise and only 21 percent do so in the United States.

Data in the United States do not follow the expectation that a focusing event in an advocate's favor will increase the chances of success. In the derivative case, the Enron scandal in which corporate executives misrepresented their account balances was a focusing event in favor of the regulators, yet industry won the debate. In the stock option case, the same focusing event was in favor of the regulators, yet again industry won the debate. In the anticloning debate, the focusing event was in favor of legislating against cloning, yet the status quo won out, meaning again that those who had a focusing event working in their favor did not succeed. In the antiterrorism legislation case, the focusing event was in favor of the regulators, but this case led to a compromise between strict crackdown measures and more moderate approaches to antiterrorism regulations related to immigration and lab security. Finally, the affiliate relationships case, which would have regulated the communications between subunits of a massive company if those entities were operating at different stages on the energy production supply chain, was impacted by the Enron focusing event, but deadlock in the case led to no victory on either side—for the regulators or industry.

In the European Union, on the one issue where a focusing event occurred the effect played out in the expected direction. The Madrid train bombings focused attention on the need for data retention regulations and were used in the arguments of pro-regulators; they won the day, with industry being forced to store volumes of data for months with no compensation. The EP passed the regulation in December 2005, as *Euractiv* reported: "The vote means that member states will have to impose on Internet service providers and telecommunication operators an obligation to store all traffic and location data for fixed and mobile telephony as well as e-mail, web browsing, instant messaging and other internet services. The data will have to be stored for a period of six to twenty-four months and must be made accessible to authorities investigating on nonspecified serious crimes. When first proposed after the March 11, 2004 Madrid bombings, the proposal had been justified through the fight against terrorism." (2005c) Thus we see evidence of focusing events aiding advocates, but there are also instances, as seen in the U.S. cases, where other factors are of major importance.

Regardless of the political system an advocate is working within, the characteristics of the issue on which the advocate is active have a significant impact on the probability of achieving lobbying success. Most clearly, the larger an issue is in scope and salience and the higher the level of conflict, the less likely lobbyists are to achieve their aims, a pattern that is even stronger in the European Union than in the United States.

INTEREST GROUP CHARACTERISTICS AND STRATEGIES

Who the advocate is and what the advocate does were also expected to matter. However the empirical evidence is spotty—some factors seem to matter while others do not. The resources of an advocate, both financial and membership, exhibit no clear relationship to lobbying success. In addition, the specialized tactics an advocate chooses to use also do not seem to have a consistent impact on lobbying success—neither the use of a consultant nor activity in a coalition exhibited a relationship to lobbying success in either bivariate analysis or when included in the multivariate model. Outside lobbying did have a significant impact in both the United States and the European Union, but in both cases use of outside lobbying techniques led to a decrease in lobbying success. This is discussed in more detail below in the description of the multivariate findings.

The type of advocate appears to have an impact on the likelihood of succeeding in lobbying goals; this speaks to the two alternative hypotheses related to democratic accountability. For clarity, the independent variable has been collapsed here to a dichotomous one: attained no success or attained any level of success. The differences between the United States and the European Union are stark in table 10.3: In the United States, citizen groups and foundations are much more likely to fail in attaining their goals, while trade/business associations and corporations are much more likely to attain some level of success (with 89 percent of corporations attaining some level of success). In the European Union citizen groups and foundations are more likely to attain some level of success, but so are trade/business associations and hired consultants.

Table 10.3 Lobbying Success in the United States and the European Union by Group Type and Position (percent)

	United States				European Union		
	No Success	Any Success	N		No Success	Any Success	N
Citizen	60	40	10	Citizen	44	56	16
Foundations	63	38	8	Foundation	33	67	3
Trade	47	53	19	Trade	39	61	46
Corporation	11	89	9	Hired	43	57	7
Government	47	53	19	Government	30	70	10
Total N	30	35	65	Total N	32	50	82
Total percent	46	54		Total percent	39	61	
For:				For:			
Status quo	19	81	21	Status quo	31	69	26
Change	59	41	44	Change	43	57	56
Total N	30	35	65	Total N	32	50	82
Total percent	46	54		Total percent	39	61	

It seems that the financial power of wealthy U.S. interests cannot be captured in the strength of their government affairs offices alone. It is not only the resources they put into lobbying that help wealthy interests win; these same groups and firms achieve influence through PACs and campaign financing. While this study does not have data on PAC contributions or soft money donations, analyzing the differential lobbying success of business and citizen interests in the United States provides additional support for the scholarly studies and common perception that money talks in Washington. This is in addition to the power wealthy business interests enjoy through their control of the means of production in society (Lindblom 1982).

Thus we see support for the fourth hypothesis relating democratic institutional design to lobbying success: the U.S. system, with direct elections that are privately funded, biases responsiveness in favor of wealthier advocates. Policymakers in the European Union who do not face elections and who do not need to do fund-raising for elections do not have the same incentives to favor wealthy advocates. As a result, their responsiveness is more balanced, with a wider range of advocate types attaining some level of lobbying success.

The other interest group characteristic that shows a strong relationship to lobbying success is whether the advocate was for or against the status quo. In the United States the Pearson chi-squared value is significant at the .01 level and in the European Union significant at the .1 level. Lobbyists fighting for the status quo are more likely to succeed in both polities. In the United States, 81 percent of advocates for the status quo succeeded in some of their goals and in the European Union 69 percent achieved some level of success. This is in line with theories of institutional stickiness (Jones and Baumgartner 2005); governments are often more likely to remain stationary rather than muster the resources and political will required to make a policy change.

It is important to note that some actors are more likely to support the status quo and some are more likely to support change from the status quo. Specifically, business interests are more likely to support the status quo, as citizen groups are often pushing for policy change such as new environmental regulations, new rules to protect consumers, or policies that prevent outsourcing jobs, to cite a few examples. Table 10.4 shows the relationship between actor type and support or opposition of the status quo. In both the United States and the European Union citizen groups, foundations, and government advocates are significantly more likely to be pushing to change the status quo, while corporations, for-hire lobbying firms, and trade associations are much more likely to be fighting to maintain the status quo. And as the previous analysis demonstrated, they will have a much easier time achieving their goals if they are fighting to maintain the status quo than the citizen groups fighting for change.

Table 10.4 Position on the Status Quo by Actor Type in the United States and the European Union (percent)

	United States				European Union		
	Change	Status quo	N		Change	Status quo	N
Citizen	90	10	10	Citizen	94	6	16
Foundation	88	13	8	Foundation	100	0	3
Trade	53	47	19	Trade	57	44	46
Corporation	33	67	9	Hired	57	43	7
Government	79	21	19	Government	80	20	10
Total percent	68	32	65	**Total percent**	68	32	82

Turning to the multivariate ordinal logit analysis we see that both issue-level and interest group–level independent variables are significant determinants of the level of lobbying success. Table 10.5 reports the findings for the ordinal logits in both systems. As suggested by the bivariate analysis, advocates fighting for the status quo are more likely to achieve their goals and advocates engaged in outside lobbying are less likely to achieve their lobbying aims. These patterns hold in both systems.

This second relationship is counterintuitive and contrary to the hypothesis that more sophisticated lobbying techniques should aid advocates in their fight. It is especially surprising considering the significant finding on the issue-level variable of salience in the U.S. case: As the salience of the issue increases in the United States the likelihood of lobbying success also increases. However this does not hold for the EU case. Moreover, as noted during the bivariate analysis discussion, the relationship between salience and success was mixed in the United States, but the percentage of advocates fully attaining their goal decreased as salience increased. This pattern held for all three categories of lobbying success in the European Union: the more salient an issue became the less likely an advocate would attain lobbying success.

So are advocates who "go public" with outside lobbying tactics behaving irrationally? As the salience of an issue increases, policymakers are forced to take more viewpoints into consideration and the advocate therefore is less likely to attain lobbying success. It may be that advocates decide to go outside to promote their position vis-à-vis their opponents, but often the opponents respond by also going outside. As more and more advocates flood the policy space with their outside lobbying communications, the likelihood decreases of any single advocate achieving its goal. It may also be the case that advocates go outside on particularly difficult issues as a last resort. This then would suggest a selection bias, where we see a negative relationship between outside lobbying and lobbying success because advocates choose to go outside only when they anticipate possible failure. They expect that inside lobbying tactics will not be sufficient to achieve their goals and thus turn to outside lobbying as a potential additional weapon that might help their cause. Finally, it is possible that groups go public to signal to their membership that they are doing something, while not expecting outside lobbying to achieve their goal. In any case, the fact that outside lobbying is related to lower levels of lobbying success may explain why groups almost always combine both inside and outside lobbying strategies, as Beyers (2004) finds in his study of European interest associations.

Turning back to the multivariate ordinal logit estimation for the U.S. case, the model also shows advocates active on high-conflict issues are less likely to succeed, in line with the bivariate analysis. In the European Union only one

Table 10.5 Ordered Logits Predicting Lobbying Success in the United States and the European Union

	United States			European Union		
	Coefficient	SE	$P > z$	Coefficient	SE	$P > z$
Business	0.424	0.574	0.460	−0.423	0.528	0.423
For status quo	1.603	0.630	0.011*	1.322	0.593	0.026*
Outside lobbying	−1.451	0.565	0.010*	−1.584	0.644	0.014*
Conflict	−0.691	0.346	0.046*	0.010	0.315	0.974
Salience	0.633	0.294	0.031*	−0.384	0.358	0.284
Scope	−0.229	0.266	0.389	−0.709	0.278	0.011*

Log likelihood = −57.448
N = 65
LR chi²(7) = 22.63
Pseudo R^2 = .1646

Log likelihood = −68.671
N = 82
LR chi²(7) = 31.65
Pseudo R^2 = .1873

issue-level factor is significantly related to lobbying success controlling for other factors: advocates active on large-scope issues are less likely to achieve their lobbying goals. This again is in line with the bivariate finding. This multivariate analysis shows that, controlling for a number of factors, variables at both the issue and interest levels matter when we seek to explain lobbying success.

CONCLUSION

It is important to recognize the overall levels of lobbying success in the two polities are not drastically different. In contrast to the view put forward by some transatlantic observers, U.S. advocates are not highly successful while their European counterparts achieve little (Michalowitz 2005, *EurActiv* 2005a). In fact, overall advocates are having an impact on policymaking at roughly equivalent levels. It is the variation in who is winning that is interesting.

The U.S. system fails to reach compromise nearly 75 percent of the time. More often than not absolute winners dominate clear losers, and on average those winners are industry. In the European Union industry wins too but so do citizen groups and foundations. The EU system negotiates compromises that allow more advocates to achieve their goals. Therefore, ironically, the less democratically accountable system may be more responsive to a broader range of interests. The more democratically accountable system appears biased in its response and that bias is pro-business. The European Union on the other hand, from these data, exhibits a higher capacity to fuse competing interests into policy compromises that allow everyone to see at least some of their goals realized. Lacking direct elections, the system finds itself also free from exploitation of the electoral process by moneyed interests.

Of course, this is an initial investigation, analyzing lobbying success of only one hundred forty-seven advocates on forty-seven issues. Larger studies will be needed to further support or question these findings and expand the analysis to investigate a larger number of contextual factors. First, it will be important to consider the position of governmental officials (Michalowitz 2004). If policymakers in a powerful DG or executive bureau are pushing for the same objective as an interest it could make their fight much easier. Similarly, if large numbers of members of the EP or members of Congress (or committee chairs, etc.) have lined up behind a certain position on an issue that support will be important in the ultimate outcome. Understanding where the preponderance of government support lies may be very important in understanding when lobbyists succeed and when they fail.

This is related to a second important factor: nongovernmental allies. Whether an advocate is alone or whether there are hundreds of groups standing with them should affect whether they are successful or not in their lobbying goals. These advocates need not be allied in an official ad hoc coalition—they may not even be communicating—but if all are pushing in the same direction, it should make a difference in whether they attain their goals in the final outcome. Future research projects collecting data on the full universe of groups mobilizing for a political debate, and collecting information on their positions, would allow social scientists to study the relationship between the number of groups with their positions aligned with an advocate and the ability of an advocate to achieve its lobbying goals.

A third factor is time. Especially in the European Union, where the policy process can be extremely long, future studies could be designed to cover a longer expanse of time, better assessing whether advocates truly ever achieve their goals. Some fights take decades, thus long-term successes would not have registered in my shorter-term study. This analysis has made clear a few points that should be kept in mind when we consider interest group influence. First, the design of the political system has implications for the responsiveness of politicians; this in turn fundamentally affects who succeeds and who does not. Specifically the coupling of direct elections and private funding of elections in the United States leads to a system with incentives for elected officials to be more responsive to wealthier actors. Second, issue context is critical and plays a large role in lobbying success. Advocates lobbying in a niche, where there are no competing advocates or public scrutiny, are at an advantage. Third, many of the factors that lobbyists believe make or break their strategy—hiring a professional lobbyist or joining an ad hoc issue coalition—have no effect at all. Other activities like outside lobbying might actually hurt their cause, as can their position on a given issue—fighting to bring about a change is more difficult than fighting for the status quo.

In addition, this chapter has provided additional evidence for viewing advocacy as a process and recognizing that decisions at one stage of the process can have implications for outcomes at another—whether advocates were fighting for or against the status quo or whether they opted to join a coalition combined with institutional, issue, and interest factors to determine lobbying success. Over time, the level of lobbying success at the end of a policy debate may determine whether an advocate mobilizes for the next related fight. For example, perhaps an advocate was promoting a new policy and succeeding only in achieving an amendment calling for a report on the topic. This may embolden the advocate to continue pushing during the next year for additional action on the topic. Stages of the advocacy process are linked affecting other stages on the same legislative fight and through time affecting advocacy throughout policymaking cycles.

All three levels—institutions, issues, and interests—must be included in any explanation of who wins, who loses, and who achieves compromised success. However, perhaps surprising to some, many of the interest-group level factors, including what tactics were used, were not as powerful determinants as the broader political and issue context. The environment in which an advocate finds himself or herself largely dictates success; while many lobbyists would be dismayed by this, it is critical that social scientists understand this characteristic of lobbying success.

Conclusion

MANY OBSERVERS HAVE suggested the U.S. and the EU policy communities are converging in their lobbying practices; others have claimed advocacy in the two systems is categorically different. This book has shown that neither extreme is accurate. American and European advocates share similarities and also display differences.

The argumentation strategies employed by American and European advocates are quite similar. The same five types of arguments can be heard in both arenas: those referencing commonly shared goals, cost and economic arguments, feasibility and workability arguments, technical and scientific arguments, and finally fairness or discrimination arguments. Only constituency arguments are unlikely to be made in the European Union. In addition, advocates in both the United States and the European Union are more likely to formulate arguments evoking commonly shared goals if they are active on highly salient issues, if they are an organization representing citizen interests, or if they are promoting a policy alternative rather than trying to block or modify one. Similarly, in both polities, if an advocate is in a blocking position he or she is most likely to make feasibility arguments. Although it might seem possible to spin a position in millions of ways, there does appear to be a finite set of argumentation types on which European and American advocates rely. The frame adopted on a given case is very much determined by issue and interest group factors.

Second, inside lobbying is similar on both sides of the Atlantic. Tactics such as letter-writing, face-to-face meetings, drafting legislative language, testifying at hearings, and contributing to consultations are all being employed by advocates in both systems. Also critical to advocates interviewed in both spheres was issue-related research: policymakers want to see advocates who bring evidence to support their claims and positions. Moreover, the tactical decisions made by advocates in both systems are driven by the policymaking procedure of the issue. Third, networking activity is nearly identical. U.S. and

EU advocates engage in exactly the same type of networking at legislative hearings, conferences, and cocktail parties, as well as in the same type of data and information sharing via e-mail, conference calls, and informal meetings.

American and European advocates differ on lobbying approaches, targeting strategies, outside lobbying activity, coalition building, and success patterns. First, lobbyists in the United States and the European Union are somewhat inclined to approach lobbying from different positions, with U.S. lobbyists marginally more likely to attempt to block policy proposals and EU lobbyists slightly more likely to work to modify proposals. From the qualitative evidence it is clear this difference in tendencies is due not to temperament but rather to institutional rules surrounding the policymaking process and the likelihood of policy change. Once the policymaking process is underway in the European Union, the probability that a policy change will result is high, as such advocates work to modify the inevitable. In the United States, there are many opportunities to kill a policy proposal; policy change is less assured and thus advocates opposed to a measure work to block it.

Second, targeting strategies are significantly different in the two polities. In the United States targeting options are more flexible, allowing lobbyists to target a large number of members of Congress and tailor their targeting strategies to include only friends or to extend to undecided and opposed policymakers, depending on the issue at hand. In the European Union, targets are much more predetermined by the policymaking procedure. Advocates are required to direct their lobbying communications to the few individuals with power over a given dossier.

A third substantial difference between U.S. and EU advocacy is the propensity to go public. Outside lobbying is much more prevalent in the United States than the European Union. Every outside lobbying tactic, including grass-roots mobilization, media outreach, issue advertisements, public education campaigns, protests, and op-ed writing, is used at a higher rate by American lobbyists. This disparity between outside lobbying in the two polities is due in part to the democratic accountability of policymakers and their related responsiveness to outside lobbying communications and in part to the strength of the media systems in the two arenas. In the United States a far-reaching single-language media system can communicate advocacy messages across the country quickly and effectively, while in the European Union separate media markets, divided by language and media outlets, inhibit the spread of pan-European communications.

American lobbyists are more likely than their European counterparts to construct highly coordinated coalitions that exist for the purpose of a single legislative debate. These are formal entities with names, secretariats, logos, and letterhead. The qualitative evidence presented emphasized how there is both a resource-sharing aspect and a signaling aspect to coalition formation in the United States. Advocates approaching electorally accountable policymakers want to send a signal that their coalition is big and broad and that they represent the views of a large majority of the public. In the European Union such cueing is not needed and resource-sharing benefits can be achieved through loose networks without the operational costs incurred with a formal coalition.

Lastly, advocates in the United States are more likely to either fully achieve their goals or achieve nothing at all and more often than not it is industry who wins. In the European Union higher numbers of advocates achieve a partial success, seeing some of their goals realized but not all. Whether advocates achieved their goals or not is not categorical evidence of interest group influence. Many factors, as this book has shown, are at play in all advocacy outcomes. It is difficult to tease out the precise effect of one lobbyist. However, determining the lobbying goals of organizations and comparing those goals to policy outcomes on specific cases allows us to begin to understand who wins and loses in the advocacy game.

While there are differences between advocacy in the United States and the European Union the data presented in this book have shown that American and European advocates respond in similar ways to issue characteristics: highly salient issues drive lobbyists in both polities to engage in more outside lobbying, high-conflict issues lead both to join coalitions, and large-scope issues impel lobbyists in both systems to employ more inside advocate tactics.

Moreover interest group characteristics, including membership and financial resources, organizational structure, and actor type, lead to similar advocacy behavior in both polities as well. For example, citizen groups in both settings are more likely to try to promote new policies, push for changes to the status quo, evoke references to the broader good when arguing for those changes, and engage in outside lobbying tactics and coalition work to get their messages across. Business interests, in contrast, are more likely to fight to maintain the status quo, blocking new policy proposals, and will convey their economic, technical, and feasibility arguments through direct inside lobbying tactics.

It should be noted that since different actors have a tendency to use different advocacy strategies, and since there are differences between the two samples in the number of the various types of advocates, such disparities could result in findings suggesting U.S.–EU advocacy differences that are an artifact of the sample differences. For example, if the U.S. sample has more citizen groups than the EU sample, then in the aggregate we will see more outside lobbying in the U.S. case, but this will be due to more citizen groups being in the sample and their tending to use outside lobbying at a higher rate, rather than due to institutional factors. As you will recall when the two samples were broken down by advocate type in chapter 3, there were in fact slightly more citizen groups in the EU sample (21 percent compared to 14 percent) as well as more industry interests in the EU sample (65 percent compared to 43 percent). The U.S. sample included more policymakers, stemming from the empirical reality that policymakers come to act as advocates and champions of the causes they take up much more often than their European counterparts.

Precisely matched samples (to each other and to the universes from which they are drawn) would be more ideal and allow us to more accurately assess the independent effect of institutions and feel more confident that system differences are not an artifact of the research design. However, as each of the substantive chapters demonstrated, through the interviews institutional design factors have been shown to be important determinants of advocacy decisions.

It is difficult to conclusively determine the degree of similarity between the U.S. and EU advocacy universes due to the lack of an EU registration requirement. We know that there are more advocates in the aggregate in the United States, and we know there is a business bias in both the Brussels and Washington advocacy communities, but direct comparisons of each actor type category are difficult. The voluntary registry launched in spring 2008 by the European Commission's Administration, Audit and Anti-Fraud Commission vice president, Siim Kallas, may be an answer to the problem, if his predictions are accurate: "The register is a huge step forward. Okay, people can say that 'look, this is voluntary and it doesn't work.' It will work. It will work. There will be a register, and the vast majority of lobbyists will join it" (*EurActiv*, May 10, 2007).

Comparing the comprehensive U.S. Lobby Disclosure Report database with the planned, similarly comprehensive EU Lobbying Register would, first, provide two excellent sampling frames for future research; second, provide data to accurately compare the two advocacy communities; and third, allow researchers to begin investigating whether U.S. and EU institutional design factors differentially affect the composition of their advocacy communities. If there are affirmative conclusions on this last point, institutional structures would be shaping advocacy in the systems in two ways—directly by influencing argumentation, tactic selection, and other strategy decisions as described in this book and indirectly by influencing whose voices are being heard in the policymaking process.

Future research agendas aside, this comparison of U.S. and EU advocacy activity has clearly shown that blanket statements about U.S. and EU lobbying should be put to rest. Reality is more nuanced. The day-to-day lives of American and European lobbyists are similar in many ways; where they differ is largely due to the design of their respective institutional systems.

THE IMPORTANCE OF INSTITUTIONS: THE EFFECT OF ELECTIONS

The Convention on the Future of Europe was tasked with drafting a treaty establishing a constitution for Europe; one of the primary aims would be make the European Union "more democratic." Criticized for decades for its "democratic deficit" and lambasted for its lack of democratic institutions, the European Union was getting ready to reform. While the constitutional process was derailed in the spring of 2005 by 'non' votes in the referenda in France and The Netherlands, constitutional advocates still hope to see the document, or at least the democratic reforms laid out in it, come to fruition in one form or another.

The constitutional reforms called for a revision in qualified majority voting so that a double majority was needed to pass an initiative; the right of citizen initiative, which would allow the public to request the Commission to initiate a policy proposal if the initiatives' organizers could collect one million signatures of European citizens; strengthening the role of the EP; and opening the deliberations of the Council to the public (Europa 2004). The proposed reforms, however, fall short of calling for direct elections of the commissioners or the members of the Council or substantial revisions to the election process of MEPs, which would result in increased electoral accountability to their constituents. This, however, may not be the worst outcome, at least in terms of the effect on the advocacy process.

The evidence presented in chapters 4 through 10 has demonstrated the impact of democratic accountability on advocacy decisions and outcomes. Whether policymakers are directly elected or appointed has bearing on how advocates approach those policymakers aiming to influence their decisions. In some ways the effect of direct elections is more innocuous: policymakers driven by the reelection motive respond more readily to constituent-based arguments and tactics devised to emphasize the preferences of constituents. However, in democratic systems that couple elections with private funding of those elections, the effect can be more nefarious where it counts: on influence. The findings in chapter 10 show that directly elected policymakers in the United States may not be responding mostly to their constituents, or even to the majority opinion, but rather to those who can help them win their next electoral race.

The bias in favor of wealthy interests, most notably industry, is magnified in the policymaking process in two additional ways beyond the resources brought to bear on a lobbying campaign. First, wealthy interests can mobilize for a larger number of issues, including small niche issues on which they face no opposition. Citizen groups with limited resources can only mobilize for the largest, most important issues. Small technical changes and regulatory rulemaking fall through the cracks with only the interested industry representatives there to have their preferences incorporated into the policymaking process. Second, industry more often than not is fighting to maintain the status quo, to prevent new regulation of their sectors. As findings in chapter 9 showed, those fighting to stand still are more likely to succeed than those pushing for a policy change. Citizen groups are often the organizations promoting a new rule or piece of legislation to regulate the noneconomic costs associated with industry. Thus, we see wealthy interests have an advantage in all democratic systems in that they are often fighting the easier battle, they are able to mobilize for a larger number of battles, and they have more resources to bring to their advocacy strategies on each of those battles. In democratic systems, with direct elections that are privately funded, they are offered additional power—the ability to influence policymakers through campaign financing support.

It is beyond the scope of this book to determine whether the power of wealthy interests is advanced by helping secure the election of friendly policymakers, through gaining access as a result of financial support, or a more base and corrupt quid pro quo of money for policy. What is clear however—from studying the advocacy of a range of actor types on a large random sample of issues in two political systems that differ in their democratic accountability structures—is that wealthy interests do succeed more than citizen interests in the United States. In many ways this is unsatisfying since it supports the generally held notion of disenfranchised voters and disillusioned citizen activists but yet again falls short of case-closed hard evidence of the power of money in the American political system.

The findings presented in this book, however, do provide one more piece of substantiation for that view. The findings related to the effect of privately funded elections on advocacy should perhaps give pause to democratic reformers who tout direct elections as the ultimate credential in democratic consolidation. In assessing the strength of democracy in a polity, we must also take into account the democratic nature of inputs and outputs. We must question who participates in the policymaking process: Who is included, who is excluded, how are preferences incorporated into policymaking? We must consider policy outcomes in light of interest group preferences: Is the majority satisfied with the resulting policy, is the public pleased with the outcome, or is it only the wealthiest who see their policy preferences reflected in the law?

The quantitative and qualitative evidence presented throughout the substantive chapters provides strong support for the idea that the democratic accountability of policymakers plays a role in the strategy decisions of advocates. Simplistic explanations of cultural differences can be ruled out. Cultural differences, manifested on an individual level, cannot explain the differences we see between U.S. and EU lobbying because these very advocates behave in similar ways when issue contexts create environments similar to the other system. For example, when U.S. advocates are active on a case that will inevitably lead to policy change they assume modifying positions, working toward a compromise. When EU advocates are active on a case that is less likely to lead to policy change they behave in the stereotypical American manner, trying to kill the proposal. Advocates in the European Union active on highly salient issues will formulate their arguments to evoke commonly shared goals, although this argumentation strategy is generally more common in the United States. Advocates in the United States active on regulatory issues will be less likely to engage in outside lobbying tactics aimed at communicating the will of the people. When U.S. and EU advocates are faced with similar issue contexts, they behave in similar ways.

Cultural differences, manifest at the system level as majoritarian and consensus-based democracies, as suggested by Lijphart, find support in the evidence presented here. Lijphart argues that highly fragmented societies will create institutional structures to incorporate the greatest number of views and work to please the largest majorities in policymaking, leading to consensus democracies. More homogenous societies do not require these same types of structures; majority rule can sufficiently account for societal preference and achieve acceptable policy outcomes, leading to majoritarian democracies.

As mentioned in chapter 2, Lijphart categorizes the European Union as a consensus democracy and the United States as a majoritarian democracy (1999, 42–47). The findings in chapter 10 fit with this categorization and provide support for Lijphart's distinctions. The European Union more often results in compromised outcomes where a large number of interests are at least partially satisfied with the policy outcome. The U.S. policymaking process is more likely to result in clear winners and losers. This is where the empirical findings, however, may diverge from Lijphart's theory; it does not appear that it is the interests in the majority that necessarily win, but rather those that are most financially well endowed. Thus, we once again come back to the role of elections and private financing of elections. Further research is needed on advocacy outcomes, to gather data on the relative support of a policy outcome by the full range of societal interests, in addition to their financial resources. In this way we could begin drawing some conclusions about whether policy outcomes in majoritarian systems are truly supported by the majority of interests or rather the wealthiest interests.

The findings presented here also may be evidence of the role of another important institutional factor that could not be studied due to this project's design: multilevel structural design. While the United States and the European Union share a similar federal structure, the EU member states retain significant power compared to the U.S. states. Some of the differences we see in advocacy activity between the two systems at the central level studied here may be due to important advocacy efforts still being taken at the national level on EU issues in the European Union (significant advocacy activity of course remains at the national level on issues that remain in the full control of national authorities).

When it comes to outside lobbying, as mentioned in chapter 8, a great deal of grassroots and protest activity remains at the national level, according to the study by Kriesi, Jochuma, and Tresch's (2005), which looks at advocacy activities in three policy areas at the EU level and the national level in seven member states. Imig and Tarrow's (2001) edited volume provides many examples of cases in which demonstrators restricted themselves to national arenas even though they were disgruntled about EU policies. Language barriers and travel costs still inhibit mass mobilization in Brussels; French farmers and Spanish fishermen must be satisfied by voicing their displeasure with EU policy in their national capitals. If we combined national- and supranational-level advocacy activities in Europe we might see more similar levels of outside lobbying, coalition activity, and other tactics in comparison to the United States.

In addition to explaining differences in absolute levels of activity at the national and supranational levels, the multilevel structure of the European Union may be used by lobbyists in an iterative way leading to qualitative difference between national- and supranational-level lobbying. Two iterative scenarios are plausible: first, advocates who successfully accomplish their goals in a national arena may try to achieve those same goals in the wider EU arena; second, advocates who fail to accomplish their goals in their national arena may move to the EU level to push their case. In both scenarios the advocacy strategies are likely to differ at the national and EU levels, with advocates using different sets of arguments and tactics depending on the arena.

Consider the first scenario. Advocates who have succeeded in getting a new proposal passed at the national level may turn their attention to getting a similar proposal adopted at the EU level, so the policy will apply not just in their home country but across the European Union. For example, Swedish environmental groups urge the Swedish government to pass a new environmental law on air pollution. Seeing success in the first battle, they move to the EU level, likely working with other European environmental advocates to pass a similar measure at the EU level. They would then also have the support of the Swedish government, which has already backed the proposal.

This would fit with Börzel's (2002) findings that show how member states try to "upload" their policies to the European Union so that they don't have to "download" new EU policies that differ from their national laws. When the Swedish environmentalists begin working at the EU level, they will likely use different arguments and tactics than they did at the national level. While during the first iteration they may have drawn on arguments about the Swedish public's support for such a measure and the need for novel responses to climate change, during the second iteration at the EU level they may focus on how effective the policy has been in the testing ground of Sweden and the practicality of the measure. Thus, what we are seeing at the EU level is only one piece of the picture; combining advocacy strategies from the two stages we may see greater similarities between the European Union, for example in argumentation, and the United States.

In the second iterative scenario, advocates may work to promote an issue at the national level and when that fails, move to the EU level to see if they can achieve their goals there. Anecdotally there are numerous examples of this, referred to as "bypassing the nation-state" or venue shopping. When advocates cannot make headway at home, if for example the party in power is not sympathetic to their cause, they can go directly to Brussels and try to press their case there. When they shift to the EU level the nature of their advocacy likely will change: they will alter their arguments, making them more pan-EU in focus and alter their strategies to be more effective for European bureaucrats. That is, European advocates may behave more like U.S. advocates at the national level; when they move to the EU level their strategies may change and depart from U.S. patterns. Thus, if we were to consider all European lobbying, combining national and supranational activities from the two stages, we might see greater commonality with U.S. patterns. This is the next big step needed in EU interest group research—studying EU advocacy on issues at both the national and supranational levels over a longer period of time.

THE ADVOCACY PROCESS AND THE INFLUENCE PRODUCTION PROCESS

This book has demonstrated the advantage of recognizing and studying advocacy as a process. Advocacy is not only the tactics advocates use or simply the arguments they make, but rather a process whereby advocates mobilize for a policy debate, determine their lobbying position, settle on their argumentation, decide on their lobbying targets, select their inside and outside lobbying tactics, choose to work alone or with others, and finally whether they achieve their goals. Breaking down advocacy into its component parts and studying the factors that drive advocacy decisions and outcomes in each of those stages allows us to better understand the entire process.

We have seen evidence of how stages of the advocacy process link to others; how decisions at one stage can affect outcomes at another. Chapters 3 and 4 suggested that the lobbying position an advocate assumes can influence argumentation strategy. Chapter 10 demonstrated how inside lobbying decisions and outside lobbying decisions can influence lobbying success. As mentioned in chapter 2, Lowery and Gray coined the concept "*the influence production process*" (2004, 164). This concept fully integrates mobilization into the process.

Mobilization is a fundamentally important aspect of advocacy but the design of this research project did not allow the study of those groups that did not mobilize.

When we shift to a longer-term perspective we see how mobilization can affect the stages of the advocacy process studied here, and how the stages of the advocacy process can in turn influence mobilization—leading to an over-time advocacy cycle. In the first half of the cycle, the mix of advocates mobilizing on a policy debate can affect the nature of discourse and debate on that issue. If a large number of environmental and consumer organizations mobilize for a debate on a new chemicals law, the dynamic is going to be very different than if they had not mobilized at all and industry was the only voice being heard. A larger number of active interests can expand the perceived scope of the issue and lead to a higher level of conflict, since citizen groups will be opposing industry; there may be more vocal advocacy tactics used, leading other advocates active on the debate also to go outside, and thus the collaborative work of one side could drive the opposition to ally. In addition, the constellation of actors that opt to mobilize for a debate can affect the ultimate policy outcome and thus the lobbying success of each advocate lobbying on the case. Returning to our theoretical case, had the environmental and consumer groups not mobilized, the industry representatives may have quietly influenced the legislative language and achieved all their objectives. With the citizen group mobilization, the lobbying success of industry may become less assured. Thus, variation in mobilization patterns can affect issue characteristics, and as this book has shown, those in turn can affect lobbying decisions and outcomes.

Looking at the second half of the advocacy cycle, the ultimate policy outcome on an issue could influence subsequent mobilization. As Kingdon (1995) said, no issue is really new—every issue on the agenda today existed in some form or can be traced back to an issue twenty years ago. Similarly, every issue being debated today will exist in some form on the agenda a decade from now. Who wins and who loses on a discrete policy issue could influence the mobilization of those parties in subsequent related policy debates. Again, take the hypothetical chemical regulation example. If the environmental and consumer protection groups mobilize and achieve some level of success, they may feel empowered by their gains to remobilize when the regulation is up for reauthorization. Or if they succeed in mandating a study, they will mobilize for the hearings and consultations surrounding the research findings. Alternatively, if they do not achieve any of their goals, they could be so disheartened that they see the case as hopeless and decide to spend their time and resources on another topic. Thus the outcomes during the advocacy process influence subsequent mobilization decisions.

This is just a simple hypothetical scenario, but the implications are clear: mobilization can affect the six advocacy decision stages studied here, which can in turn affect policy outcomes and lobbying success. Lobbying success can, over time, affect future mobilization and advocacy. Over the long term it may be helpful to think about an advocacy cycle in interest group research.

THREE SETS OF FORCES—A MODEL FOR COMPARATIVE INTEREST GROUP RESEARCH

The evidence presented in this book has demonstrated that to understand advocacy it is crucial to consider the nature of the political environment in which an advocate operates as well as the nature of the advocate itself. This research, based on observing the process of advocacy on forty-seven issues through 149 interviews in both Washington and Brussels, has made clear that the similarities and differences between the United States and the European Union are understandable, predictable, and systematic. They relate to institutional settings, issue characteristics, and interest-based factors. Importantly the relationship between these features and the advocacy process is similar in both systems.

We can indeed understand the process of advocacy better by studying advocacy activities across institutions, issues, and interests. This model can serve as a stepping off point for future comparative interest group studies; a number of avenues are possible. First, it would be possible to extend this framework to investigate the advocacy processes in other Western democracies including Canada, the member states of the European Union, other European countries not included in the European Union such as Switzerland and Norway. Do the same factors drive advocacy decisions in this large sample of polities? It may be the case that in countries with weaker traditions of lobbying we do not see as strong relationships between issue characteristics and lobbying strategy. The young democracies of Eastern Europe for example are still building their civil society communities and increasing the professionalization of their advocates.

Researching advocacy in a broader range of institutional systems would not only give us more insight on the role of democratic accountability on lobbying decisions but would also allow us to investigate other institutional factors that may play a role in determining advocacy outcomes, such as the federal or unitary structure of the state, or the presence of official interest intermediation venues. A large number of polities would also provide more leverage on the question of the role of the media in advocacy. The United States and the European Union are significantly different in this regard. Looking at a greater range of polities with variations in the reach of media systems would allow us to better understand the extent to which the media restrict or facilitate advocacy communications.

Second, more work is needed on civil society and advocacy processes in non-Western democracies. How would the model extend to Japan, India, Peru, or Kenya? When we expand to global comparison does culture play a larger role? It could be argued that while there may be differences in political culture among the Western democracies, they also have a great deal in common, sharing many of the same values and mores. Do advocacy processes in more communal societies behave in a similar way to the individualist-centered Western democracies? How does the degree of democratic consolidation affect advocacy processes? When democracy is seen as the only game in town politicians are likely to respond in different ways to civil society compared to less-stable democracies still building the foundations of democratic institutions and the culture that surrounds such institutions.

Moreover, in postconflict societies the development of civil society can be fundamentally important to the healing process, to incorporate diverging views into new policy development and to begin rebuilding the society. It is therefore important that we understand how the representatives of interests in postconflict societies mobilize and get their views across to policymakers, and whether they are successful. What barriers to mobilization exist in these societies? What implications do such hurdles have for the constellation of civil society actors in postconflict governments seeking to develop policy to begin rebuilding the society? What is the effect on advocacy decisions?

A third approach that would provide an interesting testing ground for this model and offer important insights to comparative interest group researchers is the study of transnational advocacy, that is, advocacy by groups organized at the national, regional, or global level targeted at international organizations (IOs), regional organizations, or foreign national governments. Investigating how advocates from different regions lobby a single international organization would allow researchers to investigate how differences in advocacy culture may influence advocacy strategies targeted at the officials of a single institution. Expanding that to consider transnational advocacy targeted at the UN, WTO, World Bank, and others would allow the investigation of another layer of institutional design. How does the decision-making structure of the World Bank, in which voting is weighted by member state contribution, compare to the decision-making structure of the UN General Assembly in which the one country, one vote rule reigns, and what effect do they have on the advocacy strategies of transnational NGOs, multinational corporations, and other IOs?

This project has demonstrated the leverage comparative interest group research can provide in looking at questions of institutional design. However, being limited to only two polities, it is difficult to parse out the effects of the various institutional factors that differ between the two systems. For example in chapter 8 on outside lobbying techniques, both democratic accountability and the strength of the media system differ between the United States and the European Union. The different requirements of the various outside lobbying tactics allowed us to distinguish the effects of these two system differences to some degree. Studies with a larger number of polities, with more shades of gray in institutional design, will allow more nuanced analysis of the unique effect of different institutional factors.

Future research can certainly build on these findings, but this study has amply demonstrated something that was not so clear and often argued against in the separate literatures on U.S. and EU lobbying: The systems are not completely dissimilar, they are not impossible to compare, and their differences are not based on general cultural differences. On the contrary, while there are indeed important differences in context and lobbying behaviors, these are understandable through a tripart model that takes into consideration institutional structures, issue contexts, and interest group characteristics.

Appendix:
Case Descriptions

U.S. ISSUES

1. Amendment for Commodity Futures Trading Commission Regulation of Over-the-counter Derivatives

Derivatives are financial instruments agreed upon by two private parties to limit risk; they derive their value from another asset that can include stocks, bonds, currencies, or commodities. They were not traditionally regulated by the Commodities Futures Trade Commission (CFTC). However, in response to the 2000–2001 California energy crisis, a result of Enron's online energy trading, which was not subject to CFTC supervision, an amendment was drafted to ensure that a regulatory agency would oversee the trading of energy derivatives. The goal of supporters of the amendment was to prevent another scandal like Enron through the oversight of transactions. Opponents of the regulation, largely the major financial companies and trading houses, argued the legislation was too broad and thus inadvertently covered many other kinds of derivatives. They further claimed such regulation would make derivatives less attractive financial instruments, leading to less utilization of the instruments, and would ultimately negatively impact the market.

2. Reauthorizing Federal Funding for the State Revolving Fund Loan Programs

Much of the infrastructure for water and wastewater in the United States was originally constructed through works projects of President Franklin D. Roosevelt. Over time projects have deteriorated and while local governments have worked to maintain them, patchwork repairing has become less and less feasible. The facilities are nearing the end of their functional life. Everyone agrees funding is needed to replace them, but the question remains who should pay—the federal, state, or local government. Proponents of reauthorizing federal funding for the State Revolving Fund (SRF) loan programs, which include water infrastructure organizations, labor interests, the states, the municipalities, and some environmental interests, feel that the federal government should be a larger contributor. They argue the federal government determines the standards, and places the burden on state and local governments to find the money to accomplish those goals. The SRF is a program by which the federal government gives states grants and then the states loan out money to local communities for projects. Opponents, mainly private water companies, counter that federal grants could be misused and that there are more effective ways to accomplish infrastructure replacement than grants from the government.

3. EPA Transportation Equipment Cleaning Effluent Limitation Guidelines

Tanker trucks can be seen every day on America's highways transporting liquids of all kinds in bulk—milk, orange juice, oil, and countless other products, some hazardous. When those trucks get to their destination and empty their contents, the inside of the tanks needs to be cleaned before the next use. Congress insisted that the EPA develop regulations on tank truck facilities, which would control how truck companies dispose of water used to clean the inside of trucks after transporting potentially hazardous substances. Environmental organizations pushed for this as well, although they were not active beyond the initial call for regulations. Thus the EPA was charged with the task of drawing up those regulations. Tank truck advocates argued that the regulations should not be excessively stringent. The EPA's small business office worked closely with the tank truck cleaning facilities to assess acceptable levels of substances and the types of substances that would be allowed in runoff and also to determine the process by which wastewater would be disposed.

4. Funding for Optometric Clinical Education Training

For the layperson the distinction between ophthalmologists and optometrists is unclear. Ophthalmologists are medical doctors who specialize in the eye; they can perform eye surgery as well as all the normal, routine eye exams. Optometrists on the other hand are limited license practitioners—they are not able to perform surgical procedures, but they are able to conduct standard eye exams. While physicians and those in other medical professions such as dentistry and podiatry have their graduate medical education training funded by Medicare, optometrists do not. Thus, optometrists were seeking another option to support their optometrists-in-training, asking HHS to release funds for a clinical education training program in optometry. There was no opposition to this aim, but it remained a difficult issue because it required interest by a member of Congress who could introduce legislative language in a bill that would urge HHS to act.

5. National Security Restrictions on Foreign Nationals and Laboratory Security

It seemed nearly every issue could have a national security aspect to it in post–September 11 Washington politics, but the national security debate was greatest on specific antiterrorism legislation like the Patriot Act and other related bills that had the sole purpose of making the country more secure and identifying and addressing all sources of threat. Since a number of the terrorists who hijacked the planes that crashed into the World Trade Center towers originally had gained access to the country with student visas and attended flight school within U.S. borders, it is not surprising that college campuses became a source of scrutiny for officials seeking out threats. In the fervor to respond to national security threats, some members of Congress actually called for a total ban on all student visas. This proposal did not take hold, but calls for stringent controls on student visas did. Security-concerned officials also called for monitoring foreign students from certain "rogue states" as well as surveillance of the courses being taken by foreign students; so-called sensitive areas of study would include things like nuclear chemistry and biophysics. Proponents of stricter security also argued that foreign nationals from states that sponsor terrorism have restricted access to certain dangerous substances. For example, a biologist from Syria working in a university lab would not be able to work with anthrax. In addition, labs would generally be much more stringently regulated to ensure all dangerous substances would not fall into the wrong hands—members of the university or not. The goal of all these provisions was to increase national security, and thus it was difficult for anyone to argue against it; however if antiterrorism measures were too overzealous they could have the effect of stifling education and research at America's universities. Advocates for higher education advised members of Congress and the administration to exercise moderation and balance when deciding these issues.

6. Disabled Recipients under Temporary Assistance for Needy Families Reauthorization

In the overhaul of the welfare system under the Clinton administration, welfare as it was known was abolished and TANF was put in its place. The new program's priority was to move people from welfare roles to work. In the first years of the program, the change was dramatic—huge numbers of welfare recipients became active participants in the workforce. However, it was the easiest cases that made the transition at first—those who were able to work with some training and job placement help were able to do so. In 2000 the TANF bill was up for reauthorization and while many Republicans wanted to continue seeing the shift from welfare to work, it was less and less possible. Those still on the welfare roles in 2000 were people facing serious barriers to moving into the workforce, including single parenting, drug addition, and disability. It is this last category that advocates argued would likely never be able to make the transition. Severe mental retardation is not something that can be cured; it is not something that a training or education program can help the individual overcome. Advocates argued that such individuals should not be thrown off the welfare roles when their "clock" was up. They called for revisions to the bill to allow education and training classes to count as work time, to improve the assessment process by which individuals are declared able to work, and not to sanction disabled recipients for not meeting requirements that are difficult or impossible for them to meet. These advocates did not face active opposition but the rhetoric on the welfare to work side remained a strong impediment—calling for 70 percent of recipients to get back to work.

7. Human Cloning Prohibition Act

Ever since Dolly the sheep was cloned by scientists in Scotland, proving that viable cloning was possible, bills have been introduced in Congress to ban human cloning. While none had passed by 2002 and interest had died down to some degree, the claim in December of that year by Clonaid that a mother had given birth to a baby girl clone sparked a revival of the debate. Proponents of a ban on human cloning are largely right-to-life advocates who seek to legislate against humans playing God. Joining them in this fight, however, were some environmental groups that view cloning as tampering with nature, and some women's groups who were largely involved due to the possibilities of exploitation of women in cloning research—the millions of eggs that would be needed for research would need to be harvested from women. While no groups are lobbying to clone humans for reproductive purposes, as Clonaid claimed to have done, patient advocates and representatives of the scientific community seek to keep "therapeutic cloning" legal, so that the promising research on stem cells can continue. The proponents of a complete ban and proponents of therapeutic cloning both put forward bills during the 106th Congress. Titled the Human Cloning Prohibition Act of 2002, one bill would have banned cloning for any purpose and the other bill would ban reproductive cloning, cloning to produce a living human, but would allow cloning to create embryos for stem cell research.

8. Funding for an Alternative to the EA-6B Prowler

The Electronic Attack (EA)-6B Prowler did its job for the Air Force for the past twenty years, flying out with a squadron and protecting American planes by jamming the radar of the enemy so that they could not detect U.S. jets. But after twenty years the fleet of EA-6B Prowlers began to deteriorate. They had been patched and repatched but it was becoming too costly and dangerous to continue deploying them. A new alternative needed to be developed and defense contractors were lobbying hard for the opportunity to secure the contract. The government would supply funding for research and development of a new electronic jamming platform. There was no opposition to this, although there was the standard competition between contractors to woo government officials.

9. U.S. Farm Bill

The 2000 U.S. Farm Bill was a massive piece of legislation that at its core is to provide support to farmers; this was also the fundamental point of dispute. There are those for price support, the farmer organizations; and those against, the producers who need to buy the farm commodities, the taxpayer watchdog groups who do not want taxpayer money going to pay one profession, and the fiscal liberals that think international trade should be free. While this debate on price supports continued to rage on, there were hundreds of other issues that drew the attention of literally hundreds of other interest groups. The Farm Bill included numerous other programs including provisions on topics from windmills to puppy mills, on fruit trees in the east to vegetable crops in the west, on covered bridges in New England to school lunch programs across the country. With the number of specific topics and the amount of federal money up for debate, the U.S. Farm Bill drew hordes of lobbyists to the Hill.

10. Wind Energy Tax Credit

Wind energy is one of the most promising types of sustainable clean energy production. In order to promote the further development of the industry, a tax credit for wind energy production was established, but the credit had an expiration data. Companies and industry representatives were seeking to extend the tax credit and to do so for a period long enough to provide economic stability to encourage companies to invest in the technology. Proponents of the government tax subsidies argued that the program had been successful in bringing down the cost of wind energy and thus in fostering environmentally friendly energy production. In addition, the argument that alternative forms of energy would reduce the country's dependence on foreign oil reso nated especially well in the post-September 11 political atmosphere.

11. SMART Growth and the Transportation Bill Reauthorization

U.S. transportation policy is revised cyclically. Every few years, transportation reauthorization is on the agenda, and much more is always at stake than the core topic of funding for the U.S. highway system. Also included are issues related to an assortment of environmental, traffic, transit, and safety provisions. The case at hand has to do with the concept of SMART Growth in the transportation bill reauthorization. SMART Growth is a movement and a concept aimed at recognizing the negative aspects of urban sprawl and advocating a new approach to development and growth. Proponents of SMART Growth call for preservation of open spaces and rehabilitation of urban spaces and older suburbs through restoration of housing, improvement of public transportation, and promotion of community development and engagement. Two basic factions were engaged in the reauthorization debate: on one side, the environmental lobby was working to protect natural lands and wildlife from roadway construction and to minimize urban sprawl; on the other side, the transportation lobby was seeking to foster support for transportation infrastructure construction, which provides jobs and promotes commercial industries.

12. Corporate Average Fuel Economy Standards

First passed in 1975, Corporate Average Fuel Economy Standards (CAFE) regulated the fuel efficiency of automobiles, that is, how many miles the vehicle can travel on a gallon of gasoline. In 2002, with fuel prices again on the rise and increased concern about the nation's dependence on foreign oil, the CAFE standards came up for revision. The issue was hotly contested by environmental organizations and industry representatives. Environmental advocates adamantly argued for the need to improve vehicle efficiency in order to protect the environment and alleviate U.S. dependence on foreign oil, while industry representatives contested that no further technological changes were feasible and decreasing the weight of vehicles cars could endanger passengers. Further, they claimed that consumers were clearly demanding larger SUVs and thus industry production patterns were simply a reflection of consumer taste. The positions of members of Congress were largely determined along classic partisan lines.

13. Basic Education Funding for Developing Countries

Among social science academic circles the positive benefits of educating girls seem to be common knowledge. With increased education, young women can make better decisions for themselves, have fewer children, and be better able to provide for their families. At the macro level, countries with higher levels of education of both boys and girls are more productive and have higher standards of living and lower HIV/AIDS infection rates. Moreover, early education helps develop a citizenry that can contribute to national development. However, developing countries do not have the capital to invest in the education systems that could ultimately improve the situation of their countries; thus the need for external aid becomes clear. The United States has provided assistance to developing countries for basic education, which includes early childhood education through early secondary school, but advocates argue that more funding needs to be set aside for this area of developmental aid. They highlight the positive ripple effect that occurs when money is spent on education and argue that it is more effective and efficient to fund a solution at the source rather than treat the symptoms.

14. PURPA Repeal within the Energy Bill

Certain industries produce energy in addition to consuming energy during their production processes—for example, producing chemicals and plastics requires a great deal of heat and produces a great deal of steam. Instead of allowing the steam to be released through a smokestack into the environment, the energy in that steam can be harnessed through a turbine and in doing so produce electricity. Companies that were able to engage in such "cogeneration" were able to put their electricity out on the electrical grid trough the Public Utilities Regulatory Provisions Act (PURPA). The electric utilities felt it was unfair that they were forced to buy energy from these cogeneration facilities and called for the repeal of PURPA in the form of an amendment to the Energy Bill. Opponents to PURPA argued that they were forced to buy energy when it was not needed, and at high prices ultimately passed on to consumers. Proponents of PURPA countered that cogeneration facilities were still not secure in the newly liberalized energy market and needed a period of protection by the PURPA regulation. This protection was important considering the environmental benefit of cogeneration.

15. Recreation Marine Employment Act

There are thousands of small marinas across the United States, on lakes, rivers, and in coastal towns. They are recreational facilities for boats used for waterskiing, fishing, and sunbathing. Representatives of the recreational marine industry were working to make a political issue of the hefty insurance these small marinas were being forced to buy to be in compliance with U.S. law. This longshoreman insurance was intended to protect dockworkers of large industrial ports, longshoremen. The recreation marine industry was calling for legislation to exempt them from this insurance. It argued the cost of the insurance was putting small mom-and-pop operations out of business and thus people were losing jobs. The industry established a coalition of organizations to promote the bill and succeeded in finding a member of Congress to sponsor the bill.

16. Federal Public Safety Officers Amendment to the Affordable Housing for Americans Act of 2002

The Affordable Housing for Americans Act included a provision that would provide housing assistance to police officers so they could be located in communities and help control crime by being a constant presence in the neighborhood. For an unknown reason the legislative language was written to pertain only to local law enforcement. Federal officers were lobbying to be included as well. They faced no opposition. Their exclusion was a technical mistake and a technical correction was made to the legislative language through this amendment.

17. Regulations on Relationships among Affiliated Gas and Electric Producers, Pipelines, and Distributors

In the modern world of corporate America, mergers have become commonplace. In the energy sector this has led to large companies with many subunit companies, or affiliates, engaging in activities throughout the energy production process. So, for example, one large company may have an affiliate that is mining natural gas in one state, another affiliate processing that gas, another moving the gas through a pipeline across states, and another distributing the natural gas to consumers. While mergers cut redundancies and increase efficiencies, they can also lead to situations in which individuals along the line of production could be privy to information they should not know. A distributor that knows about disruptions in the gas supply before its competitors do (because it has a sister company mining gas) could unfairly benefit in the energy market, in a manner akin to insider trading in the stock market. To ensure against such unfair market activity, and in response to the Enron scandal and its effects on the California energy market, the Federal Energy Regulatory Commission (FERC) proposed a rulemaking to regulate what type of information various members of a large company had access to. Industry representatives came down both for and against the proposal since some would benefit while others envisioned considerable costs imposed by the new rules.

18. Math and Science Education Funding for K-12

The United States has seen declining test scores on standardized tests over the past few decades. This is especially marked in math and science education, traditionally more difficult subjects for students to learn. To correct this dangerous trend, advocates were calling for special funding of math and science programs that would provide extra training for grade school and high school teachers, build contacts between education and business institutions, and generally strengthen the resources devoted to math and science education. Industry, professional, and educational lobbyists argued that the nation's economic health depended on technological superiority and that superiority came from well-trained students in U.S. universities. However, if math and science were not supported from an early age, from kindergarten through high school, American students would be less and less likely to major in math- and science-intensive subjects in college. Ultimately, this self-reinforcing process would mean the country would fall behind in technological competitiveness. Proponents of math and science funding did not face opposition, but did face the ubiquitous problem of finite budget resources.

19. NIH Funding for the Cystic Fibrosis Clinical Research Network

Patient advocates, pharmaceutical manufacturers, and scientists of the National Institutes of Health (NIH) all contributed to the founding of the Therapeutics Development Network, a network of universities, research institutes, and pharmaceutical companies working to develop new treatments for cystic fibrosis. The network achieved considerable advances in medications and streamlined the process of clinical trials. Although the network had been in existence for many years, advocates were seeking more funding from NIH in addition to promoting the structure of the clinical trials network as a model for other disease groups. There was no opposition to their position but there is always the impediment of finite funding for the thousands of diseases that need attention.

20. Stock Option Expensing

When a manufacturing company buys new machinery or a service industry firm hires new partners, the money spent on those acquisitions goes into the company's accounting as an expense, ultimately affecting the bottom line and net profits. However when CEOs and rank-and-file workers are given stock options—the option to buy stock at a certain price at some point in the future—this form of compensation does not get figured into the company's books. Following the Enron/Worldcom scandals, in which the companies' true financial health was masked so investors would not be alarmed, regulators, citizen groups, and some industry advocates began calling for the expensing of stock options—allowing options to be included as expenses on a company's books. Proponents argued it was necessary to protect shareholders. Opponents claimed since stock prices change from hour to hour, there is no clear way to determine how much stock options are worth and thus it is impossible to expense them.

21. Reform of the Food Quality Protection Act

The aim of the Food Quality Protection Act was to regulate the level of pesticides used on food. Through scientific testing and regulations of farming use of pesticides EPA ensured human consumption of pesticide residue was not at dangerous levels. The EPA felt the policy was a success. However industry advocates argued that the way EPA made its decisions about what pesticides were approved and about what levels were acceptable was not transparent. They claimed it was unclear which pesticide companies would receive clearance and which would be denied. They called for modifications to the scientific methodology used by EPA in the regulatory process.

EU ISSUES
1. Data Retention

The measures in this controversial proposal have been compared to those found in the U.S. Patriot Act. The European-level regulation would require sectors of the telecommunication industry—fixed telephony, mobile telephony, and internet service providers—to retain all traffic data for a certain time period. Traffic data are information on where people go on the internet, what they buy, whom they call, who calls them, where they call from, and so forth. Retention of traffic data would allow law enforcement authorities to consult the stored information, if the need arose, to track down criminals. The legislation was a Council framework decision that was promoted by four member states—Sweden, Ireland, France, and the United Kingdom. Since it was a justice and home affairs issue it required a unanimous vote by the member states and limited the input of the EP since it follows a consultation procedure. The major stakeholders were representatives of the telecommunication industry and law enforcement, in the form of national law enforcement agencies, the EU-level organization EUROPOL and the international-level organization INTERPOL. Two focusing events occurred that had an impact on the debate: the Madrid train bombings in March 2004 and the London Tube bombings in July 2005.

2. Outermost Regions

While the visibility and importance of regions in EU politics is quite established, with the existence of the committee of regions and the seemingly constant influx of representations from new European regions to the European capital, one set of regions receives considerably less attention—the ultraperipherical regions (UPC) or more simply "the outermost regions." These are regions that are far removed from the Continent, the overseas territories, and departments of the European member states. The UPCs include the four French overseas departments of Guadeloupe, French Guiana, Martinique, and Reunion (in the Indian Ocean); the Spanish autonomous community of the Canary Islands; and the Portuguese autonomous regions of the Azores and Madeira. These regions are defined as part of the European Union by the foundational Treaties and receive structural funds to aid in their development. With the enlargement of the European Union to twenty-five in May of 2004, the regions were concerned that their structural fund support would be diluted and were seeking to ensure their continued funding. These regions argued that they faced unique obstacles such as tropical climate and diseases, narrowness of surface area, reliance on single cash crops, and proximity to undeveloped countries.

3. PHARE Funds

The mark of EU financial support may sometimes seem quite ubiquitous, from building projects in regions with structural fund development, to independent European films, to NGO publications. In Europe acknowledgments thanking the support of the European Union are often seen. All of the various EU grant programs involve a detailed application process that actors seeking support must navigate. One of the myriad grant programs is the PHARE small projects funds, a program to foster development in the regions previously referred to as candidate countries, now known as the new member states. One organized interest was working in 2004 to get a small slice of those funds for a program of conferences to foster business relationships between Western European member states and the ten new member states.

4. REACH

After two years of discussing a green paper on the topic, the Commission released a draft regulation on European chemical policy called REACH, an acronym for Registration, Evaluation, Authorization, and Restriction of Chemicals. The legislation would force the European chemical industry to register thirty thousand chemicals. As a draft regulation it goes through the normal process of codecision, making its way through the Commission, Council, and EP. The chemical industry is clearly one of the largest players in this debate, but many other industrial sectors that use chemicals in the processing and manufacturing of other products also have a stake in the outcome. On the other side, the Group of 8, the green lobbying alliance, was lobbying vigorously supporting the Commission proposal with issue ads, press campaigns, and inside lobbying. Due to the massive scope of the regulation and the uncertainty of its feasibility the Commission called for a test run of the proposal. Beginning November 1, 2004, selected companies from various industry sectors would follow the registration procedure for nine chemicals to inform decision makers of the regulatory burden.

5. Automobile Market Liberalization Implementation

A directive was passed in 2003 that incrementally liberalized the aftermarket automotive industry. In 2006 the regulation was to move to the next level, whereby an automobile dealer that had been accepted as a car dealer anywhere in the European Union would legally be allowed to open a business in any other member state. After 2010 the directive would cease to regulate the aftermarket auto industry and there would be a totally free market. In 2004 trade organizations most affected by the liberalization of the market were monitoring the implementation of the directive very closely—whether member states were transposing it quickly and correctly into national law and whether businesses in the member states were complying with the new rules. In cases where there appeared to be noncompliance the interested organizations would notify the Commission. It was then in the Commission's hands to assess if there was indeed evidence of noncompliance and take action against the member states or compel a member state to take action against a wayward business. Thus EU industry associations were acting as de facto watchdogs of the implementation of the directive in the process of protecting their own interests.

6. Social Dialogue on Crystalline Silica in the Workplace

Crystalline silica is a group of minerals composed of one atom of silicon and two atoms of oxygen; the chemical formula is SiO_2. It has been used by humans for thousands of years to produce things like glass, cement, and ceramics and today is used in the high-tech industry to produce silicon chips. When it is in its raw material form it appears as powder or sand. Prolonged exposure to respirable particles of crystalline silica has been shown to result in a lung disease referred to as silicosis. Considering the danger to worker health, advocates argued some type of EU regulation of the level of silica in the workplace was necessary. Regulation could take the form of an official piece of legislation from the European Union or a social dialogue agreement worked out between employers and employees, endorsed by the Commission. Each regulation option has pros and cons on both sides of the debate. Some industry representatives would have preferred the more straightforward EU legislation route, where some minimal level of compliance had to be met. On the other hand, the social dialogue route was more flexible and private actors had more say in the development of the agreement. Due to the limited resources of the EU institutions, if industry can self-regulate in certain sectors, this is often embraced by the Commission; such was the case in regulating the level of crystalline silica in the workplace. The parties involved ultimately opted for a social dialogue process that put in motion a series of meetings between employers drafting a proposed social dialogue agreement, followed by additional meetings with union representatives. Meetings of a working party of industry representatives were held leading up to a series of meetings with labor to negotiate a level of regulation acceptable to both sides.

7. Services Directive

One of the primary agenda items of the Barroso Commission, which came into office in November 2004, was the realization of the Lisbon agenda—a blueprint for making the European Union the most competitive and dynamic market by 2010. A keystone in that process, the new Commission argued, was the opening of the market on services. The directive on services in the internal market was the legislative framework that would bring it about. Considering the scope of the proposed directive and the share of the European market that services constitutes, it is not surprising that debate was highly charged. The "principle of origin" was by far the most contentious point. This principle states when a service provider wants to operate in another member state then the provider must comply with the regulations in his or her home country. Thus, if a foreign service provider, such as a Danish travel agent, was active in Spain, that provider would be required to follow only Danish regulations. While this principle would simplify and thus foster the provision of services across borders, many trade and professional associations as well as member states' governments held strong reservations about the feasibility and accountability of a system that would ultimately be based on mutual trust that foreign service providers were complying with the regulations of their home nation.

8. Services of General Interest Framework Directive

The European Parliament, always eager to increase its role in the legislative process, has increasingly used various types of communications to compel the Commission to introduce legislation on a topic. It did just this when it called on the Commission in early 2001 to draft a green paper on a framework directive in the area of "Services of General Interest." The concept of services of general interest varies across member states and does not even exist in some. However the Commission, EP, the economic and social committee, and the committee of the regions all considered the topic in various communications and reports in 2003 and 2004 with the aim of creating harmonized EU policy in the sector. The Commission's green paper states "[i]t covers a broad range of different types of activities, from certain activities in the big network industries (energy, postal services, transport, and telecommunications) to health, education, and social services, of different dimensions, from European or even global" (COM(2003) 270).

The green paper's aim was to launch a debate on EU-level action in the area of services of general interest. It emphasizes the need to balance the tenets of the internal market (specifically rules against state aid) with the need to ensure the smooth and efficient provision of basic services to European citizens. The green paper encourages discussion on the proper level of EU regulation in this area, and on whether a general framework approach or an approach by sector would be preferable. Central players in the debate are, of course, the corporations and organizations of corporations providing services of general interest. A major provider of services of general interest was actively trying to block the progression of EU legislation in this area, preferring that the idea remain in the "idea stage" of the green paper and not progress toward an actual proposed directive from the Commission.

9. Getting Public Health on the EU Agenda

As early as the 1997 Amsterdam Treaty, public health had a place in EU law. Article 152 of the Treaty called for "[c]ommunity action, which shall complement national policies, shall be directed towards improving public health, preventing human illness and diseases, and obviating sources of danger to human health" (Amsterdam Treaty, Title XIII). However, as of 2004, the European Union was still not actively legislating in the area of public health, nor was the issue receiving much space on the agenda. Advocates of increased EU legislation related to public health took the Intergovernmental Conference on the new Treaty Establishing a Constitution for Europe as an opportunity to promote the place of public health on the EU agenda and to advocate for increased ability of the EU institutions to legislate in this area. They worked to get more concrete language and commitment by the European Union to become more active in this area. Although the debate was often misdirected, focusing on the "hot" issues of bioterrorism and communicable diseases like SARS, advocates were successful in getting two full pages of treaty space devoted to public health. However, changes in the treaty were only one part of the much broader campaign. Their efforts were welcomed by the public health commissioner (of the Prodi Commission), David Byrne, who was supportive of EU-level action in this area and initiated an open consultation to foster discussion on the topic.

10. Community Clause in Aviation Agreements

In the international aviation industry there are bilateral agreements between countries, which lay out the rules governing the activities of the carriers of each nation, including how many flights are allowed, how often, to what destination, by what carriers, and so forth. Every country that is a member of the European Union separately negotiates these bilateral agreements with the countries to which it flies. In 2002 the ECJ ruled that one clause in those bilateral agreements, the "national clause," is illegal. It states that a national carrier can be designated to fly certain routes; for example, Spain could designate Iberia to fly the Madrid–New York route. Such clauses are in breach of the EU Treaties, which say there can be no discrimination or preference based on nationality.

The bilateral agreements favor the national carrier and discriminate against carriers from other member states. The Commission is now trying to get member states to replace that national clause with a community clause that says a carrier from any member state can be designated to fly certain routes. However, since the ECJ ruling the member states have refused to alter their bilateral agreements because doing so would result in considerable conflict with their national carriers. The Commission's next step is to begin infringement proceedings against the member states in the ECJ to force them to change their agreements.

11. Development Heading in the EU Budget

Every year the Commission proposes a budget for the European Union and the Council and EP vote on that proposal. In addition, the Commission proposes seven-year financial perspectives, which provide a fiscal blueprint for the years ahead. In 2004, the EU institutions were considering both the annual budget and the 2007–2013 financial perspectives.

Advocates of EU aid to developing countries have been working for years for a technical change in the structure of EU budget language, which would in turn result in a real-world change in how the European Union deals with certain developing countries. Countries in Latin America, Asia, and the Mediterranean have traditionally been under Heading 19 – External Trade in the EU budget, but advocates wish to see these countries shifted to Heading 21 – Development. They argue the heading influences the objectives or the philosophy of the European Union's approach to the countries in each area. If a country is under external relations, then interactions surround trade and focus on the economic interest of the European Union as a trading block. If it is under development it is a different philosophy, focusing on aid to the developing country to build schools and foster local economic growth. While it might appear such a seemingly technical revision would face little opposition, this is far from the case. There are certain member states that trade with nations in these regions and are very aware of the real-world changes that would result from this technical shift. These member states have an economic stake in the continuation of the status quo. National pressure is sufficiently strong that officials in the Council and MEPs across political groups are toeing the national line.

12. Cold Storage Room ETA

While major pieces of legislation are usually passed via the visible process of co-decision, volumes of regulations are being implemented through a process that receives considerably less attention from academics, observers, and the media. Standard setting, through various standard-setting bodies, is being conducted on nearly everything imaginable, with the intent to make the internal market work more efficiently. One example of these countless consultations and subsequent regulations is cold storage rooms, structures that keep things, most often food, cold. To keep workers safe inside, and the food processed within them safe, acceptable criteria were debated and agreed upon by the competent regulatory bodies from each of the member states. Every aspect of the cold room was considered, from the impact capacity of the structure, to the flammability of the walls, to the durability of the unit, to the ventilation. Not only were the acceptable characteristics and levels agreed upon but so too were the techniques to assess those characteristics harmonized. With the standardization of cold room regulations, cold rooms manufactured and sold anywhere in the European Union would be of the same quality.

13. Aromatic Oils

While the name conjures up the scent of harmless patchouli, aromatic oils are in fact the common name of polycyclic aromatic hydrocarbons (or PAHs). These oils are used in converting plastics and rubber, especially for car tires. But more importantly a number have been proven carcinogenic, mutagenic, and reprotoxic (damaging to reproduction). As a result, EU law calls for the phasing out of these oils in the production of automobile tires (by amending a directive passed in the 1970s on dangerous substances, 76/796/EEC). While the tire industry sees the proposed policy as a foregone conclusion, it is simply requesting a longer phaseout period to buffer the economic impact on business. However, the industry is not speaking with a wholly unified voice; there are members of the industry working independently for an outright exemption to the legislation. Their claim is that certain specialty automobiles require specialty tires that can only be manufactured with the use of aromatic oils, such as race cars and Hummers with bulletproof tires. The oils have been proven to increase the traction of tires in wet conditions; thus advocates argue that while the oils do constitute some level of risk to human health as carcinogens, tires created without them could lead to more immediate health risks from an auto safety standpoint. Debate on the proposed directive was conducted through the codecision procedure.

14. Codex on Fruit Juice

As globalization continues to progress and global markets become ever more intertwined, global dispute resolution through international institutions like the World

Trade Organization (WTO) becomes critically important. Minimizing and solving disputes is aided by global standards, which provide a foundation of a basic level of practices for producing, packaging, marketing, and selling products in the world's markets. A fundamental area of standard setting is in the foodstuff sector. An international standard setting system, the Codex Alimentarius, was organized by the Food and Agricultural Organization of the United Nations and the World Health Organization (WHO) in 1963. However due to the increasing need for clearly defined standards by organizations like WTO, and at the organization's impetus, the process of negotiating and setting standards had been catapulted forward in the last decade. Within the food industry standards for specific sectors are negotiated by ad hoc task forces hosted by a member country. In the case of fruit juices, of concern to some organized EU interests, working groups were hosted by and held in Brazil, with member countries from around the world meeting, debating, and deciding the standards for fruit juices. At the table were the major juice producers and processors including the United States, Brazil, Germany, France, and Italy. In addition to individual nations, the European Commission was also present and was also granted a vote, to represent the trading block as a whole. Thus, lobbying on the part of the sector was necessary not only in national capitals but also in Brussels to ensure the Commission was in line with the European fruit juice industry representatives.

15. Reduced VAT for Construction

The value added tax (VAT) is a sales tax found on goods and services throughout the European Union. There is a normal rate, set at a minimum of 15 percent but the actual rate varies across member states. In France, for example, it is 19 percent, in Belgium 21 percent, and in Germany 17 percent. The first VAT directive was in 1967; after a number of rounds of revisions, in 2004 it was referred to as the 6th Directive on VAT. In that version there were reduced VAT rates on certain products; these derogations are found in Annex H; in Eurospeak it is referred to as Annex H of the 6th Directive. While Annex H includes social housing, the construction industry was actively lobbying to have all private building maintenance and repair services included as well. Due to difficulties in the building sector, advocates argued that reducing the VAT in construction could bolster the industry, create jobs, and discourage consumers from turning to the black market in construction. They were successful in getting the Commission to propose a framework by which member states could experiment with reducing the VAT in certain sectors, construction being one of them, to study the effect on growing the economy in those sectors. The authorization was given in 1999 to conduct studies through 2002. After the three-year period member states were to report their findings to the Commission. The summary of results was to form the basis on which the Council would rely in their decision to make a permanent change to the VAT directive's Annex. Since the VAT is part of the financial affairs portfolio, it is governed by the unanimity rule in the Council; the Parliament has no formal role in the debate. The Council became deadlocked because of the need for unanimity and the unwillingness of some member states to approve of the change. The Commission decided to bypass the gridlock by extending the experimental period one more year, until 2003.

16. CAFE—Clean Air for Europe

CAFE is the acronym denoting a Commission initiative to develop a package of legislation for cleaner air across the European Union. By 2001 numerous directives were up for evaluation and renewal and the Commission decided to consider them together under one framework. The goal was the adoption of a thematic strategy on air pollution by 2005 designed to protect the environment and human health. In order to draft this substantial air quality program the Commission established a secretariat and organized a steering group composed of member states, MEPs, and interest groups that met several times a year up to the 2005 deadline. The working groups were organized into the areas of target setting and policy assessment, particulate matter, and implementation. External research institutes contributed to the scientific work, developing models and running simulations on various regulatory scenarios. In addition to the environmental lobby, industry advocates included those from heavy industry, the energy sector, and the automobile sector. Industry activity was coordinated by the pan-EU business association UNICE.

17. Package Environment Indicator Amendment on Packaging and Packaging Waste

The first Packaging and Packaging Waste Directive was passed in the early 1990s, with the goal of minimizing the environmental impact of packaging. In 2004 the directive was up for reevaluation. Some advocates and the rapporteur in the Parliament were pushing for a PEI—a Package Environment Indicator—amendment to the directive. The PEI would be a mark on packaging indicating its environmental impact. The idea is if a discerning consumer were faced with two products the consumer would choose the one with more environmentally friendly packaging. This is similar to energy efficiency labels on appliances.

Although the amendment did not gain enough support, the final version of the 2004 revision included a requirement for a study to be completed by June 30, 2005, assessing the implementation of the directive, and considering additional measures that could be used to minimize packaging and packaging waste, including a PEI. Industry advocates continued to communicate to policymakers that the PEI was unworkable; it was unclear how the "environmental performance of packaging" could be measured.

18. NGO Cofinancing Amendments

The annual EU budget covers a large range of policy areas, and the language that gets approved in the annual budget has far-reaching consequences for subsequent decisions throughout the year. While previous budget language had been favorable to NGO foundations, the language changed in the 2004 budget proposal; NGOs were working to introduce four amendments to change the language back to the original, specifically regarding how the European Union cofinances and cooperates with NGOs for development.

19. Consumer Credit Directive

While the debate on the Consumer Credit Directive (CCD) could often be found in the Brussels news throughout 2002, 2003, 2004, and 2005 it was not exactly new—the four-year-long debate concerned the revision of the original Consumer Credit Directive of 1987 (87/102/EEC). The goals of the original and the revision are ultimately an internal market in consumer credit, in which EU citizens could compare credit lenders across the European Union and decide where they would like to borrow from, without barriers. However, the specific rules that would bring such an internal market to fruition were hotly debated, with the Commission, the Parliament, the banking industry, and consumer advocates all weighing in. There was strong disagreement between the institutions, with the Parliament arguing the Commission's proposal was underdeveloped and outdated. In addition, there was a classic industry versus citizen group battle, as banking representatives attempted to protect their interests while consumer protection organizations sought to protect the public.

20. Communication on Business Organization

What is a fundamental issue to one organization may not seem to be an issue at all to others. A subnational business organization was lobbying the European Commission to issue a communication regarding the organization of an influential pan-European business lobby, of which the subnational group was a member. Essentially, an internal dispute of a business association led to the weaker party expanding the scope of conflict by reaching out to the European Commission. The hope was that the Commission could put some pressure on the Eurogroup to change its ways, but without the Eurogroup knowing of the subnational group's activities. Needless to say, due to the clandestine nature of the appeal, no other organizations were active on this case.

21. Self-Regulation of Alcohol Ads

The tobacco industry was dealt quite a blow when the Commission passed regulations restricting the advertising of tobacco products. Producers of alcoholic beverages did not want to find themselves subject to similar regulations and thus began working early on to draw up an industry code of conduct and to speak with the relevant Commission officials about the feasibility and desirability of industry self-regulation. In 2004–2005 there was a mix of legislation and self-regulation. Public health advocates and alcohol prevention organizations were arguing that self-regulation did not work and that stricter regulations needed to be put in place. They emphasized that alcohol is not like any other commodity, its use has effects not only on the user but also on those around the user, with alcohol often leading to alcohol-related injuries. With the aim of reducing alcohol consumption they argued against all lifestyle advertising, that is, ads should not show situations that symbolically represent the lifestyle one could live if one consumed the product. They also called for restrictions on when alcohol ads could be shown on television (i.e., after a certain time in the evening) or during sporting events, notorious for alcohol-related injuries. Representatives of the alcohol industry were arguing for continuation of the status quo, claiming that industry codes of conduct and the public education campaigns industry supports are sufficient controls.

22. Telecom Liberalization Implementation

The classic story is that in some European countries like England and Belgium, it used to take up to nine months to get a phone, and then when you got it, you could have it anywhere in your house as long as it was in the hallway. The days of bad telephone service subsided with the opening of the market, but the process is not yet wholly complete in the European Union. Industry organizations continue to monitor the liberalization of the telecommunication sector across EU member states and notify the Commission whenever they detect a member state's failure to implement the EU regulations or a company in breach of EU law. This was the activity of advocates interviewed on this case.

23. Integrated Product Policy

Whether it is a simple wooden bench or a complex Blackberry with Bluetooth technology, all products have a history and a future. The aim of integrated product policy is to recognize the entire life cycle of a given product and consider its environmental impact at each stage. From extracting raw resources, through manufacturing, packaging, and sale, to use, and ultimately disposal, the manufacturing of products can damage the environment. By working to minimize that damage at each step of the way, we can create more environmentally friendly goods. While the goal seems commendable, how to attain it remains a matter of debate. The Commission released a green paper on the topic in 2001, followed by stakeholder consultation and another communication in 2003, but as late as 2005, the way forward was still unclear. Many environmental organizations are seeking clear legislation from the Commission to compel industry to act, while industry would prefer softer policy instruments like ecolabels and voluntary agreements. A turf battle between DG Environment and DG Enterprise has further stalled development of a coherent integrated product policy.

24. Regulation of Live Animal Transport

Millions of animals are transported across Europe for slaughter and consumption every year. Animal welfare activists argue that the duration of these trips can be extremely long and the conditions the animals endure are characterized by lack of water, food, ventilation, and climate control. Activists have continued to push hard for Commission regulations on transportation conditions, midtransit breaks to allow animals to be fed and watered, and maximum driving times. Activists argue that this is not only an animal welfare issue but also a consumer health concern, as incidents of BSE (mad cow disease) and avian influenza have increased over the past decade. A healthier animal means safer meat. The livestock industry and the livestock transportation industry argued that while conditions are not optimal, the best policy option was not new regulations but stronger enforcement of existing rules. This line of thinking led to the innovative monitoring method of placing GPS on trucks transporting live animals so they could then be tracked by the European Union's satellite Galileo.

25. Piracy of Conditional Access TV

Television viewing has come a long way from the days of bunny ears and three channels. Today satellite and cable television bring hundreds of channels into people's homes. Conditional access television is a system whereby only viewers that pay for the service can have access to the channels. However the system is not foolproof. Television piracy is done by unscrambling the channels and stealing the service. The conditional access industry, which includes the service providers and the producers and suppliers of conditional access technology and hardware, is monitoring the implementation of the Conditional Access Directive, and continues to push for stricter EU regulation against conditional access piracy. The industry is also working to promote a culture of antipiracy before the EU institutions. It faces no opposition to its arguments; but finds gaining the attention of policymakers for this fairly arcane topic difficult.

26. Trafficking in Children

It is estimated that 1.2 million children are trafficked globally each year, and one million children are forced to enter the sex trade, according to Save the Children International. To work to decrease the number of children abducted, abused, and exploited, the European Union has launched a number of initiatives, including a Council Framework Decision in 2002 combating trafficking in human beings; a European conference in late 2002 on preventing and combating trafficking in human beings, which led to the Brussels Declaration and the 2003 Framework Decision on sexual exploitation of children and child pornography. In 2004 further action was seen on the topic with the May 26, 2004, roundtable on EU action against child trafficking and related forms of exploitation and the October consultative workshop on the report of the experts group.

There are two different approaches to combating the international phenomenon of child trafficking: One, a law enforcement approach that focuses on border control and on catching and prosecuting the traffickers is supported by member state law enforcement and international organizations active in the area of migration. The second is a more holistic approach, which includes consideration of the rights of the child; the root causes of trafficking including abject poverty, which leads parents to sell their children; public communication campaigns to raise awareness; and rehabilitation and reintegration of children who have been victims of trafficking. This latter approach is the approach being advocated by human rights and children's rights organizations.

References

Anderson, Jeffrey J. 2002. Europeanization and the transformation of the Democratic polity, 1945–2000. *Journal of Common Market Studies* 40 (2002): 793–822.

Arnold, R. Douglas. 1990. *The logic of congressional action.* New Haven: Yale University Press.

Austen-Smith, David, and John R. Wright. 1994. Counteractive lobbying. *American Journal of Political Science* 38:25–44.

Avner, Marcia. 2002. *The lobbying and advocacy handbook for nonprofit organizations.* Saint Paul, Minn.: Amherst H. Wilder Foundation.

Bacheller, John. 1977. Lobbyists and the legislative process: The impact of environmental constraints. *American Political Science Review* 71:242–63.

Bachrach, Peter, and Morton Baratz. 1962. The two faces of power. *American Political Science Review* 56:947–52.

Bauer, Raymond A., Ithiel de Sola Pool, and Lewis A. Dexter. 1963. *American business and public policy: The politics of foreign trade.* New York: Atherton Press.

Baumgartner, Frank R., and Bryan Jones. 1993. *Agendas and instability in American politics.* Chicago: University of Chicago Press.

Baumgartner, Frank R., and Beth L. Leech. 1998. *Basic interests: The importance of groups in politics and in political science.* Princeton, N.J.: Princeton University Press.

———. 2001. Interest niches and policy bandwagons: Patterns of interest group involvement in national politics. *Journal of Politics* 64:1191–213.

Baumgartner, Frank R., and Christine Mahoney. 2004. Social movements and the rise of new issues. In *Routing the opposition: Social movements, public policy and democracy,* eds. Helen Ingram, Valerie Jenness, and David S. Meyer, 65–86. Minneapolis: University of Minnesota Press.

Benford, Robert, and David A. Snow. 2000. Framing processes and social movements: An overview and assessment. *Annual Review of Sociology* 26:611–39.

Bentley, Arthur F. 1908. *The process of government.* Chicago: University of Chicago Press.

Berry, Jeffrey M. 1989. *The interest group society.* 2nd ed. New York: HarperCollins.

Beyers, Jan. 2002. Gaining and seeking access: The European adaptation of domestic interest associations. *European Journal of Political Research* 41:586–612.

———. 2004. Voice and access: Political practices of European interest associations. *European Union Politics*. 5:211–40.

Boin, Arjen, and Paul t'Hart. 2003. Public leadership in times of crisis: Mission impossible? *Public Administration Review* 63(5): 544–53.

Bomberg, Elizabeth, Laura Cram, and David Martin. 2003. The EU's institutions. In *The European Union: How does it work?*, eds. Elizabeth Bomberg and Alexander Stubb, 43–68. Oxford: Oxford University Press.

Borchardt, Klaus-Dieter. 1999. The ABC of community law. 5th ed. Luxembourg: Office for Official Publications of the European Communities. www.europa.eu.int/eur-lex/en/about/abc_en.pdf.

Börzel, Tanja A. 2002. Pace-setting, foot-dragging, and fence-sitting; member state responses to Europeanization. *Journal of Common Market Studies* 40:193–214.

Bounds, Andrew, and Laura Dixon. 2007. Brussels to toughen rules on lobbyists. *Financial Times*, October 9, 2007.

Bouwen, Pieter. 2002. Corporate lobbying in the European Union: The logic of access. *Journal of European Public Policy* 9(3): 365–90.

Boyd, Chris. 2002. Lafarge and global warming. In *European Union lobbying: Changes in the arena*, ed. Robin Pedler, 57–86. Palgrave: Basingstoke.

Browne, William P. 1995. Organized interests, grassroots confidants, and Congress. In *Interest group politics*. 4th ed., eds. Allan J. Ciglar and Burdett A. Loomis. Washington, D.C.: CQ Press.

Burnstein, Paul. 2003. The impact of public opinion on public policy: A review and an agenda. *Political Research Quarterly* 56: 29–40.

Burson-Marsteller/Wirthlin-Europe. 2003. *A guide to effective lobbying of the European Commission*. Spring.

Bush, Evelyn, and Pete Simi. 2001. European farmers and their protests. In *Contentious Europeans: Protest and politics in an emerging polity*, eds. Doug Imig and Sidney Tarrow, 97–124. Lanham, Md.: Rowman & Littlefield Publishers.

Byrd, Robert C. 1987. Lobbyists. An essay by the senate majority leader. September 28. www.senate.gov/legislative/common/briefing/Byrd_History_Lobbying.htm.

Caldeira, Gregory, and John R. Wright. 1990. Amici curiae before the Supreme Court: Who participates, when, and how much? *The Journal of Politics* 52:782–806.

Campbell, James I. 1994. Couriers and the postal monopolies. In *Lobbying the European Union. companies, trade associations and issue groups*, eds. Robin H. Pedler and M.P.C.M van Schendelen, 123–48. Aldershot: Dartmouth.

Cater, S. Douglass. 1964. *Power in Washington*. New York: Random House.

———. 1959. *Fourth branch of government*. Boston: Houghton Mifflin.

Cawson, Alan. 1992. Interests, groups and public policy-making: The case of the European consumer electronics industry. In *Organized interests and the European community*, eds. Justin Greenwood, Jurgen R. Grote, and Karsten Ronit, 99–118. London: SAGE Publications.

Christiansen, Thomas. 1996. A maturing bureaucracy? The role of the commission in the policy process, in *European Union, power and policy-making*, ed. Jeremy Richardson, 135–54. New York: Routledge.

Clark, Peter B., and James Q. Wilson. 1961. Incentive systems: A theory of organizations. *Administrative Science Quarterly* 6:129–66.

Coen, David. 1997. The evolution of the large firm as a political actor in the European Union. *Journal of European Public Policy* 4(1): 91–108.

———. 1999. The impact of U.S. lobbying practice on the European business-government relationships. *California Management Review* 41(4): 27–44.

———. 2002. Business interests and European integration. In *L'action collective en Europe*, eds. Richard Balme, Didier Chabanet, and Vincent Wright, 255–72. Paris: Presses de Sciences Po.

———. 2004. Environmental and business lobbying alliances in Europe: Learning from Washington? in *Business in international environmental governance: A political economy approach*, eds. D. Levy and P. Newell, 197–220. Cambridge, Mass.: MIT Press.

Cohen, Michael, James March, and Johan Olsen. 1972. A garbage can model of organizational choice. *Administrative Science Quarterly* 17:1–25.

Composition du Bureau du Parlement, January 16, 2002. www.europarl.eu.int/orgpresi/default_en.htm.

Congressional Record. 109th Cong., 1st sess., 2005. Resume of congressional activity. Daily Digest. February 15, D97.

Cook, Timothy E. 2005. *Governing with the news: The news media as a political institution*. 2nd ed. Chicago: University of Chicago Press.

Corporate Europe Observatory. Curbing corporate lobbying power. October 25, 2004. www.corporateeurope.org/barroso.html.

Cowles, Maria Green. 2001. The transatlantic business dialogue and domestic business-government relations. In *Transforming Europe. Europeanization and domestic change*, eds. Maria Green Cowles, James A. Caporaso, and Thomas Risse, 159–79. Ithaca, N.Y.: Cornell University Press.

Cress, Daniel, and David Snow. 1998. Mobilization at the margins: Organizing by the homeless. In *Social movements and American political institutions*, eds. Anne Costain and Andrew McFarland, 73–98. Lanham, Md.: Rowman & Littlefield Publishers.

Cronin, David. 2005. London's Washington wish-list. *European Voice* June 30–July 6: 34.

Dahl, Robert A. 1956. *A preface to democratic theory*. Chicago: University of Chicago Press.

———. 1957. The concept of power. *Behavioral Science* 2:201–15.

———. 1961. *Who governs?* New Haven: Yale University Press.

De Bièvre, Dirk, and Andreas Dür. 2007. Introduction: Researching interest group influence on policymaking in Europe and the United States. *Journal of Public Policy* 27(1): 112.

Dinan, Desmond. 1999. *Ever closer union: An introduction to European integration*. 2d ed. Boulder: Lynne Rienner.

———. 2005. *Ever closer union: An introduction to European integration*. 3rd ed. Boulder: Lynne Rienner.

Downs, Anthony. 1957. *An economic theory of democracy*. New York: Harper and Row.

Dür, Andreas. 2005. How to assess power and influence? Paper presented at the
    CONNEX research group 4, Civil Society and Interest Representation in EU-
    Governance, Leiden, The Netherlands, April 14–16.
Edwards, Geoffrey. 1996. National sovereignty vs. integration? The Council of Min-
    isters. In *European Union, Power and Policy-Making.* Ed. Jeremy Richardson. New
    York: Routledge.
Eising, Rainer. 2005. Patterns of interest intermediation in the European Union. Paper
    presented at the CONNEX research group 4, Civil Society and Interest Repre-
    sentation in EU-Governance, Leiden, The Netherlands, April 14–16.
Esterling, Kevin M. 2005. *The political economy of expertise: Information and efficiency
    in American national politics.* Ann Arbor: University of Michigan Press.
EurActiv. 2005a. EU and US approaches to lobbying. February 17, 2005. www.euractiv.com
    /Article?tcmuri=tcm:29-135509-16&type=LinksDossier.
———. 2005b. Clean air strategy seeks balance between health and business concerns.
    September 21, 2005. www.euractiv.com/en/environment/clean-air-strategy-seeks-
    balance-health-business-concerns/article-144604.
———. 2005c. Data retention: Parliament caves in to council pressure. December 14,
    2005. www.euractive.com/en/infosociety/data-retention-parliament-caves-coun-
    cil-pressure/article-150891.
———. 2007. Interview: Kallas confident on lobbyists' register and new initiatives. 10
    May 2007. http://www.euractiv.com/en/pa/interview-kallas-confident-lobbyists-
    reegister-new-initiatives/article-163701.
Eurelectric. 2005. EURELECTRIC takes issue with elements of EU thematic strategy on
    air pollution and legislative proposal on air quality. Press release. December 2.
Europa. 2004. A constitution for Europe. http://europa.eu.int/constitution/en/
    lstoc1_en.htm.
———. 2005. Codecision step-by-step. European Commission. www.europa.eu.int/
    comm/codecision/index_en.htm.
———. 2006. Europa glossary. www.europa.eu/scadplus/glossary/index_en.htm.
European Commission. 2003. Green paper on services of general interest. Presented
    by the European Commission. Brussels, May 21, 2003. COM(2003) 270 final.
European Environmental Bureau. 2005. Air thematic strategy is far too weak, says EEB.
    Press release. September 21.
European Parliament. 2004. Co-decision step-by-step. www.europarl.eu.int.
———. 2005. The European parliament's new website is aimed primarily at the
    citizens of the European Union. September 10. www.europarl.eu.int/news/
    public/focus_page/008-977-255-9-37-901-20050819FCS00976-12-09-2005-
    2005/default_en.htm.
European Public Affairs Directory. 2004. 14th ed. Brussels, Belgium: Landmarks
    Publishing.
European Voice. 2005. Why the fine art defies digits and definition. Editorial. *European
    Voice* September 22–28.
Fenno, Richard F., Jr. 1978. *Homestyle.* Boston: Little Brown and Co.
Fligstein, Neil, and Alec Stone Sweet. 2002. Constructing polities and markets: An in-
    stitutionalist account of European integration. *American Journal of Sociology*
    107:1206–43.

Follesdal, Andreas, and Simon Hix. 2006. Why there is a Democratic deficit in the EU: A response to Majone and Moravcsik. *Journal of Common Market Studies* 44(3): 533–62.

Fritschler, A. Lee. 1975. *Smoking and politics.* 2nd ed. Englewood Cliffs, N.J.: Prentice Hall.

Gabel, Matthew. 2003. Public support for the European parliament. *Journal of Common Market Studies* 41(2): 191–202.

Gais, Thomas, and Jack L. Walker, Jr. 1991. Pathways to influence in American politics. In *Mobilizing interest groups in America,* ed. Jack L. Walker Jr., 103–22. Ann Arbor: University of Michigan.

Gerber, Elizabeth R. 1999. *The populist paradox.* Princeton: Princeton University Press.

Gillingham, John. 2003. *European integration 1950–2003: Superstate or new market economy?* Cambridge: Cambridge University Press.

Goldstein, Kenneth M. 1999. *Interest groups, lobbying, and participation in America.* New York: Cambridge University Press.

Greenwood, Justin. 1994. Pharma and biotech. In *Lobbying the European Union: Companies, trade associations and issue groups,* eds. Robin H. Pedler and M.P.C.M van Schendelen, 183–98. Aldershot: Dartmouth.

———. 1997. *Representing interests in the European Union.* New York: St. Martin's Press.

———. 2002. *Inside the EU business associations.* New York: Palgrave.

Griffith, Ernest S. 1939. *The impasse of democracy, a study of the modern government in action.* New York: Harrison-Hilton Books, Inc.

Grossman, Emiliano. 2004. Bringing politics back in: Rethinking the role of economic interest groups in European integration. *Journal of European Public Policy* 11(4): 637–54.

Guyer, Robert L. 2003. *Guide to state legislative lobbying.* Gainsville, Fla.: Engineering The Law, Inc.

Habermas, Jürgen. 2001. Why Europe needs a constitution. *New Left Review* 11 (September–October): 5–26.

Hall, Richard L. 1998. Lobbying as informational subsidy. Paper presented at the annual meeting of the Midwest Political Science Association, Chicago, April 12–14.

Hall, Richard L., and Alan V. Deardorff. 2006. Lobbying as legislative subsidy. *American Political Science Review* 100(1): 69–84.

Heaney, Michael T. 2004. Reputation and leadership inside interest group coalitions. Paper presented at the annual meeting of the American Political Science Association, Chicago, September 2–4.

Heclo, Hugh. 1978. Issue networks and the executive establishment. In *The New American Political System,* ed. Anthony King, 87–124. Washington: American Enterprise Institute.

Heinz, John P., Edward O. Laumann, Robert H. Salisbury, and Robert L. Nelson. 1990. Inner circles or hollow cores? elite networks in national policy systems. *Journal of Politics* 52:356–90.

Hix, Simon. 1999. *The political system of the European Union.* New York: St. Martin's Press.

Hix, Simon, Amei Kreppel, and Abdul Noury. 2003. The party system in the European parliament: Collusive or competitive? *Journal of Common Market Studies* 41(2): 309–31.

Hix, Simon, Tapio Raunio, and Roger Scully. 2003. Fifty years on: Research on the European parliament. *Journal of Common Market Studies* 41(2): 191–202.

Hojnacki, Marie. 1997. Interest groups' decisions to join alliances or work alone. *American Journal of Political Science* 41:61–87.

———. 1998. Organized interests' advocacy behavior in alliances. *Political Research Quarterly* 51:437–59.

Hojnacki, Marie, and David C. Kimball. 1998. Organized interests and the decision of whom to lobby in Congress. *American Political Science Review* 92:775–90.

———. 2001. PAC contributions and lobbying contacts in congressional committees. *Political Research Quarterly* 54:161–80.

Hooghe, Lisbet, and Gary Marks. 2003. Unraveling the central state, but how?: Types of multi-level governance. *American Political Science Review* 97(2): 233–43.

Hula, Kevin. 1995. Rounding up the usual suspects: Forging interest group coalitions. In *Interest group politics*. 4th ed., eds. Allan J. Cigler and Burdett A. Loomis, 239–58. Washington, D.C.: CQ Press.

———. 1999. *Lobbying together: Interest group coalitions in legislative politics.* Washington, D.C.: Georgetown University Press.

Imig, Doug, and Sidney Tarrow, eds. 2001. Mapping the Europeanization of contention: Evidence from a quantitative data analysis. In *Contentious Europeans: Protest and politics in an emerging polity.* Lanham, MD: Rowman & Littlefield.

Jacobson, Gary C. 2004. *The politics of congressional elections.* 6th ed. New York: Longman.

Johnson, Charles W. 2000. How our laws are made. U.S. House of Representatives. January 31. http://thomas.loc.gov/home/holam.txt.

Jones, Bryan D., and Frank R. Baumgartner. 2005. *The politics of attention: How government prioritizes problems.* Chicago: University of Chicago Press.

Jordan, Grant, and Darren Halpin. 2004. Olson triumphant? Recruitment strategies and the growth of a small business organisation. *Political Studies* 52:431–49.

Kallas, Siim. 2007. Kallas confident on lobbyists' register and new initiatives. *EurActiv.* Interview. May 10. www.euractive.com/en/pa/interview-kallas-confident-lobbyists-register-new-initatives/article-163701.

Keating, Michael, and Liesbet Hooghe. 2001. By-passing the nation state? Regions and the EU policy process. In *European union, power and policy-making.* 2nd ed., ed. Jeremy Richardson, 239–56. New York: Routledge.

Kernell, Samuel, and Gary C. Jacobson. 2006. *The logic of American politics.* 3rd ed. Washington, D.C.: CQ Press.

King, Tim. 2005. To register or not—the debate rages. *European Voice* September 22–28: 24.

Kingdon, John W. 1995. *Agendas, alternatives, and public policies.* 2nd ed. New York: HarperCollins.

Klandermans, Bert, Marga de Weerd, José Manuel Sabucedo, and Mauro Rodriguez. 2001. Framing contention: Dutch and Spanish farmers. In *Contentious Europeans:*

Protest and politics in an emerging polity, eds. Doug Imig and Sidney Tarrow, 77–98. Lanham, Md.: Rowman & Littlefield Publishers.

Kohler-Koch, Beate. 1994. Changing patterns of interest intermediation in the European Union. *Government & Opposition* 29:166–89.

Kollman, Ken. 1998. *Outside lobbying: Public opinion and interest group strategies.* Princeton, N.J.: Princeton University Press.

Krehbiel, Keith. 1998. *Pivotal politics: A theory of U.S. lawmaking.* Chicago: University of Chicago Press.

Kreppel, Amie. 2002. *The European parliament and supranational party system.* Cambridge: Cambridge University Press.

———. 2005. Understanding the European parliament from a federalist perspective: The legislatures of the USA and the EU compared. Paper prepared for the EUSA 9th Biannual International Conference, Austin, Tex., March 31–April 2.

Kreppel, Amie, and George Tsebelis. 1999. Coalition formation in the European parliament. *Comparative Political Studies* 32:933–66.

Kriesi, Hanspeter, Silke Adam, and Margit Jochum. 2005. Comparative analysis of policy networks in western Europe. Paper presented at the CONNEX Research Group 5, Social Capital as Catalyst of Civic Engagement and Quality of Governance, Academic Workshop, May 20–22, Bled, Slovenia.

Kriesi, Hanspeter, Margit Jochuma, and Anke Tresch. 2005. Going public in the EU. Changing strategies of western European collective political actors. Unpublished working paper.

Lahusen, Christian. 2002. Commercial consultancies in the European Union: The shape and structure of professional interest intermediation. *Journal of European Public Policy* 9:695–714.

Latham, Earl. 1952. *The group basis of politics.* Ithaca, N.Y.: Cornell University Press.

Leconte, Cecile. 2005. Between an emerging European political space and the gatekeeping role of national party elites: Which prospects for the Europeanization of domestic political spaces? Paper presented at the CONNEX Research Group 5, Social Capital as Catalyst of Civic Engagement and Quality of Governance, Academic Workshop, Bled, Slovenia, May 20–22.

Leonard, Dick. 1988. *Pocket guide to the European community.* New York: Basil-Blackwell.

Lijphart, Arend. 1999. *Patterns of democracy: Government forms and performance in thirty-six countries.* New Haven: Yale University Press.

Lindblom, Charles E. 1982. The market as prison. *The Journal of Politics* 44(2): 324–36.

Long, Tony, Liam Salter, and Stephan Singer. 2002. WWF: European and global climate policy. In *European Union lobbying: Changes in the arena,* ed. Robine Pedler, 87–103. Palgrave: Basingstoke.

Lowery, David, and Virginia Gray. 2004. A neopluralist perspective on research on organized interests. *Political Research Quarterly* 57(1): 163–75.

Lowi, Theodore J. 1969. *The end of liberalism: Ideology, policy, and the crisis of public authority.* New York: W. W. Norton.

Maass, Arthur. 1951. *Muddy waters: Army engineers and the nation's rivers.* Cambridge: Harvard University Press.

Madison, James. 1787. Federalist #10. www.constitution.org/fed/federa10.htm.

Mahoney, Christine. 2003a. Influential institutions: The demand side of lobbying in the European Union. Paper presented at the American Political Science Association annual meeting, Philadelphia, August.

———. 2003b. The structure and bias of the interest group system in the European Union. Master's thesis. The Pennsylvania State University.

———. 2004. The power of institutions: State and interest-group activity in the European Union. *European Union Politics* 5(4): 441–66.

Majone, Giandomenico. 1998. Europe's democratic deficit: The question of standards. *European Law Journal* 4(1): 5–28.

Malone, Margaret Mary. 2004. Regulation of lobbyists in developing countries, current rules and practices. Institution of Public Administration: Dublin, Ireland.

Marks, Gary, Richard Haesly, and Heather A. D. Mbaye. 2001. What do subnational offices think they are doing in Brussels? Paper presented at the European Community Studies Association meeting, Madison, Wisconsin, May 31–June 3.

Marks, Gary, and Doug McAdam. 1996. Social movements and the changing structure of political opportunity in the European Union. *West European Politics* 19(2): 249–78.

———. 1999. On the relationship of political opportunities to the form of collective action: The case of the European Union. In *Social movements in a globalizing world*, eds. D. della Porta, H. Kriesi, and D. Rucht, 97–111, Basingstoke: MacMillan.

Martin, Andrew, and George Ross. 2001. Trade union organizing at the European level. In *Contentious Europeans: Protest and politics in an emerging polity*, eds. Doug Imig and Sidney Tarrow, 53–76, Lanham, Md.: Rowman & Littlefield Publishers.

Maskell, Jack. 2001. Lobbying Congress: An overview of legal provisions and congressional ethics rules. *Congressional research service report for Congress*, Code RL31126. Congressional Research Service: www.senate.gov/reference/resources/pdf/RL31126.pdf

Mayhew, David. 1974. *Congress: The electoral connection*. New Haven: Yale University Press.

McAllister, Richard. 1997. *From EC to EU: An historical and political survey*. New York: Routledge.

McCarthy, John D., and Mayer N. Zald. 1978. Resource mobilization and social movements: A partial theory. *American Journal of Sociology* 82:1212–41.

McCarty, Nolan, and Lawrence S. Rothenberg. 1996. Commitment and the campaign contribution contract. *American Journal of Political Science* 40:872–904.

McCormick, John. 1999. Environmental policy. In *Developments in the European Union*, eds. Laura Cram, Desmond Dinan, and Neill Nugent, 193–210. New York: St. Martin's Press.

McGrath, Conor. 2000. Comparative lobbying practices: Washington, London, Brussels. Working paper.

———. 2005. *Lobbying in Washington, London, and Brussels: The persuasive communication of political issues*. Lampeter, Wales: Edwin Mellen Press.

McKissick, Gary J. 1995. Interests, issues, and emphases: Lobbying Congress and the strategic manipulation of issue dimensions. Paper presented at the annual meeting of the Midwest Political Science Association, Chicago, April 6–8.

McLaughlin, A., G. Jordan, and W. A. Maloney. 1993. Corporate lobbying in the European community. *Journal of Common Market Studies* 31(2): 191–212.

Membres de la Conference des Presidents, January 14, 2002. www.europarl.eu.int/orgpresi/default_en.htm.

Menon, Anand. 2005. The limits of comparative politics: International relations in the European Union. Paper prepared for the EUSA 9th Biannual International Conference, Austin, Tex., March 31–April 2.

Merriam-Webster English Dictionary. 2006. Online version. www.m-w.com.

Michalowitz, Irina. 2004. *EU lobbying—principals, agents and targets: Strategic interest intermediation in EU policy-making.* Munster: Lit Verlag.

———. 2005. Service bureaux of decision makers or successful spin-doctors: Assessing interest group influence in the EU and the US. Paper prepared for the EUSA 9th Biannual International Conference, Austin, Tex., March 31–April 2.

Milbrath, Lester W. 1963. *The Washington lobbyists.* Chicago: Rand McNally.

Mitchell, James, and Paul McAleavey. 1999. Promoting solidarity and cohesion. In *Developments in the European Union,* eds. Laura Cram, Desmond Dinan, and Neill Nugent, 174–92. New York: St. Martin's Press.

Moe, Terry M. 1980. A calculus of group membership. *American Journal of Political Science* 24: 593–632.

Moravcsik, Andrew. 2002. In defense of the democratic deficit: Reassessing the legitimacy of the European Union. *Journal of Common Market Studies* 40(4):603–34.

New York Times. 2005. The lobbying-industrial complex. Editorial. *New York Times* August 26. 18.

Olson, Mancur, Jr. 1965. *The logic of collective action.* Cambridge: Harvard University Press.

Pedler, Robin H. 1994. Fruit companies and banana trade regime. In *Lobbying the European Union: Companies, trade associations and issue groups,* eds. Robin H. Pedler and M.P.C.M van Schendelen, 67–92. Aldershot: Dartmouth.

———. 2002. *European Union lobbying: Changes in the arena.* Palgrave: Basingstoke.

Pedler, Robin H., and M.P.C.M van Schendelen, eds. 1994. *Lobbying the European Union: Companies, trade associations and issue groups.* Aldershot: Dartmouth.

Pijnenburg, B. 1998. EU lobbying by ad hoc coalitions: An exploratory case study. *Journal of European Public Policy* 14(2): 95–145.

Pinder, John. 1988. *European community: The building of a union.* Oxford: Oxford University Press.

Pollack, M. 1997. Representing diffuse interests in EC policy-making. *Journal of European Public Policy* 4(4): 572–90.

Princen, Sebastiaan, and Bart Kerremans. 2005. Opportunity structures in the EU multi-level system. Paper presented at the CONNEX research group 4, Civil Society and Interest Representation in EU-Governance, Leiden, The Netherlands, April 14–16.

Riker, William H. 1986. *The art of political manipulation.* New Haven: Yale University Press.

Romer, Thomas, and James M. Snyder, Jr. 1994. An empirical investigation of the dynamics of PAC contributions. *American Journal of Political Science* 38:745–69.

Rothenberg, Lawrence S. 1988. Organizational maintenance and the retention decision in groups. *American Political Science Review* 82:1129–52.

Rucht, Dieter. 2001. Lobbying or protest? Strategies to influence EU environmental policies. In *Contentious Europeans: Protest and politics in an emerging polity,* eds. Doug Imig and Sidney Tarrow, 125–42, Lanham, Md.: Rowman & Littlefield Publishers.

Sabatier, Paul A. 1988. An advocacy coalition framework of policy change and the role of policy-oriented learning therein. *Policy Sciences* 21:129–68.

Salisbury, Robert H. 1969. An exchange theory of interest groups. *Midwest Journal of Political Science* 13:1–32.

Salisbury, Robert H., John P. Heinz, Edward O. Laumann, and Robert L. Nelson. 1987. Who works with whom? interest group alliances and opposition. *American Political Science Review* 81:1211–34.

Sandholtz Wayne, and Alec Stone Sweet. 1998. *European integration and supranational governance.* Oxford: Oxford University Press.

Saurugger, Sabine. 2005. Associative democracy and the democratic legitimacy of the European Union. Paper presented at the CONNEX research group 4, Civil Society and Interest Representation in EU-Governance, Leiden, The Netherlands, April 14–16.

Scharpf, Fritz.W. 1999. *Governing in Europe: Effective and democratic?* Oxford: Oxford University Press.

Schattschneider, E. E. 1960. *The semi-sovereign people.* New York: Holt, Rinehart and Winston.

Schlesinger, Joseph. 1994. *Political parties and the winning of office.* Ann Arbor: University of Michigan Press.

Schlozman, Kay Lehman, and John T. Tierney. 1986. *Organized interests and American democracy.* New York: Harper and Row.

Schneider, Gerald, and Konstantin Baltz. 2003. The power of specialization: How interest groups influence EU legislation. *Rivista di Politica Economica* 93 (January–February): 253–83.

Schneider, Volker. 1992. Organized interests in the European telecommunications sector. In *Organized interests and the European community,* eds. Justin Greenwood, Jurgen R. Grote, and Karsten Roni, 42–68. London: SAGE Publications.

Siaroff, Alan. 1999. Corporatism in 24 industrial democracies: Meaning and measurement. *European Journal of Political Research* 36(2): 175–205.

Smith, Mark A. 2000. *American business and political power: Public opinion, elections, and democracy.* Chicago: University of Chicago Press.

Smith, Richard A. 1984. Advocacy, interpretation, and influence in the U.S. Congress. *American Political Science Review* 78:44–63.

Snow, David E., Burke Rochford Jr., Steven K. Worden, and Robert Benford. 1986. Frame alignment processes, micromobilization, and movement participation. *American Sociological Review* 51:464–81.

Stevens, Handley. 2004. *Transport policy in the European Union. the European Union series.* London: Macmillan Press Ltd.

Stone Sweet, Alec. 2003. European integration and the legal system. In *The state of the EU.* Vol 6. Oxford: Oxford University Press.

Stone Sweet, Alec, and Markus Gehring. 2004. Environmental protection. In *The judicial construction of Europe,* ed. A. Stone Sweet, 199–235. Oxford: Oxford University Press.

Streeck, Wolfgang, and Philippe C Schmitter. 1991. From national corporatism to transnational pluralism. Organized interests in the single European market. *Politics & Society* 19(2): 133–65.

Stubb, Alexander, Helen Wallace, and John Peterson. 2003. The policy-making process. In *The European Union: How does it work?*, eds. Elizabeth Bomberg and Alexander Stubb, 136–55. Oxford: Oxford University Press.

Tauber, Steven C. 1998. On behalf of the condemned? The impact of the NAACP legal defense fund on capital punishment decision making in the U.S. Court of Appeals. *Political Research Quarterly* 51:191–219.

Thody, Philip. 1997. *An historical introduction to the European Union.* New York: Routledge.

Thomas, Clive S., ed. 1993. *First world interest groups: A comparative perspective.* Westport, Conn.: Greenwood Press.

Thomas, Clive. S., and Ronals J. Hrebenar. 2000. Comparing lobbying across liberal democracies: Problems, approaches and initial findings. Paper presented at the American Political Science Association, Washington, D.C., August 31–September 3.

Truman, David B. 1951. *The governmental process: Political interests and public opinion.* New York: Alfred A. Knopf.

Urwin, Derek W. 1995. *The community of Europe: A history of European integration since 1945.* 2nd ed. New York: Longman.

Van den Polder, Rene. 1994. Lobbying for the European airline industry. In *Lobbying the European Union: Companies, trade associations and issue groups,* eds. Robin H Pedler and M.P.C.M van Schendelen, 103–22, Aldershot: Dartmouth.

Van Schendelen, M.P.C.M, ed. 1993. *National public and private EC lobbying.* Aldershot: Dartmouth.

Walker, Jack L., Jr. 1983. The origins and maintenance of interest groups in America. *American Political Science Review* 77:390–406.

Wallström, Margot. 2005. Grass-roots change for Europe, the future of the union. *International Herald Tribune,* June 21, p. 9.

Watkins, Michael, Mickey Edwards, and Usha Thakrar. 2001. *Winning the influence game: What every business leader should know about government.* New York: John Wiley & Sons.

Watson, Rory, and Michael Shackleton. 2003. Organized interests and lobbying in the EU. In *The European Union: How does it work?*, eds. Elizabeth Bomberg and Alexander Stubb, 88–110. Oxford: Oxford University Press.

Wawro, Gregory. 2001. A panel probit analysis of campaign contributions and roll call votes. *American Journal of Political Science* 45:563–79.

Weiler, Joseph H. H., Ulrich R. Haltern, and Franz C. Mayer. 1995. European democracy and its critique. *West European Politics* 18(3): 4–39.

Wessels, Bernhard. 2000. Interest groups in the EU: The emergence of contestation potential. Draft paper for the conference Dimensions of Contestation in the European Union, Chapel Hill, April 30–May 2.

Whitford, Andrew B. 2003. The structures of interest coalitions: Evidence from environmental litigation. *Business and Politics* 5:45–64.

Wöll, Cornelia. 2005a. Lobbying in a transatlantic comparison, opportunity structures and lobbying content in the US and EU. Paper prepared for the EUSA 9th Biannual International Conference, Austin, Tex., March 31–April 2.

————. 2005b. Lobbying in the European Union: From sui generis to a comparative perspective. Working Paper. Köln, Germany: Max Planck Institute for the Study of Societies.

Wright, John R. 1985. PACs, contributions, and roll calls: An organizational perspective. *American Political Science Review* 79:400–414.

Index

Index

Hix, Simon, 22–23, 38, 47
H_2O Coalition, 174
Hojnacki, Marie, 45, 51, 111, 169–70
Honest Leadership and Open Government Act of 2007, 17
Hrebenar, Ronald J., 63
Hula, Kevin, 169
Human Cloning Prohibition Act of 2002, 224

Imig, Doug, 214
See also democratic institutional designs

See also advocates
EU policymaking procedures and, 24

Jochum, Margit, 152, 163, 214
Jones, Bryan, 117, 126
Jordan, Grant, 43

Kallas, Siim, 141, 210
Kerremans, Bart, 25
Kimball, David C., 45, 51, 111
King, Tim, 29
Kingdon, John W., 35, 168, 216

Printed in the United States
205473BV00001B/112-126/P

9 781589 012035